THE LAST OF
THE FIRST

Also by Spike Mays

Reuben's Corner
Fall Out The Officers
No More Soldiering For Me
Five Miles From Bunkum
(with Christopher Ketteridge)
Last Post
The Band Rats
Return To Anglia

THE LAST OF THE FIRST

SPIKE MAYS

JANUS PUBLISHING COMPANY
London, England

First published in Great Britain 1997
by Janus Publishing Company
Edinburgh House, 19 Nassau Street
London W1N 7RE

British Library Cataloguing-in-Publication Data.
A catalogue record for this book is available from the British Library.

ISBN 1 85756 325 5

The right of Spike Mays to be identified as the author of
this work has been asserted by him in accordance with the
Copyright, Designs and Patents Act 1988.

Cover design Harold King

Photosetting by Keyboard Services, Luton, Beds
Printed and bound in England by
Antony Rowe Ltd, Chippenham, Wilts

Contents

1

Jack Overhill

I saw Jack Overhill's writing before I saw his face. Both have been important and dear to me over twenty years. His first letter was congratulatory and inquisitive. First, he praised my first book, *Reuben's Corner*, then began questioning me about my maternal grandfather's place of work. Grandfather Reuben Ford was dead. For sixty years he had squatted in a corner of The Bonnet Inn each day, to take his midday pint, bread and cheese and a slice or two of raw onion. He had his own pint pot, white with blue rings, his own stool and his own corner. He was a farm labourer and horse-keeper at Overhall Farm.

Even when The Bonnet was filled to capacity and grandfather was not present, no one was allowed to sit on his stool. If someone was sufficiently misguided as to try, that someone would be warned off pretty sharp...

'Yew marn't sit there, my owd met. That's Reuben's Corner!'

Jack Overhill's letter praised my book and the title. I had written that The Bonnet Inn stood on the boundaries of three East Anglian counties: Essex, Suffolk and Cambridgeshire, smack at the bottom of Overhall Lane, a deep-rutted, flint-capped cart-track leading to Overhall Farm.

Village gossip had it that in the distance of unrecorded time strange folk infiltrated the hamlet or passed through it in search of work. Journeymen, tramps, gypsies and tinkers. Most of them had no proper name. Possibly because they had not met up with a font of christening and had hailed from a long line of bachelors. Without surnames, some were taken on at Overhall Farm and afterwards were known as The Overhallers.

Peter Layng, a Cambridge genealogist, had told Jack his name stemmed from Overhall Farm, two miles from the village of Ashdon. Peter gave him two hundred names from the parish records around Haverhill – with the variants of Overhill, Overill, Overall, Overhall, going back as far as 25th March, 1561, when James Overhall was born and baptised at the Anglican church of Shudy Camps, quite near to Castle Camps and Bartlow, Cambridgeshire, where stands the famous 'Three Hills' burial ground of ancient marauders from Rome.

It seems unlikely that Jack had Roman blood in his East Anglian veins, and I am not unduly concerned about his origin; but I am determined to lift up the bushel under which Jack's life and labours have been hidden, his literary life lost for far too long.

Robert Malster, another East Anglian pen-pusher who was not behind the door when writing talent was dished out, surprised and pleased us a good ten years ago when he wrote a well-merited tribute to Angus Wilson (a fellow East Anglian writer) on the publishing of his book *Writers of East Anglia*.

Robert stated that Angus's book, an anthology, shows how rich a heritage of literature we have in our lovely region. Quoting Angus Wilson, Robert continued with these words: 'A very good anthology could be written by people recording their childhood.'

Both Robert and Angus can say that again, but I'll let the pair into a secret... There's not a lot of sense putting down one's head to write such books when publishers prefer to 'cash in quick' with torrents of tomes on sex, batteries of books from BBC's alleged personalities on cooking, and tirades of trash on old and new BBC and ITA programmes – *ad nauseam*.

Some East Anglians have already recorded their childhood in the permanence of the written word. I, for one, have been guilty of this enormity on two occasions; first in my book *Reuben's Corner*, and later in Michael Watkins' *The East Anglian Book*. Because the latter was so beautifully produced when it came to light in 1971, I would like to repeat a bit of its blurb...

'Take a company of distinguished East Anglian writers: Hammond Innes, Ronald Blythe, James Wentworth Day, Norah Lofts, John Hadfield, Adrian Bell, Spike Mays, Allan Johnson, Simon Dewes. Add Norfolk's greatest living painter, Edward Seago, Peter Pears, co-founder, with Benjamin Britten, of the Aldeburgh Festival; an eminent churchman, the Bishop of St Edmundsbury and Ipswich; a humorist poet, Paul Jennings; an interior decorator, Mary Gilliat; a sportsman, Logie Bruce Lockhart; an historian, W. G. Arnott; a sailor, Bob Roberts; a broadcaster, John Seymour; a farming journalist, Rintell Booth; an antiques expert, John Steel; a gardener and steam engine enthusiast, Alan Bloom; a naturalist, Alan Savory; a ghost hunter, Eric Rayner; a cartoonist, Giles...

'Allow the editor, travel writer and co-editor of the *East Anglian Magazine*, Michael Watkins, to stir gently – and the result should be a literary "bombe surprise".'

Well now! The book was published and turned out to be an East Anglian love story.

To my regret, one East Anglian author did not appear in its pages, but I am pleased Robert Malster made mention of him, because that man is my very good friend, Jack Overhill.

Jack has put down his childhood in the permanence of excellent writing, and a lot of the childhood of his forebears. His father was born on 11th May, 1863, in Haverhill, Suffolk, and was taught shoemaking by *his* father. For a time he lived in Castle Camps, Cambridgeshire. Then he moved to Cambridge in his late twenties to become a journeyman boot and shoemaker for bespoke shops. His productivity was not confined to footwear, for he sired thirteen children; six boys (Jack was one of them) and seven girls. He died in 1941, aged 78.

Friend Jack was born four years before me, in 1903. His parents separated when he was five, and he was brought up by his father, with whom he lived alone from the age of eleven. The industrious Jack performed six jobs out of school hours – 35 hours a week for three shillings a week. He won a scholarship to the Cambridge Higher Grade School, left school at 14 to learn his father's trade. He should have stayed until he was 15, but the home fires had to be kept burning.

For ten years he learnt shoemaking, but also went to night school for three years without missing a lesson, where he learnt Pitman's shorthand and book-keeping, commercial arithmetic and English.

He married at the age of 20 (on £2 per week) and produced a son and a daughter. Jack took a Pitman's Shorthand Teacher's Diploma at 20, became a clerk for seven years, and then a bookmaker. He graduated, B.Sc. (Econ.), as an external student of London University; became a teacher of shorthand and typewriting at Cambridgeshire Village College and a Lecturer in Economics at the Cambridge College of Arts and Technology.

Jack is no stranger to the 'media'. He has made 55 broadcasts for the BBC. His fiftieth, 'A Regular Snob' was broadcast twice by the Third Programme and then on the Home Service. No mean effort, for it was non-scripted and lasted for one hour. In 1968 it was included in *Good Talk* (Gollancz), the first anthology from BBC Radio. And there, squatting before a nest of microphones, was my old friend, the old snob (shoemaker) rubbing shoulders and matching wits with Sir Bernard Lovell, Professor A. J. Ayer, Sir Gavin de Beer, FRS, and our East Anglian friend, René Cutforth.

Eighty-five, straight as a bean-pole and not much thicker, a lifelong teetotaller and non-smoker, he walked several miles a day. Much of the proceeding to places on foot was connected with his daily visits to the River Granta. All the year round for 63 years, he ignored babblings about pollution, breaking the ice to enter the wet stuff so as not to miss his daily dip – even diving into it just before dark on a wintry day. He summed it up with a BBC broadcast, 'I Like It'.

He married Jess on a May morning, 1923, whipped her off to Sheeps Green bathing place, had a swim as she watched him, and from then made it their annual ritual, a procedure they repeated on their Diamond Wedding Day.

Reg Mansfield, a Cambridge swimming coach, estimated in a local newspaper article that Jack had dived into the Granta 20,000 times. He was the Royal Life Saving Society representative for 21 years, and regards that as his personal contribution to social services.

He founded the Granta Swimming Club in 1934, which flourished for 50 years until expanding to become the Cambridgeshire Club.

I will not enlarge further on these perishing aquatic capers; they quake and shudder me. My object in writing about this truly remarkable man is to invite attention to his literary qualities. But each time I meet him I'm reminded of a military rest camp at Sidi Gaba, about three horse's lengths from Ras el Tin Lighthouse, one of the seven wonders of the world, near Alexandria.

Every trooper in my squadron could swim and play water polo, bar me.

Swimmers took me to a jetty on which was a warning notice, typical of military police intelligence.

> OTHER RANKS ARE NOT ALLOWED TO
> ENTER THE WATER UNTIL THEY HAVE
> LEARNED TO SWIM

Ignoring the notice, and with contemptuous disregard for my salvation, my fellow troopers slung me in. I was fished out by an Arab, with a boat-hook.

During one of Jack's periodic telephone calls from Trumpington, he told me when he was first bitten by the writing bug. He wrote a short story, 'The Ruined Abbey' (now in the Cambridgeshire Collection at the City Library). He wrote it in the small kitchen of his home, where it was bitterly cold and without a fire, starting on a Sunday morning in December 1916. One hour a day ... His father told him to get on with it; he might turn out to be another Dickens. Three weeks later he left school and began to learn his father's trade, shoemaking.

He didn't get his short stories accepted, so he wrote a novel, *Romantic Youth*, about Cambridge University life. It was published, and Morley Stuart, editor of the *Cambridge Daily News* and an authority on Cambridge in fact and fiction, said in a long review, 'Sixty novels have been written about Cambridge University, but all by University men and he is an elementary schoolboy'. That said it all.

Heartened, Jack set about writing novels. He turned out a dozen, but only two were accepted for publication. *The Snob*, the life-story of a shoemaker, after twenty rejections, hit the headlines in the national newspapers. John Betjeman was one of those who fell over themselves in praising it. Daniel George, the leading critic, said in *Tribune* that it was the best book about our working class in print, and backed it up in BBC broadcasts on the Home and Overseas Services.

The Mille of Trumpington, an historical novel, had 25 first-rate reviews, but it was not made into a film, as rumour had it.

Queen Street – a novel about a cul-de-sac of four-roomed cottages, twelve a-side, with a cobble-stoned roadway and broken flagstone paths, period 1911 to 1938, with 200 characters – came in for special notice. Neil Bell, the author of scores of novels and hundreds of short stories, said of it in a letter to him:

> *Queen Street* is more than a novel. It is a powerful and vivid sociological documentary. You are in a class by yourself as a proletarian writer and as sure as tomorrow's sunrise your books will be published. No one else is quite like you or half as good in the astonishing vividness of your visual memory and your unfaltering eye for the revealing detail. When your books will be published, no one can say. One day they will be digging out all you wrote about a scene and people gone for ever from the earth. Just as now they are digging out and publishing every scrap of Boswell. Story-tellers are ten-a-penny. Their work – and Tressell's – is but a drop to your full moon as an almost blinding light upon life as it was lived by millions at the turn of the century. You have the full

moon. Why cry for the penny-dip? You may be dead when it all comes about, but you may well live to see it. You haven't really the faintest notion what you've accomplished, simply because you've hankered to be a novelist. All the novels written in our time, bundled together, aren't worth *Queen Street* alone. No one in the future can write a history of our times who does not know your work. So stop being so bloody humble. There's no one you need to look up to.

Yours, Stephen
(Neil Bell)

Jack came under the spotlight when Joyce Wilson, a reader for London Weekend Television, top-graded *Queen Street*. That led to his going to the South Bank to discuss a weekly series. The material and approach were very appealing, but the huge cast of characters was against it and it faded out.

Relatives and friends think a publisher's reader got the idea of television's 'Coronation Street', 'Crossroads' and 'EastEnders' from *Queen Street*. The typescript was making the round of publishers from 1939, years before they came into focus, so there's no telling.

There was also a bit of excitement when the galley proofs of *The Money Bug* arrived. Alas, it didn't last long. The publishers went bust and didn't even pay the advance royalty!

An extract of Jack's novel *Back Street Boy* was included in *Writers of East Anglia*. Angus Wilson, the editor, said in the preface that Jack was a case of talent ignored and publishers should be ashamed of themselves. He called on Jack, had tea with him and his wife, and stayed an hour showing professional interest in the mass of material of Jack's writing life.

Thinking he was 53 and had plenty to say, he wrote his autobiography, *No Mother Love*. Publishers wanted cuts. The odd thing about it was they all wanted different cuts. But how can you cut your life? What happened, had happened. It joined his growing list of rejected typescripts.

He still kept at it, and when he was 59 got down to writing

a series of books about his own life and times. He'd had the idea for years, and during the war had written three of them. He rewrote those three and kept on in earnest. He had no thoughts of their being published but often thought of my contempt for the breed that flourished on sex and violence, and spoke about it to my credit.

Jack wrote one volume a year for 15 years, completing the series on Sunday 15th April, 1978, when he was 75.

The Cash Chronicles, the collective title, is an honest record of his life and times with a local, national and world background since the turn of the century ... 600 people, 150 place-names, changed and indexed ... Like all his literary output, including the typing, it is his own work from beginning to end.

'How the devil did you manage it as well as working for a living?' I asked quite recently.

'Getting to bed late and getting up early. Jess used to call me from upstairs, sometimes when the sun had just decided to get up.'

Wrapped in his writing, he lost touch with time. He also lost a loving Jess, who died suddenly in December 1985. He had taken her a cup of tea, to her bed, every morning for 43 years. The thought of it gave a mite of balm to his grief. He still grieves and now is far from well, following torture at the hands of a dentist lasting seven weeks.

'Supposed to be extractions, Spike ... He broke off most of the crowns of my teeth, then dug down to yank out the roots, and they got infected. A better description would be "excavation".'

He still grieves about the loss of Jess, and his dogs, and always will; but his published books and typescripts are now in the Cambridgeshire Collection, safe at the City Library. He gave me a copy of the letter of acknowledgement.

1st April, 1986

Dear Jack,

For nearly twenty years I have been aware of your writings on the Cambridge scene and have become increasingly conscious of their importance in chronicling an aspect of local life that has not been recorded before. Their value to future historians will be immense.

I am especially proud to be allowed to make *The Cash Chronicles* available to those researchers and hope that I can ensure that their importance is realised.

Thank you for such an important donation, and thank you also for your friendship and inspiration over the last twenty years.

Yours sincerely,
Michael Petty,
Senior Librarian, Local Studies

His daughter Jess is 64.
His son Jack is 61.
He has five grandsons.
Two great-granddaughters.
For 66 years (1921–1987) he had seven dogs; retriever, springer spaniel and five collies. He says they were the salt of the earth. 'There's no bad dogs, only bad dog-owners.'

2

The Donkey Wallopers

On Sunday 6th May, in the Senior NCOs Mess, Hyde Park
Barracks, a pack of old war hounds were baying. Some were
grey of mane, others bald of bonce. All were happy. We had
got more than halfway through, 'Wrap Me Up in My Old
Stable Jacket' and were wondering how we could clean up
our next ritual ditty... that plaintive cry to riding school
instructors, sung to the melody of a haggis-bashing love song,
'My Bonnie Lies Over the Ocean...' Our version was a bit on
the ripe side... 'Oh give back my stirrups to me!' Our Ladies
were with us... We did not want them to hear words they
might not have understood!

We were halted in our melodic stride by a yell...

'Belt up!'

This courteous request for silence came from the throat of he
who had enlisted with me in March 1924. Born in Welsh
Abergavenny, he served with the Regiment for 50 years, under
various pseudonyms... 'Spud, Dixie, Taffy, Taff and, because
he ain't all that far out of mother earth, Short-Arse.' Rumour
had it that he suffers still from Duck's Disease; a painful
bruising of his undercarriage. Each time he steps off a pavement from the kerb, he suffers a bump to his rump, poor chap!

Never mind!... Spud was tall enough to stand alongside
a lovely, gracious lady, beautifully dressed in smiles and
powder blue, to represent us at the Combined Cavalry
Memorial Service, Hyde Park.

We did not really mind him chipping in, poor dab. He only wanted to ask a question.

'Do you know what the Queen Mum told me?'

Major C. W. J. Lewis looked wholly pleased. His eyes shone like a chestnut newly shelled.

'Her Majesty said that I must have worked long and hard to lick you lot into shape, for it's the best Combined Cavalry turnout she had seen!'

We replenished his water bottle. He beamed and continued... 'I could have told her no organisation was needed. All you noisy shower needed was the first notes of our March from our Band; then you'd behave like gentlemen for a change... Who wants a refill?'

Like old Kipling's Judy O'Grady, our Ladies soon picked up the words and joined us in song. Afterwards they paid us a tribute from the USAAF: by proxy or intentional eavesdropping. My wife was one witness, my sister another, plus a bevy of beauties who had cantered down with us from the villages of Suffolk, Norfolk, Essex and Cambridgeshire. A spot of East Anglian craft had secured enclosure places for them; smack opposite the Queen Mum and Spud Lewis. They had overheard songs of praise from a Yankee contingent who had popped along from their nuclear-studded aerodromes to see ancient Donkey Wallopers marching dismounted and certainly not 'disunited'.

'Gee! Those old guys can march better than our young guys in uniform. With funny hats and umbrellas! They sure look proud!'

We felt proud. There were reasons...

Through disbandment and amalgamation, many old cavalry regiments have lost their individuality and autonomy. Guidos, Colours and Badges have blended, but the cavalry spirit is indestructible, for 'Cav muck in'.

Each year the tradition continues in Hyde Park, usually in May, when sunshine filters green leaves – to caress bible-black bowlers, rapier-like brollies, and those familiar faces above breasts bristling with campaign and long service medals.

Few are late on parade. We muster under our own Association banners. Pipes are pocketed, cigarettes stubbed. Ears prick and eyes light up as the bands strike up with a march. A rapid shaking of hands; a raising of bowlers to the Ladies and a wink to old pals... 'See you for a stirrup cup in the Mess.'

You march once more with Old Comrades, to the music of one of the cavalry bands. After the march-past and salute, you halt at the bandstand to see the padre's medalled surplice stirring in the breeze. You hear the voices raised in unison, old bandsmen in full harmony, for that hymn... No need to look at the printed programme, we know the words and what they signify...

'O, God, our help in ages past...'

Above the hooting and blasting of motor horns and exhausts we hear the Chaplain's fine enunciation as he reads the lesson; then we sing for our lost comrades the wonderful words of 'O, Valiant Hearts'.

You keep a sharp eye on the Household Cavalry Trumpeters as, so slowly, they raise the bannered trumpets to sound that military lullaby, 'Last Post'.

Pigeons swoosh and swirl in flight at that first note, when all should be still and silent, but resume the pavement peckings and coo-ings that follow our intoned remembrances...
'THEY shall grow not old, as WE that are left grow old. Age shall not weary them, nor the years condemn... At the going down of the sun, and in the morning, we will remember them'.

Then follows that silence when two short minutes seem to be lifetimes. Thoughts gallop back over the years; mostly about old friends, draped and empty chairs and permanent parting. Before you can blot out memories, or collect scattered thoughts, the pigeons are on the wing ... the Trumpeter is sounding Cavalry Reveille, 'Rise, Soldiers, rise, and put your armour on!'

Then we think of our dearest friends, those with a leg at each corner. How we all loved them (before horsemen became sardined into tinny tanks and armoured cars). Some of us recall memories in the words of Julian Grenfell, one of our officers, who was killed in action 14 days after he had paid this tribute:

INTO BATTLE

The naked earth is warm with Spring
And, with green grass and bursting trees,
Leans to the sun's gaze glorying,
And quivers in the sunny breeze.

And life is colour and warmth and light
And a striving evermore for these;
And he is dead who will not fight,
But who dies fighting has increase.

In dreary, doubtful, waiting hours
Before the brazen frenzy starts,
Our horses show him nobler powers...
O, patient eyes, courageous hearts!

The thundering line of battle stands
And in the air death moans and sings;
But Day shall clasp him with strong hands
And Night shall fold him in soft wings.

We lacked Grenfell's poetic splendour, but not his capacity for sincerity and concern for the loss of friends, two-legged and four; and paid our tribute in words of our barrack room ballads, sung at many a departure – in many lands...

Wrap me up in my old stable jacket
And say a poor Trooper lies low.
Then six Royal Dragoons will soon carry me
To that place where the best horsemen go...

Look at the horses! Bloody great horses!
But no oak box, all lined with lead.

Only relations, bloody-well howling...
Ain't it grand to be bloody-well dead!

One of our best singers of regimental cavalry songs was
'Heigho' ... alias RSM Charlie Bowles. He was such a good
horseman that one could not be sure where Charlie left off
and the horse started. He hailed from Norfolk, but his voice
was not as flat as his county. When suitably lubricated with
quarts of ale (Heigho seldom drank pints!) he could imitate
trumpet calls so well that brigade trumpeters could scarce tell
the difference. We always heard his favourite song after a
funeral...

Heigho! Many a year ago...
We rode along together you and I, my old Shako;
And we didn't give a button
If the odds were on the foe...
Ten, twenty, thirty, forty, fifty years ago.

It is well over 50 years since I last heard him sing that song. It
was in Cairo, when a lance-corporal and his love committed
suicide in some Gippo hotel. Half the lovelorn troopers of our
HQ Squadron were on the verge of suicide; leaning over the
railings of Main Barracks, Abbassia, they heard not one
nightingale. From the depths of the NCOs' Mess, night after
night, came the shrieking of a Lancashire lass, all about
Whippoor Wills and Blue Heaven. Not all that encouraging
for lusty lads confined to monastic living. That was at the tail
end of 1928, before the advent of 'Amalgamation'.

I still have the old shoulder badges, '1R.D.' ... insignia of
1st Royal Dragoons.

Some of us were stationed on the Curragh (Dublin Race
Course), others were midway poised twixt Athlone and
Aoughrea, at Ballinasloe.

'The Shinners', as we called them, were on the march ... to
remove the British Administration, by passive resistance, or
aggressive resistance, and to establish in its place an Irish
Government.

Now the 'Shinners', or Sinn Fein, had been at it since they were founded in 1905 by one Arthur Griffiths. The name means 'We ourselves' or 'We are it'. Even before the British Army had been forced to plumb the strange depths and shoals of reorganisation, resulting in disbandments, reductions and amalgamations, the old numerical titles were dropped and many new county titles substituted. After Adolf Hitler's War, most county regiments were reduced to a single battalion, then merged into large regiments of three or more battalions.

Cavalry amalgamations preceded those of the infantry, and by the same process our regiments lost much of their autonomy and identity. Many of these 'War Office Weddings' were held in low regard by old sweats weaned on 'regimental pride'.

Irish regiments suffered more than most, particularly with disbandments. We should not forget that when old Kaiser Bill's War began in 1914, those Irish regiments came swiftly to our aid. Catholics and Protestants flocked to the recruiting offices and Redmond, the Irish Parliamentary Leader, offered his National Volunteers to fight the common enemy, Germany. We won! We dreamed (of that land fit for heroes to live in!), and Parliament put the problems of Irish Home Rule into cold storage. The sooner we forget it, and David Lloyd George, plus his Black and Tans, the better.

Because our soldiers are back in the Emerald Isle – with rubber bullets versus IRA rockets, and the slaughtering of horses and men in Hyde Park (where we hold Remembrance Services) – it has occurred to me that it might help if we put the job of looking after that land in the right hands. We would be cantering on the right rein.

Why not reinstate the Irish Army? Why not reform the disbanded regiments and un-amalgamate the amalgamated? Electricity, gas, oil and Guinness might flow full spate, with a tidy ration of Goodwill.

Take a peep at their nicknames...

4th (Royal Irish) Dragoon Guards ... The Buttermilks – Mounted Micks; 5th (Royal Irish) Lancers ... The Daily

Advertisers – The Redbreasts; 6th (Inniskilling) Dragoons ...
The Old Inniskillings – The Skins; 8th (King's Royal Irish)
Hussars ... St George's – The Cross Belts – The Twenty-
Fives; Irish Guards – Bob's Own – The Micks – O'Leary's
Lads; The Royal Irish Regiment (18th) – The Namurs –
Paddy's Blackguards; The Royal Inniskilling Fusiliers (27th) –
The Skins; The Royal Ulster Rifles (83rd) – Fitch's Grenadiers
(late Royal Irish Rifles); The Royal Ulster Rifles (86th) –
Irish Giants (late Royal Irish Rifles); The Royal Irish Fusiliers
(87th) – Faugh-a-Ballagh Boys – The Eagle Takers – The Old
Fogs; The Royal Irish Fusiliers (89th) – The Rollickers –
Blayney's Bloodhounds; The Connaught Rangers (94th) –
The Garvies); The Leinster Regiment (100th) Canada – The
Crusaders – The Centipedes – The Beavers; The Leinster
Regiment (109th) India – The Poonah Pets – The Steel
Heads; The Royal Munster Fusiliers (101st) – The Dirty
Shirts; The Royal Munster Fusiliers (104th) – Bengal – Delhi,
1857; The Royal Dublin Fusiliers (102nd) India – The Blue
Caps; The Royal Dublin Fusiliers (103rd) – Bengal – The Old
Toughs.

It is a great pity that Major Michael O'Leary (Victoria
Cross) died in 1961. He would have made the world's finest
recruiting officer for a new Irish Army. Mind you, he was
only an unpaid lance-jack on 11th July, 1915, the day he
earned his decoration. According to the citation...

'He rushed up along a railway embankment above the
trenches, shot down five Germans behind their first barricade
in the trench, then three more trying to work a machine-gun
at the next barricade fifty yards farther along the trench, and
also took a couple of prisoners.'

By his high gallantry he saved two leading companies of
the Coldstream and Irish Guards from heavy casualties.

He was the first Irish VC in the Kaiser's War, the first for
the Irish Guards. He and his parents conducted a recruiting
campaign, a private one, the like of which has never been seen
before or since.

An 'O'Leary Fund' was set up to look after the widows and
orphans of Irish soldiers; July 11th 1915 was set up as

O'Leary's Day and a recruiting drive started, with the hero as the figurehead.

Among their nicknames, the Irish Guards have one in his honour ... 'O'Leary's Lads'.

I have friends in The Micks and some who served as Donkey Wallopers in the old Irish cavalry regiments now disbanded. They deplore the terrorist ruination of their lovely country. Colonel Jiggs Jaeger ... Director of Music, Irish Guards, Senior Director of Music (British Army), then, until he died (after composing and arranging the music for the installation of HRH The Prince of Wales at Caernarvon) Director of Music, The Royal Military School of Music, Kneller Hall. He had a profound love for Ireland and its soldiers. A brilliant musician, who could play the Posthorn Gallop on the barrel of a Lee-Enfield rifle (and on the hollow shaft of a golf club), he was a master raconteur. He told marvellous stories...

The best I know of them was typical, and true...

3

2609406

'Wanna cuppa char, Metty?' asked a bricklayer working on the new Church Field Estate, already beginning to ruin the pristine splendour of our lovely old village ... 'We are just about to drum up!'

I joined the party of three ... one bricky, one chippy and the 'Char Wallah' (tea boy) who had served in The Suffolks, 12th of Foot or 'Dutty Dozen', in India before the partition and in old Hirohito's war. I call it Hiro's because the 'Char Wallah' had helped to make that railroad on which many Suffolk lads lost their liberty and lives.

'Why do you call it "drumming up"?', said I (testing him out).

'Ain't got a clue, met ... D'ye want sugar?'

I said that *I* knew, but had no time to spare and, if he listened, his bloody awful estate would never get built.

I had been let into the secret of Drumming, which led to 'Drumming Up', by No. 2609406. He was not a freemason (left-handed bricklayer) or even a member of the Mafia and such gatherings. He was, and is, my brother, Leslie Gordon. Junior to me in age, but slightly senior to me in Army Service ... but only by fourteen days, when he joined the Drums of the 1st Battalion, Grenadier Guards, in February 1924. Before he left us in the village, working on the land for ten bob a week, our father John Mays, who had soldiered in the Suffolks before the Kaiser's War, gave No. 2609406 (to be) a tip or two...

'Allus do as you're told, boy. Keep your kit tidy, your bowels open, never be late and watch out for the Drum Major!'

From what Les endured later, and my personal perusal of ancient military musical documents, it appears that my father's enjoinder was more than justified.

Once upon a military time, Drummers were considered to be a cut above the common swaddie. They existed long before the rank of drum major was instituted and sometimes took advantage of their alleged supremacy. They were careless, neglectful and inattentive on parade, and it is believed that the rank of drum major originated from the wishes of military authorities to 'drum them up' and make them conform to military discipline. They were Masters of Bands, Masters of Music or Music Masters. Most were of French or German extraction, who used to absent themselves in times of war.

The earliest evidence of the institution of the rank of drum major seems to be that given by Farmer in his *History of Military Music in England*. Although the function was the same as that of today, the title was not. These officers first appeared in the reign of Edward VI (1547–1553) when Benedict Browne was sergeant trumpeter and Robert Bruer was 'master drummer'.

According to another recorder, Brigadier Sir John Smythe, the 'master drummer' title was changed to drum major in 1591.

Thus, in those early days were created all ranks and titles that we have today, including trumpet major and drum major.

There was not a military rank for leaders of regimental bands, but an interesting and revealing account of the duties of the drum major is given in *The Principles of the Art Militaire* (Henry Hexhan 1973).

'Every Regiment ought to have a drumme Majour to whom when it is watch time, the other Drummers are to repair, there to create a call, and to march with his company that is appointed for the Guard. A Drumme

Majour ought to be a grave man, able to instruct the other Drummes to beate a true march and other points of warre, to see the Drummes that beate upon a march to be duly relieved, and also to speak divers tongues and to be wise and cautelous what he shall speake to an enemy'.

Towards the end of the eighteenth century the drum major's exalted position began to decline. There had been some public outcry about floggings and other brutalities. From time to time it was found necessary to hold courts martial at the drum head. According to recorder Thomas Simes (1788) his duties included beatings upon skins other than drum skins ... 'to have with you your apparatus for punishing ... and it should be an established rule, that a man who receives lashes, or more, should pay 2d; and if punished a second time for another offence, 6d. No cat to have more than nine tails. Further, you are to carry the letters to and bring them from the Post Office. You are every morning to see that the drummers sweep and clean the officers' mess and men's necessary houses.'

The drum major did not only supervise the flogging of soldiers, but was obliged to teach his drummers how to flog them, with both hands.

For adult soldiers the punishment by flogging persisted in the army until the 1880s, but enlisted boys were flogged by the drum major up to 1903.

Nevertheless, the drum major of the twentieth century maintains an important disciplinary position and can command a regimental reverence amounting almost to adoration.

His precision of drill and leadership, as well as his prowess as a musician, are of great significance.

On parade he must be immaculate in turnout, an example to all others. Like the lilies of the field, drum majors in full ceremonial dress are more glorious to behold than was ancient Solomon. Before the appointment of drum major in the late 16th century, the senior drummer or 'sergeant' drummer, wore no distinctive multi-coloured sash, but a standard pattern leather drummer's 'carriage', a belt with metal or leather loops that secured the two drumsticks when they were not being used for drumming. Later, the sash became more elaborate by the addition of embroidered battle honours, and gradually the drumsticks were reduced in size to make room for more embellishments. Today, while very small, the sticks are an essential part of the sash, as a symbol of the drum major's original appointment.

The sash might have a royal cypher and arms as well, and the colour of the ground is taken from the unit's uniform facing colour, or branch of the service.

Badges, devices and honours must conform strictly with regulations, or be raised in sterling silver with coloured silk edges of gold and silver lace; and between the rows are heavy gold or silver fringes on which are looped the miniature drumsticks.

Now, m'dears! If this ain't enough to stir with envy the minds of onlooking, adoring ladies, there is more... The manly breasts, sturdy shoulders, brawny arms and clever hands of both drum and bugle majors bear other insignia of authority. From shoulder tabs are draped aiguillettes, all silk-plaited in the regimental colours, their ends finished off with tapered metal tags plated in silver or gold.

Twixt elbow and shoulder are worn the arm badges, in the form of gilded drums, or silver-plated bugles; and there, too, are worn the chevron bars of gold and silver, 'dressed' on the coloured ground of the regimental facings.

Some wear dress cords in gold bullion; others, ornate shoulder epaulettes, or drum major's 'wings'. All wear gloves – some of snow-white doeskin; others, pipe-clayed gauntlets with white cuffs. The 'dandies' have been known to affect gauntlet over-cuffs, which they slip over the dress-gloves and gauntlets, keeping them in place with elastic bands to ensure that their 'under-gloves' are immaculate for parade inspection.

Now then ... All this glorious tarting-up had its origin in the most primitive instrument, the drum. When brother Leslie (No. 2609406 Drummer L. G. Mays, 1st Battalion, Grenadier

Guards, Wellington Barracks) was given leave to sound Last Post and Reveille at Ashdon Church for the Armistice Memorial Service, he was tarted up in red, wearing a bearskin and smothered with that braid worn by soldiers of the Household Division who proceed slowly to places (on foot). He had a drum on his sleeve and Father told him all about its origin.

It was the invention of an over-inquisitive monkey. A langur monkey, in a dhobi ghat near Delhi. The ape had tapped on a banyan leaf which the sun had welded over half a coconut shell. Hearing strange noises the ape kept tapping away. Then, quite baffled, India's first drummer tore off the welded leaf – to find out where the music was coming from.

There is one drum that the Silent Service (Royal Navy) seldom ceases to brag about (and rightly so!). The Matelots reckon that Drake's Drum is the most famous of all. That it beats spontaneously whenever Great Britain is in danger. Then, her former one-eyed, one-armed owner (an owd East Anglian boy) will set sail from the Port of Heaven (if that's where sailors end up!) to drum her enemies away and repeat his former performance after playing bowls.

Hang on a minute! ... It's all right. I thought I heard Drake's drum a-beating. It was the memsahib rattlin' teaspoons ... It's 'Drumming Up' time!

4

Doctor William Palmer

Tonight, with a mite of luck, I shall be in the Community Hall, Linton, Cambridgeshire, playing whist. Over the last few years about half a dozen of us Suffolk and Essex 'foreigners' venture forth on Monday nights to the weekly whist drive.

It is a welcome change from glaring at the goggle-box, for we are in the very best of company, and during play, before and after play and in the tea interval, we have a good old gossip; mainly about who once knew whom, what they did, and why, and how much better life used to be in neighbouring villages half a century and more ago.

Last time out, we nattered about doctors and nurses who tended the sick, lame and lazy in the villages of Lindon, Ashdon and Bartlow, and about Mrs Fisher.

Whatever its superstitions may have been, Ashdon, like most villages, had one female upon whom every family relied. Mrs Fisher, of Ashdon, who was given two apt titles, 'mole catcher' and 'body snatcher', was a tiny tot of a woman.

A widow for many years, she lived alone in a cottage on the brow of Knox Hill. The majority of Ashdon's babies were delivered by her, usually without a doctor in attendance. 'Me time's comin', but I shall be all right. I've seen Mrs Fisher and got bespoke!'

Not only would she deliver the child, but for days after the birth she would tend the other children of the family, run

23

errands, do the cooking and washing until the vitality of the mother was restored.

She also performed the 'last offices', as she called them, the 'laying out' of the dead. We did not boast a district nurse until 1918. When Miss Cant arrived at Clematis Cottage she had few possessions other than her heavy bicycle and 'that owd bag o'trickery'.

She had to serve several parishes and cycled many miles in all weathers at all times of the day and night, along the unlit, flint-strewn roads and tracks.

It was a pleasure to see her in her blue uniform, speaking to old labourers on the fields. They would touch their peaked caps, and say, 'Mornin', nuss, dear. A good day to ye!' And Pudden would say to old Barnet, 'Ain't she a little beauty? She's one o' we!'

The nearest doctor lived at Saffron Walden, and drove the five miles in a pony trap. He came in emergencies, by urgent request, often put off till the last moment because the household could not muster the half-crown fee. Visits and prescriptions had to be paid for, of course, plus a bit extra for a night call.

My mother's doctor, Dr William Palmer, practising in Linton, Cambridgeshire, started a 'round'. He first came to minister to Ashdon on a bicycle, then, not to be outdone by 'they posh owd quacks from Bunkum' (Saffron Walden), he bought a pony trap.

Soon, he opened a surgery in Ashdon in a room behind the bar of the Rose and Crown, taking a partner, Dr Gill. Attending twice weekly, Dr Palmer was conscientious and benevolent, and endeared himself to the old and ill, to whom a bedside manner was a mystery. 'A proper Christian' and 'a real genuine poor man's doctor, boy', said the farmworkers who flocked to his surgery.

A second surgery was started at the White Horse, just over the Crown Hill, by Dr Thelwell of Saffron Walden, and when he died it came under the charge of Dr Hepworth, also of Saffron Walden.

These two came in posh new motor cars, all bright and

beamy with acetylene headlamps. There was but one motor car owner in our village, and all at once Dr Palmer hurled himself into the realms of internal combustion on a pop-popping motor bike. He was big physically, but his was but a puny machine. He looked somewhat lugubrious and discon-solate as the Saffron Waldeners overtook him in their shiny limousines.

Paying the doctor was a problem for farmhands, whose wages averaged 12 shillings a week. It was worse after retirement age, for they received no pension before Lloyd George's National Insurance Act of 1911.

'If it worn't fer the cost o' that owd wooden box w' brass handles an' payin' fer that owd hearse, undertaker, top hats, wreaths, parson and gravediggers' fees, I'd be better orf a-dyin', bor. Nobody wants ye arter you've wukked out yer guts on the land!'

But a local branch was formed of a benefit society, the Loyal Order of Ancient Shepherds (The Shepherds' Club).

Lodge meetings were held in the dub room of the Rose and Crown and subscribing members were entitled to medical attention and a few shillings a week for a limited period. Dr Palmer was mainly responsible for treatment and the clerical work.

When bluff Dr Gill returned to Ireland, Dr Palmer took a new partner, Dr Wilson, who lashed out and bought a brand new motor car (chauffeur-driven!).

Nothing, not even Palmer's potent pills, could have given our villages more pleasure than to see him being driven in style along the narrow country roads and lanes.

But his splendour was short-lived. From a travelling sales-man came the story that Palmer was about to retire. 'Oi reckon owd Palmer's bin took over by one o' they Scotsmen... Now we'll hev ter pay fer bloody treatment in advance!'

As is usual in country villages, the news carrier was correct. The practice was taken over by a magnificent Scot, Dr A. M. Brown, who came to love Ashdon as much as his patients loved him. It is a long time since he retired to a new house in Scotland, which he named 'Ashdon', and now he is dead.

'A worthier candidate for wings and a halo never existed', was the Ashdon opinion.

Ashdon has been fortunate in doctors, but some of the older folk of the village, and certainly some of Linton's whist drivers, still cherish William Palmer's memory, and not only because he used to write about our village in the *Cambridge Chronicle*, with his friend Cyril Fox...

'It's all owd pills an' pellets nowadays, an' I fair rattle as I walk to the surgery ... Palmer's owd Jollop were the stuff. That made weak men strong an' strong men impossible ... Yew just ask the gals!'

Jasper the gamekeeper was knocking on a bit, well over his allotted span of three score years and ten when he attended Palmer's surgery.

'Mornin' doctor! ... I want some of your Jollop. I reckon my virility ain't much cop!'

'Now Jasper! You must put your mind on higher things and take things easy. Sit in your armchair and read some good books.'

'HELLABIT! I've been hale an' hearty all my life, but my virility has let me down. There's suffin else ... I'm a paid up member of the Shepherds' Club, and entitled to Jollop free of charge'.

The doctor mixed him up a tidy bottle. 'Take it in water after meals. Now then, as a point of medical interest, tell me when you first noticed this sad state of affairs.'

'What affairs?'

'Your loss of virility.'

'Recently, doctor!'

'How recently?'

'Once last night, and twice this morning.'

5

John Evans

When I had ripened to 81 years of age on 5th August 1988, I read my birthday cards and realised that I was getting on a bit and should make the most of the days that seemed numbered. So, in my best Suffolk handwriting and in the lingo of the Leek, I wrote a greeting to a dear old friend ... 'PEN BLWYDD HAPUS A DYMUNIAD DA'.

No one could have had a dearer, and certainly not older, old friend because on 19th August 1988 my old friend – already the oldest man in the world – would receive from Her Majesty the Queen another telegram, who had sent him half-a-score. This next one would be his eleventh. Not because he was eleven, but 111! And the Queen sent it to Welsh Wales and created a precedent for Telecom ... it was delivered *on time!*

Buck House's secretary must have had one helluva job with John Evans' address. It resembles a Chinese weather report in Gaelic cipher: Brynhawdd, Llewitha, Fforestfach, Swansea.

My family know it and love it. Privileged members and ex-members of the Household Cavalry have paraded on John's front lawn on occasions of consequence. Some were tarted up in full ceremonial dress and armed with swords. These were youngish serving soldiers of English origin who could not wrap their tongues around John's address. To them it became (and always will be) 'Taff's Caff'.

Vera, my Welsh wife, was born in Loughor, quite near

Fforestfach and midway between Swansea and Llanelli. My second son lies there permanently, after the Swansea Blitz.

Amwell, John's son, served many years in my old regiment, The Royal Dragoons. Amwell married Betty, one of Vera's closest friends. By the friendship of the women and the comradeship of their old cavalry husbands, there was forged a very strong link. As an old Suffolk Punch farm labourer I soon recognised and was impressed by the warm companionship of the miners and steelworkers of Glamorgan and Carmarthenshire. They possessed the same qualities as the East Anglians and gave a generous interpretation of that old phrase 'Galon y Sais wrth Gmro'.

Gwlad y Gan (Land of Song) is the only title for Welsh Wales. There is music in the lilt of the language, in the air, the hills and in the labyrinthine burrows of the Rhondda. I used to sing with miners in The Fountain, a pub in Pontardulais where pints of Buckley and Felinfoel ale would be pumped in readiness for the choir before they emerged from choir practice in a college half a mile away. They could be heard before they entered to have a sing-song after practising for a brace of hours.

Before I say more about the oldest Welsh Nightingale in the World, and his singing, I will quote from the Welsh Press.

Western Mail, Thursday 7th July 1988:
TREAT FROM DOWN UNDER
FOR OLDEST MAN IN THE WORLD...

The world's oldest man, 110-year-old former Swansea miner Mr John Evans, got a musical treat from Down Under yesterday.

A 40-strong Australian choir on its way to the Llangollen International Festival stopped at Mr Evans' cottage in Fforestfach, Swansea, to sing him some of his favourite Welsh songs.

The Sydney-Welsh Choir lined up on the lawn in front of the house and launched into *Myfanwy* and other Welsh favourites.

Despite his 110 years, a remarkably fit Mr Evans repaid the compliment by singing a Welsh song he learned 90 years ago.

'He loves singing and he claims it makes him feel years younger', said his son Amwell, 74, who shares the miner's cottage with his famous father.

'My father was thrilled when he heard a choir was going to sing just for him. He loves Welsh songs and hymns, they remind him of his younger days!'

A spokesman for the Sydney-Welsh Choir, which contains a number of Welsh exiles, said they could not pass Swansea without honouring the world's oldest man.

'We had learned stories in the international Press that John likes Welsh singing so we decided to give him a taste of Welsh singing Australian style.

'He proved he can still get through a tune himself and we were all amazed at his alertness and the good shape he was in', the spokesman said.

South Wales Evening Post, Thursday 7th July 1988
NOW JOHN SINGS FOR THE CHOIR

In a strong, clear voice, 110-year-old John Evans sat on his front lawn and sang a hymn for an audience of 44 choristers who had travelled half way round the world to sing for him.

John, the world's oldest man, is distantly related to a member of the Sydney Male Choir which had flown from Australia to compete in the Llangollen Eisteddfod.

The 44-strong choir journeyed from Cardiff by coach especially to sing for John outside his home at Fforestfach, Swansea.

Surrounded by choristers, family and friends, he sang along with them as they harmonised in true Welsh style. Then, for him, those Welsh favourites *Myfanwy* and *Gwahoddiad*, along with Negro spiritual *Play on Your Harp*. In return, a smiling John sang *Lead Kindly Light*, a hymn he had learnt only last year. The Choir, in Britain for a five-week tour, sang in Los Angeles on the way over and had given concerts in Cardiff.

29

Choir president, David Hutton, who hails from Tenby, received a portrait of John to take back to Sydney, and presented John with the latest album.

Obviously delighted at the tribute paid to him, John told the choir, 'I don't know how to express myself with all this kindness shown to me'.

*   *   *

John knew how to express himself when his son Amwell married Betty. In Suffolk they would say, 'That wor more'n' weddin'. I reckon it wor a weddin' and a half!'

The 'splicing' was solemnised in Fforestfach's chapel, 'Bethlehem Cadle', as rain gushed down and umbrellas sprouted.

Smack on time, for in the cavalry punctuality is the first morality, there sounded a trumpet call. It was 1330 hours precisely. There were no Household Trumpeters, but the organist played *The Trumpet Call* (Purcell) and my heels clicked together and my thumbs seemed to shoot as if by magic behind the seams!

There followed that wonderful hymn *Calon Lan* – to me, the sound of Wales:

> Nid wy'n gofyn bywyd moethus,
> Aur y byd na'i berlau man;
> Gifyn wyf am galon hapus,
> Calon onest, calon lan.
>
> Calon lan yn llawn daioni,
> Tecach yw na'r lili dlos;
> Does ond calon lan all ganur –
> Canu'r dydd a chanu'r nos.

If I could have been the Director of Music for the world, I would have scrubbed all our stupid national anthems and made *Calon Lan* the international national anthem. If all the world kept to its precepts our hymns could be scrubbed as well, for this world would then be cured of its worst affliction

The Gee-Gee disease … double G for Greed and Grasp! Roughly translated, the hymn means, 'I ask not for riches or wealth, but for a pure heart, whiter than the purest lily' (Tecach yw na'r lili dlos) and the ability to sing by day and night. Nowadays we have but one love. It is spelt with the sterling sign, and its music is played on every TV programme – straight from the Stocks and Shares Band, on computerised cash registers. DYDD and NOS!

Vows made, ring adjusted, blessings given, and singles made into a new half-section, we blessed them again with the wedding hymn, *Love Divine, all Loves Excelling* – followed by a morsel of Handel's *Largo*. Betty and Amwell were wed.

Five days were needed for the celebration. That is how and why Taff's Caff galloped into life. Upon the front lawn of Llewitha stood a monster marquee, similar to those used by Maharajahs for the Delhi Durbar. Before a riding master could crack a whip, the Blues and Royals became 'Quarterblokes'. Provisions, mostly moist, appeared on long tables groaning with the weight of splendid Welsh fodder. To ensure there was light enough to sing, motor headlights were focused to shine inside. Coaches were ready to whisk us off to the Gower Hotel, to Llanelli Ballroom for dancing, to other places for wine and song. Late or early, we always reported back to Taff's Caff and Guard Commander John Evans.

Bulbs flashed, cameras clicked. It seemed that all of Wales had to be photographed; in singles, pairs, groups; with relations, without relations and dogs, and birds and cats.

John Evans declined

'Better to take my dog for a walk!'

We insisted!

'Only if Vera is standing with me!'

Vera was in Tyrcoed, Loughor, the old home. We whisked John to Loughor, brought him back and dressed him for the camera. We made him a Blue and Royal. How spruce he looked. Good enough for guard mounting with scarlet-plumed helmet, snow-white sword-slings and lily-white gauntlets – but in the position for 'sloping swords' he was out of order.

31

He stood, at the slope, with his sword on his left shoulder. Major Spud Lewis, MBE, who enlisted with me in March 1924, took John to task. 'That man there ... your sword should be on your right shoulder. Change it!'

But John was insubordinate.

'I will NOT! For sixty years I worked down the mines. Every day I carried my pick and used it with my left hand. What is good enough for the pick is too good for the sword!'

Born at Llewitha in 1877, he first went to work as a miner at the age of 12 and remained a miner until his enforced retirement at 73. His memory and voice are as clear as the song of the thrush when he speaks of his life and international events most of us have only read about: the Battle of Rorke's Drift, Gordon's death at Khartoum, Queen Victoria's diamond jubilee, the sinking of the *Titanic*, Scott's ill-fated Polar expedition and the World Wars. He was around for the birth of the motor car and has marvelled at the greatest technological achievements and changes, most of all the trip to the moon.

But his voice saddens when he begins to speak of the demise of the coalfield and he sometimes sings a Welsh lovesong of sadness to cheer himself and his listeners. A good song, one used 'on the box' to advertise Guinness ... *Myfanwy*.

Even for his 111th birthday party he refused to break the practice of a lifetime. A total abstainer and non-smoker, he celebrated with a good strong cup of tea, a hunk of birthday cake, and enough puff to blow out eleven cake candles, one for every decade of his life.

John attributes his long life to his religious faith, music and song, and total abstinence from alcohol and tobacco, aided and abetted by herbs from the wild garden of Llewitha.

Mrs Evans cured many folk of ailments that sometimes baffled medics and vets, and saved Vera from a threatened amputation of perhaps an arm, or certainly a finger, into which a broom-handle splinter had entered and declined to leave. For weeks she was in agony. She became as white as a ghost, thin as a hayrake and completely dejected.

'Go to Llewitha!' said her brother Islwyn. 'Let Mrs Evans see it. See it before they lance it again!'

In less than a week the splinter was out and the roses were back in Vera's cheeks.

'How did she do it when the quack failed?' I asked.

'With ointment she made from her garden herbs, after washing them with soft soap and rainwater and drying them in front of the wood fire.'

If you ever go to Llewitha you will smell the goodness, not only of the herb garden, but of all the occupants.

6

Boy Waller

Boy Waller served with me in the band of the Royal Dragoons. I was Boy Mays. In the army you remained 'Boys' until you had reached the age of eighteen years. That was in 1924. Today such striplings are entitled to be classified as 'Young Musicians'.

At one of our Combined Cavalry Memorial Services in Hyde Park, everybody seemed to be present bar Boy Waller. Half the old cavalrymen of Great Britain were looking for him, or asking about him. Just because he had put a brace of Life Guards back a few horses' lengths the year before.

A few of us Old Royals were having the annual natter, refighting old battles, licking old wounds and counting each other's medals.

Then, without a 'by your leave, gentlemen', a couple of Life Guards gatecrashed into our throng, cocked up their ears and began listening, for a change, to intelligent conversation.

One Life Guard laughed at one of our jokes; without our permission.

'You, sir!' said Waller, fixing him with a bloodshot eye. 'Who the hell told you to laugh? You have not been formally introduced! Who and *what* are you?'

'I was once the Band Corporal Major. I knew you had been in the Band of the Royals, so I thought I would come over. I hope you don't mind.'

'DON'T MIND?' yelled Waller. 'You have the nerve to say that *standing up*? You should be on your bended knees, grovelling and supplicating!' And lo and behold, the Tinner (Life Guard) loved it and knelt and bowed his head and put his palms together like a Hindu blessing, a Moslem. After the Memorial Service and march back to Hyde Park Barracks, with all the cavalry bands playing and leading their individual regiments, we had a grand reunion party, to which the Tinner was invited.

But that was way back in 1978. We have not clapped eyes on Boy Waller since. Some said he had retired to dwell in Suffolk. Others thought he had kicked the bucket, but there was no mention of his passing in the regimental journal, *The Blue and Royal*.

He was very much in evidence at Shorncliffe in 1935. The Royals returned to Blighty and were stationed there just after a spell in Meerut, about 40 miles north of Delhi. We were under the command of Lieutenant-Colonel A. D. Wintle, MC, FRSL, an old friend of mine who took more boredom out of the 1950s and '60s than any other Englishman. I took part in the eleven-year war he waged against the law, and we won at the last fence, the House of Lords, where we made legal history.

Wintle lost an eye, most of his left hand, and the use of his right knee in the First World War, gaining the MC and a citation: 'For marked gallantry and initiative of the highest order'.

Wintle was a strict disciplinarian. He licked his wounds and licked the Law Lords, but Boy Waller had put him back a few horses' lengths when they met on the barrack square, at Shorncliffe – by a deliberate contravention of Part 1 Orders. The Adjutant had made it dear that in no circumstances would anyone cross the holy of holies, the barrack square, unless they were being doubled across it, marched, trolled, cantered or galloped across it in the course of drill or some other useful military enterprise, even if only by an unwanted, unpaid, acting NCO.

But Wintle's one eye had the shock of its life and almost crashed through the glass of his monocle.

Across that square slouched Boy Waller, his hands deep into the pockets of the filthiest pair of canvas trousers East of Suez. His head was bent, his feet inadequately encased in tattered remnants of gym shoes and he was whistling as he meandered un-Dragoon-like towards the NAAFI canteen.

'WALLAH, ATTENTION!' Wintle's bark halted the tramp and his whistling. Hands shot from the pockets. He stood to attention. '*Sir!*'

'Come here, Waller!' Waller doubled, halted and saluted.

'Why are you crossing the square? Why are you wearing those disgusting shoes and trousers? Have you nothing useful to do?'

An unwavering, cheeky voice replied, 'It's quicker across t'square. I've nowt t'do 'cept sup tea, an' NAAFI tea don't deserve ceremonial dress, SIR!'

Always fair, Wintle appreciated the humour and logic, but decided that Waller should be gingered up.

'You will get dressed in walking-out order and report to my office in ten minutes!'

In ten minutes Waller knocked on Wintle's door. He was closely inspected, given instructions and one half-crown.

'As you have nothing useful to do for yourself, you will now do something useful for us both. With this money you will "march" to the Post Office and buy me one half-penny stamp. You will march to attention there and back. Off you go!'

Salutes were swapped. Waller marched off to attention, properly dressed and carrying his walking-out whip, with blancoed tab and regimental crest.

Hours later, Wintle opened his door to another knock. 'Oh, it's you again Waller. You have not deserted as I had hoped. Where's my stamp?'

From the nearside pocket of his smart Bedford cord riding breeches, Waller produced a pill box; inside, wrapped in cotton wool, one half-penny stamp. He handed it over.

'Thank you! Where is my change?'

From the offside pocket of his smart Bedford cord riding

breeches, Waller tugged out a Barclay's bank bag containing 59 half-pennies.

'Your change, sir. Care to check it?'

'No thank you, Waller, I'll take your word for it; but why have you been so long?'

'Tooker long time to round up them ha'pennies, sir!'

Two weeks later Waller was on HQ Parade. He had to wait because the Squadron was always paid in alphabetical order. There were only two 'W's in HQ Squadron, but Wade had been paid. When his name was called, Waller took three paces forward and saluted the paying officer. He had applied for credit payment, to have a 'big pay' for his weekend leave. The salute was returned by the paying officer, one Aldred Daniel Wintle, MC, who said:

'I was told you wanted a big pay, Waller. You will be pleased to learn that you are getting the biggest big pay in military history. Since you prefer to deal in half-pennies I have arranged with the Bank of England that you should be paid in your favourite coinage!'

Sixteen blue-line Barclay's bank coin bags (each containing 100 half-pennies) were shoved towards the young soldier.

'Your *big pay*, Waller!' said Wintle. 'Care to check it?'

Not a muscle twitched as Waller replied, 'No thank you, sir. I'll take *your* word for it!'

The sequel occurred during the 1939–45 war. Wintle had been released from imprisonment in the Tower of London, following his trial by court martial. He had been found not guilty of threatening to shoot his senior officer in Intelligence (MI5). He was bound for Liverpool and awaited a train connection at Crewe.

Along the platform he spotted a tall, smart, gentlemanly figure in immaculate mufti. He walked swiftly towards him.

'Bless my soul if it isn't Boy Waller of the Royal Dragoons!'

The sartorially splendid gentleman clicked his heels and stood to attention. With eyes a-twinkle he replied, '*No sir!*' Captain Waller, Royal Electrical and Mechanical Engineers. Care to check it, sir?'

'No, thank you, Captain!' replied Wintle with a grin. 'I'll take your word for it!'

Most of the few of us who survived those wonderful years would like to contact Waller. His name has escaped the obituary column of our regimental journal, *The Blue and Royal*. Is he in Heaven, or down in Hell? Young Waller, who we all loved so well!

7

Clarky Cooper

I was that surprised on that Saturday morning you could have knocked me over with a Chieftain tank.

At 1100 hours precisely, just as the sun broke through London's murky rainclouds, Her Majesty the Queen arrived (smack on time, as usual) at Horse Guards for the Trooping the Colour of the 2nd Battalion of the Scots Guards, on her official birthday.

What a magnificent show it was! With a war-disabled major of the Royal Lincolnshire Regiment (The Moonrakers) I stood wet-footed in a large puddle by the Inner Line of Sentries (North), outside the Admiralty building. There were five of us in a convoy, all East Anglians.

We felt mighty proud and about ten feet tall; prouder than Polstead peacocks when we heard a hairy, colourful American speak loudly to his blonde. 'Say, honey, this is the only country in the world where they can lay on a show like this.'

East Anglian blacksmith Charles Cooper crept into the act when the Household Cavalry marched past. Two of the Blues and Royals wore black plumes and carried axes. All the others (apart from the Band) wore scarlet plumes and carried swords. My old mate from Cavendish, who was not all that well informed about the Household Cavalry, looked flummoxed when I told him the axe bearers were farriers and wore a horseshoe badge on their sleeves.

Later, over noggins in the Senior NCOs' Mess at Hyde Park

Barracks, I told him about two farriers of consequence. The first, Shoey Dempster of the Royal Dragoons at Beaumont Barracks, Aldershot. In 1925, having left the Band and just passed out at riding school, full of pomp and circumstance I took my new sabre squadron horse to the forge.

'Slap some new shoes on my charger. All round!' said I to Farrier Corporal Dempster.

'Who the hell do you think you are? Bloody band rat! Been in the army about ten minutes and start layin' down the law like some red-tabbed brigadier. Call me "corporal"! Stand to attention and look at them badges!'

Above his chevrons were two badges of brass. A shoe, the insignia of the farrier. A spur, the badge of the Rough Rider.

'What about them?' said I, feeling a bit scared.

'What about 'em? I'll tell you what about 'em, young shaver. I'm the only cavalryman in the whole bleedin' world what's allowed to wear them two badges. I am a rough-ridin' farrier and I shoe war 'orses at the bloody gallop!'

Despite this extraordinary prowess, Shoey Dempster could not hold a candle to Clarky Cooper, who, when I was a schoolboy at Ashdon, used to let me pump his forge bellows and give me horseshoe nails for boring holes in conkers. He could not shoe horses at the gallop, but he was a wheelwright, blacksmith and farrier as well. He also functioned as the village undertaker, making sturdy oak coffins which he boasted were so strong they would last a lifetime, but his main work was the repairing of tumbrils, dog-carts, wagons, wheelbarrows and wheels, combining carpentry, paint-making and painting.

Two-storeyed and well lit by windows glazed with oddly assorted panes, his workshop was enormous. The working length occupied the whole of the ground floor, where tools of all sorts lay to hand: handsaws, pad-saws, bow-saws, rip saws and coping saws, each with its purpose. There were all kinds of knives, planes, spokeshaves, long-handled augers and endless templates. Some planes were concave, some convex; tri-planes, jack planes, block planes, smoothers. Chisels of all widths and queer distortions stood in racks. There were sledgehammers, ball-payne hammers, block-and-nail hammers of the Warrington pattern, beechwood mallets, and always a big mallet made of apple wood and bound with iron hoops, the beetle for driving in stakes and splitting logs and hard-grained timber.

His oldest tool, the adze, was razor-edged and Clarky could true rough timber with it as expertly as a carpenter with a plane, but its main use was for taking off the bulk of unwanted rough wood and roughly shaping the work.

Wagons and tumbrils were painted in colours usually chosen generations before; traditionally each farmer kept to his own. It was simple for us to determine the owner of a field by the colour of the farm carts. The Haggers of Overhall Farm used a deep blue. Ashdon Place Farm had used a light blue, but when the Luddingtons came to Walton's Park and its farms, they brought with them their own colour, Cambridgeshire Beige.

Wheelwrights bought the pigments from the county town and ground and mixed their own paint. First, they went over every inch of woodwork with smoothers and fillers, then on would go the priming of white or pink, a coat of flat, and two good coats of colour, and to finish off and make the wagon shine in the sunlight, two coats of clear varnish. Finally, they would carefully paint in signwriting the name and address of the farm. Then, there would stand a magnificent wagon; sturdy, wheeled and iron shod, and shining. Fit to last one hundred years.

Charles (Clarky) Cooper junior had his smithy on the Radwinter Road, adjoining his father's yard. His cottage stood opposite the Baptist chapel, whose congregation sometimes objected to Clarky's 'strong wuds'. His work was exacting and arduous, but wielding heavy hammers was a fine exercise and he revelled in his extraordinary strength and rippling muscles.

There was scarcely an implement used in agriculture that Clarky did not have to make, repair or renew. Farm labourers came with problems, for most of them had to find their own tools. They asked for left-handed scythes, wider or narrower hoe blades to chop out weeds from the wider or narrower drillings; men with big arms would demand longer scythe blades, and gamekeepers and poachers asked for long-bladed curved spades to dig out rabbits and ferrets.

He sharpened scythes and sickles, axes, and every type of edged tool, often replacing the broken or split old stales. He made pitchforks and four-tined forks, plough spuds, coulters, shears, drills and harrows, sometimes renewing the entire set of teeth for worn-out harrows.

To watch him throwing nuggets, busily attending his fire by throwing coals through small jets of water from a long-handled ladle – all the while manipulating his bellows with his left forearm, blowing cascades of sparks up the forge chimney – was a sight for sore eyes. In desperate haste, he withdrew white-hot metal from the furnace and pounded it with mammoth blows, making bigger sparks fly.

As a farrier he had no equal; stripped to the waist and wearing a hide apron, perspiration streamed down his magnificent torso, the rivulets showing white against the smoke and grimes on his flesh.

Shires, Suffolk Punches and Clydesdales stood stock still as he nailed heavy shoes onto their horny hooves. Clarky never had to renail a shoe that he had put on. A cloud of acrid smoke rose from the scorching horn as he moulded a hot shoe to the hoof preparatory to the final fixing. He cleaned the frogs and blackened and polished each hoof until it shone.

Horses leaving Clarky's forge seemed to hold their heads higher and lift hairy fores like ballet dancers, as if proud to show to the village their clean feet and bright new shoes. Children's ponies, the shepherd's hairy cob, and the elegant hunters of the gentry, were brought from miles around to the expert who knew them all.

In spare moments he shaped new shoes to hang on the forge battens ready for use, and he always sang when making shoes for the shire horses.

Leaning on the doorpost of the smithy, hands thrust deep into the pockets of his hide apron, he would watch a pair of newly shod Suffolks go clip-clopping down Radwinter Road, smile that kind of smile that meant nothing to anyone but himself, nod his head, and take a deep breath (perhaps it was a sigh) before turning to the murk and heat of the forge where many another job awaited him.

His smithy was the meeting place of the unemployed and the sick, who would congregate there in muffled old coats, some with sacking thrown over their shoulders. There were no pensions then, no health service. They came for the comforting warmth of Clarky's in the nip of winter. Perhaps to admire his strength, so different from theirs.

But Clarky was our hero, idol and delight, who let us boys pump his bellows and gave us bright new horseshoe nails to bore holes in our shiny conkers; and made steel runners for our home-made toboggans and iron hoops and guiders. He was our friend.

But never a word durst we mention to parents about our friend and the visits.

Clarky used to drink and swear suffin terrible. We all hoped we would grow up to have muscles like him, and be able to drink and swear even better.

8

Poddy and the Parson

Harking back, over half a century, I can recall when our village choirs took time off to oil their tonsils and rest their vocalising cords. Anthems, hymns, psalms and songs of praise! Our human larks and nightingales had been hard at it, first rehearsing with particular fervour for the Harvest Festivals, then singing the lot at full throttle on that important Sunday when loudly and fervently was raised the song of Harvest Home. Our churches looked more like God's gardens than God's houses on that day, and were sights for sore eyes.

Flowers and fruit festooned the altars. On walls, pillars, pew-ends and window sills were spread the good things from the earth from farmers' fields and cottagers' gardens alike. Corn-dolly sheaves were plaited and interwoven 'twixt brass chain links supporting the old (but now new and 'electrified') brass oil lamps.

Long before the due hour, men and boys had already donned bible-black cassocks and lily-white surplices. Some would have turned down the corners of pages, more readily to find the selected hymns. All were toting their books and anthem sheets; some would be softly humming snatches of hymns or psalms, running themselves up and bursting to sing about God and Goodness. Bells would be pealing across fields and meadows to farmers and farmhands, their downy, multi-coloured ropes dancing to the weight of the cast metal bells soaring so strongly that they sometimes would take the lighter bell-ringers with them.

Whole families would be flocking to church. Children first (for Sunday school), then the parents. A brief pause at the central aisle, an almost imperceptible bow to the altar, then in the pew a rustling of skirts (jeans had not been invented) and gropings for hassocks. Knees and heads would be bent in prayer and eyes shut tight, while some merely shaded their eyes to hoodwink the parson, or to see who was present or who had bought a new hat. All would kneel until the bells were silent and the organ began to pipe out the opening bars of the processional hymn. Then... off knees, fill the lungs with clean East Anglian air and out with the song: 'Come, ye thankful people, come...

Always an important day in the lives of country folk (before bulldozers and developers poked in their grasping and ruination), it seemed to me that it was more important in our village churches over 60 years ago, when we gave far more thanks for the very little we had.

Memory tells me that farmhands' voices seemed more powerful and women's eyes more moist.

After Harvest Thanksgiving, flowers, fruit, vegetables and money were taken to the old, sick and poor, but all was not completely gathered in terms of toil for choirboys, of which I was one. Christmas was coming up the straight. New anthems required more choir practice. Hymns and chants were different and shoals of carols were bunged in for make-weight.

Although pleasant and rewarding to walk two miles back and forth to church in spring and summer (four times a week), the going was hard for poor old Shanks's pony in the tail end of autumn and in winter.

Church Hill would often be thick-carpeted with snow drifts. There were no snow ploughs and only one motor in the village, whose driver was taken to task and threatened with police prosecution for dangerous speeding (tearing through the village at nearly twenty miles an hour). Snow or not, we arrived at church, breathless and sweating, with scarce enough puff to croak a demi-semi-quaver, let alone those lung-busting breves used in psalms and anthems!

Most of the Ashdon choirboys, and sometimes just us few from Bartlow Hamlet, would band together for proper carol singing. No one was in charge of us ... no choirmistress, no parson. We were *free* and would walk miles to the remotest village ends and widely separated farms and sing louder than we did in church. We sang as loud as we felt.

For these warbling excursions we made our own lanterns, old jam jars with stuck-in candles and handles made from binder string. We would set off on wintry nights, all jam-jarred and collection-boxed. Muffs, scarves, woollen helmets, winter-warmers and leggings made from old oat sacks were the garments we made and wore to keep out the cold. Villagers could see us before they heard us, for even our puny candlelight could so easily be seen in our lovely lightless land.

It must have looked a pretty straggly torchlight procession from a distance, particularly to those Londoners who had left to dodge the German Gothas and Zeppelins; but close-up it could not have looked more Christmassy, all red of cheek, our frosted breath blowing pink and yellow through soft candle-light.

Farmers were the best payers: Tillbrooks, Furzes, Haggers and the Webbs. Usually they would invite us in, particularly if they had been at the bottle. We liked that, for we could sing to them in the warm, save our candle power and get silver coins instead of copper, plus hot mince pies and ripe Blenheim Orange apples – all brown-pippy and mellow through ripening on soft oat straw in the loft.

Between Christmas and the New Year there was always a spate of choral singing and bell practice. On one occasion the Reverend Hartly (once a chaplain in the Royal Navy and not too clever at mixing with young country folk), got very frosty and doubled practice night attendance. Rumour had it that old Starchy Williams, village undertaker and bass soloist, had complained that boys laughed at his Adam's apple when he sang in our choir. Hartly thought we should be gingered up.

With that end in view we were ordered to report to the

parish church, where the campanologists were ringing out wild bells, instead of the Sunday School building. There were plenty of flying clouds and several degrees of frost on that wintry night; enough to crisp the top of a thick blanket of snow.

Poddy Coote, the leading choirboy, who later worked with me on Ashdon Place Farm (where we used to sing hymns and psalms for our bird-scaring), hatched a plot.

When everybody else was wending their way back to home and fireside, there was one who was not. Lo and behold, it was undertaker Starchy Williams. By some unaccountable circumstance he found himself all alone – locked in the belfry.

And when all the Christian folk of Ashdon had gone upstairs, were on their knees a-saying prayers, including the Reverend Hartly, a sound rang through that wintry night. One wild bell alone was ringing out to the wild sky. It was not the customary toll for calling people to church, or of sending the departed to Heaven ... more of a feverish, frantic clanging.

When the Reverend Hartly arrived back at the church, after plodding half a mile in deep snow, to set Starchy free, he had to make the same trip all over again, in reverse (twice). He had forgotten to bring the key.

'*Retribushun!*' said the leading choirboy. 'That's what it were, retribushun!'

Poddy might well have been right, but retribution or commonsense, or both, or neither, something worked. Our doubled choir practice was halved forthwith.

Many years afterwards I was stationed in Main Barrack, Abbassia, Cairo, with the Royal Dragoons. We formed a carol party for the Christmas of 1929. Most of the choristers were Bandsmen. We sang to all and sundry and then proceeded to decorate one dining hall for our Christmas din-dins.

Not a sprig of holly was available in the land of the Sphinx. We made our own by cutting big shiny leaves with scalloped edges; by pinning red beads to leaf stems we made our Gippo holly more realistic than Suffolk holly, without getting scratched. We disregarded mistletoe; we had no one to kiss.

Being Dragoons, ever the masters of improvisation, but not permitted to pin Christmas cards on bug-ridden barrack walls, we swiped saddle-blankets and draped them from rafters, as back-cloths.

We then assembled the artistic minority. Before old King Fuad I could say 'Cleopatra', pictures prettier than Picasso's appeared on the blankets in every known colour, in dyed cotton wool which, like good horse dung, will stick on anything.

Cavalry chargers could be discerned dragging laden sleighs round the Pyramids, through mountains of pale pink snow, through forests of orange-tinted pine trees and brigades of Gippo cavalry. Plum duffs dripped with pale blue custard, and our officers were caricatured over our regimental motto, *Spectemur Agendo* ('by our deeds we are known').

As an ex-chorister, my day was made by a brace of carols. One was extremely rude and told a workhouse master what to do with his lovely Christmas pudding; the other was handwritten on regimental paper by a Trooper unable to attend as he was serving fourteen days in the Cairo clink:

> Hark the Herald Angels shout
> Six more days and I'll be out!
> Happy Xmas, Jock

My thoughts flew straight back from Cairo and its sunshine to that East Anglian night of a frantic bellringer ringing in 'Retribushun'.

Poddy was to blame for it all. As leading choirboy he could command or suggest. One night he told brother Les and me to swap choirstalls with the two Fisher brothers. The Fishers sat opposite, with a good view of old Starchy the undertaker, who sat behind us.

'Keep an eye on Starchy when he sings the Trinity Hymn. Watch 'is owd throat!'

Starchy had a huge Adam's apple. The first three words of the Trinity Hymn (No. 160, Ancient & Modern) are 'Holy'. 'Holy, Holy, Holy, Lord God, Almighty!' At the first syllable of the first 'Holy' Starchy's Adam's apple shot out of his surplice, and dithered. At the second syllable it bolted down his cassock like a rabbit dodging a ferret.

Brother Les and I laughed out loud – in church! We got tickings off and a good hiding. So, now you know!

9

Rats!

On a very wet, golf-precluding day in August 1974, after reading the letters in the *East Anglian Daily Times*, my misery intensified.

According to some cunning calculation, two gentlemen postulated that England had become far more musical, and London the musical centre of this wicked world.

In some respects they were not far off the mark. Much was mentioned about long-playing records and the outpourings of music of all kinds and at all times by radio and television. Countless columns had been concocted concerning the performances of continental composers and conductors. Arts Councils eulogised upon the pennies they have poured out to produce concerts or to have music taught in schools, universities, and even in prisons.

Now, this is very laudable. But it would appear that these cunning calculators, whose knowledge of music is so profound, have either put a foot wrong, or have taken too many bars' rest to pen a mite of praise for certain persons who have made positive contributions to British music.

Throughout the regiments of the British Army, among the Royal Marines and the Royal Air Force, bandmasters and directors of music have deservedly received high acclaim. The bandmaster's influence is felt in all ranks, not merely by those under his immediate charge, his band and band boys. But over the years, ever since regiments started bands, there have been hosts of highly skilled musicians of whom but a comparative few became bandmasters. Thousands were trained for the Army at the Royal Military School of Music, Kneller Hall, Twickenham, at the Royal Marine School of Music, Dean, Hampshire, and at Music Services of the Royal Air Force, Uxbridge, Middlesex.

Many more were not mentioned. The highest proportion were orphans, sons of servicemen killed in action. They became known as 'band rats'. My brother Leslie was one, I was another.

Although there are not now as many Army bands as there used to be, due to the reduction in regiments and many amalgamations, there are still 23 staff bands, and 55 cavalry and infantry bands with establishments which comprise 27 officers appointed Directors of Music, 68 Warrant Officers Class 1 (Bandmasters) and over 2700 Bandsmen, 41 Bandswomen and 58 Gurkha Bandsmen.

These calls have been handed down over the years since the trumpet, bugle (and the drum) were first used as a method of command and/or communication, both for parades, ceremonials and the sterner business of battle.

Each regiment has its own regimental marches (quick and slow), and the system applies also to Scottish regiments and their pipes, and to quite a library of 'associated music'.

Many a British regiment has become famous with the general public not only by virtue of its music but of its nickname. Both music and the saucy old soubriquets are positive indications of the many bands and band rats, who, over the years, have beaten drums, fingered fifes, blown trumpets, bugles and all other musical instruments, to play the music of regiments other than their own. The nicknames alone are music for professional soldiers, for many a regimental march had its origin in a nickname. Some portray a regimental eccentricity; a peculiarity of dress; some battle honour, victory or defeat, or massacre in the field. Others sprang from folklore of counties in which the regiment was raised – our good old English country music. When we played the march of the Wiltshires (The Moonrakers) I used to think of crafty smugglers who posed as straw-chewing country bumpkins as they tried to rake the moon's reflection from the top of a pond in which they had immersed stolen brandy – to baffle the boffins of HM Customs and Excise.

When we played the march of the Lincolnshires (The Poachers) I thought of my brother and I, creeping through Langley Wood with an old Bobby's lamp and a net ... on a moonlight prowl for roosting pheasants.

There was much to learn and remember from our musical bible, *The Rudiments of Music* by Davenport. If one was asked to define 'staff, or stave', nothing other than 'The five lines and four spaces upon which the pitch of a note is fixed' would save a good clout on the ear. And if you answered 'a sound' when asked to define a note, you would get two clouts round the ear'ole, all because old Davenport had ruled that a note was not a sound, or row, or noise, but a sign: 'A note is a sign used to represent the relative length of a musical sound'.

But that was merely the beginning. Each regiment had its own regimental call, the trumpet or bugle call which preceded every routine call and field call. Each call has its own jingle to aid the process of recollection, mostly humorous and to the point. For example, *The Mail Call*: 'Letters from Lousy Lou, boys. Letters from Lousy Lou!' *The Guard Call*: 'Come and do a picquet, boys; come and do a guard. 'Tisn't very easy boys, 'tisn't very hard'. Never has a cavalry trumpeter sounded the wrong call for 'Extend'. When that call is sounded, one rides, and with the bit rein, instead of posting in the saddle, one sits down and bumps to the command of the bugle, for bugles are used for field calls: 'Arse-holes, bobbin' up and down ... Arse-holes bobbin' up and down'.

The Royal Military School of Music, Kneller Hall, Twickenham, which introduced me to the delightful friendship of Colonel Jiggs Jaeger, Director of Music, Irish Guards, Senior Director of Music, British Army, then Director of Music, Kneller Hall, also introduced me to another ex-band rat who became my firm friend, Wing Commander 'George' Sims. Jiggs and George were good friends, colleagues and rivals; together they had conducted memorial services at Westminster

Abbey. After one such occasion Jiggs invited George to Wellington Barracks. Seeing that George was about to doff his cap on entering the mess of the Irish Guards – as an officer and gentleman of the RAF – Jiggs quickly corrected him.

'You don't take off caps and coats here, George. Do exactly as you are like, for you are at home – as long as you don't spit on our carpet or pee in the grate.'

When the Royal Air Force was first constituted, in April 1918, it was not really complete. They could fly better than some birds but had not a note of music for singing. They had no band; not one band rat's name was on its ration strength. Before long they mended their ways by gathering the support of semi-official bands formed on a voluntary basis and managed to achieve establishment in July 1918 at the Royal Air Force School of Music in Fitzjohn's Avenue, Hampstead.

The same month of July saw the formation at Blandford, Dorset, of what is reliably reported as the progenitor of all the semi-official bands which were made up to some extent from part-time volunteer musicians, but in the main from ex-regular soldiers and Royal Marine musicians who had transferred to the RAF while awaiting demobilization from old Kaiser Bill's War.

The School of Music was attended by a number of men of the other services who played in these semi-official bands and remained in Hampshire until pressure of numbers forced a removal to Uxbridge, Middlesex. When, in 1931, Amers retired as Director of Music, the appointment passed to a Donkey Walloper, an ex-cavalryman once in the band of the 21st Lancers. He was Flight Lieutenant R. P. O'Donnel, MVO, who, like George Sims, had transferred to the RAF from the Royal Marines, where he had served for twelve years in the Royal Yacht *Victoria and Albert*. But even before this he had been bandmaster of the 21st Lancers. As one cavalry recorder put it: 'He thus brought to the flying service a combination of experience gained in the two services from which the Royal Air Force itself emerged'.

O'Donnel was born in India. He received his musical education at the Royal Irish Academy of Music and at Kneller

Hall. He founded the RAF Symphony Orchestra at the beginning of Hitler's War, was responsible for forming the Command Bands and the five-piece dance bands at most operational stations, toured with the RAF Symphony Orchestra and the Central Band and was also a member of the Advisory Council of Music, ENSA.

Like George Sims and Jiggs Jaeger, he had a lively and mercurial wit and a profound affection for his musicians, and was convinced that in this funny old world there were only two categories of people, those who had been in the services, and those who had not. 'Soldiers' – and all kinds of servicemen – were those who knew the true meaning of friendship and sincerity, the rest were not all that important.

On his retirement in 1949, O'Donnel's baton was handed over to George Sims, alias Wing Commander A. E. Sims, MVO, OBE, LRAM, ARCM. George was christened Albert Ernest but from the day of his enlistment in the Royal Marines in 1911 he was known as 'George' to his shipmates and the name stuck. One day in his Uxbridge home, named 'The Hermitage', George told me about the appellation. Years ago there was a spicy newspaper called the *Pink 'Un*, which printed saucy stories about Edwardian London and was dutifully read by all matelots. The proprietor was his father's cousin, George R. R. Sims. Thus Albert Ernest became, and stayed, George.

Among George's many musical contributions to the RAF are 'of the RAF' and include their quick march, *A Royal Occasion* and the slow march, *Superna Petimus,* whose title is the motto of the RAF College. For the Coronation of HM Queen Elizabeth, he composed a special ceremonial slow march whose name could not be bettered: *Elizabethan Echoes.*

The old RAF Electrical and Wireless School (now No. 1 Radio School) was not neglected, for George wrote a march for those electrical wizards to match the sparky insignia on their sleeves. He called it *Sparks,* and it also doubles as the Technical Training Command March and the Halton Apprentices March. He also wrote a march for the Royal Air Force Regiment, naming it after their regimental motto *Per Ardua.*

Perhaps the most interesting of George's many compositions were two of considerable cunning (known in the cavalry as the art of improvisation). One was musical, the other artistic and unusual.

When those slick, sleek ceremonial drill units of the RAF are rehearsing their square-bashing routine for ceremonial occasions and a senior officer is 'standing in', for a Royal event it is not permissible to play the National Anthem for a mere 'stander-inner' at the saluting base. Drill instructors found that their men were much put out by a silence, so George composed the *Courtnedge Lament*, a piece which has the same number of bars and rhythm as *God Save the Queen*. George's artistic achievement is the unique badge of the Central Command Band, with its motto, *Aere Invicta*. The design was inspired by the gift of a lyre bird. No other band has such a badge and the *Courtnedge Lament* is not likely to be heard by the general public. Incidentally, 'Courtnedge' was the name of the drill officer.

One of my proudest possessions is the original drawing of the lyre bird. George gave it to me in 'The Hermitage' after we had listened to some band practice of the Central Command Band.

'What do you reckon, Spike?'

'It is a very good band, George.'

'It is, *very* good, and it is a musical band!'

We got on very well, possibly because we had both been band rats. That's about all we had in common. I was a swede-bashing son of the East Anglian soil, and George almost a Mancunian, for he was born at Newton Heath, but we shared something in our boyhood. We had warbled in the choir.

At 15 he went straight from school and became a bandboy in the Royal Marines, to serve at sea during the Kaiser's War, taking part in the battles of Jutland, Heligoland Bight and the Dogger Bank.

Some do say that O'Donnel invented the nautical story about George. Others swear it is true. Anyway, it was related that when George was riding the waves, one day he was conducting the Royal Marines Band as they played *A Life on the Ocean Wave* ('is better than going to sea'), not only because it happened to be the regimental march of the Royal Marines, but because it was Trafalgar Day and they were playing a tribute to an old East Anglian matelot, Nelson.

Unfortunately, the cornet soloist was not such a good sailor, and was so seasick that his bumper-up (second cornet) had to take the solo. Due to rough seas and nervousness at this unexpected honour, the rendering could have been better. Later a stoker approached George.

'Hey, Bandy, I thought Nelson was shot!'

'Of course he was shot. From a French frigate. Why do you ask?'

'By the way Titch played that solo, I thought he was strangled!'

I was told by a bandmaster guest at Kneller Hall that the bands of the RAF were so poor in traditional music that they swiped what they now possess from British regiments – even a regimental march, an unforgivable crime. Now, this happens to be true. Mind you, the RAF are quick to point out that this was but a positive indication of the comradeship between the two arms of the service. It is certainly true about the fellowship which exists between the RAF College, Cranwell, Lincolnshire and the Royal Lincolnshire Regiment, for in the college's first term in 1920 they swiped that regiment's march, *The Lincolnshire Poacher* and persisted in using it until 1932 when, to placate some of the critics, George Sims, then the college bandmaster, wrote a special march for Cranwell College. Closed during the war, the college did not open again until 1949 and it was then that the College Commandant wrote to Major-General Griffin, Colonel of the Lincolnshires, asking leave to continue playing 'The Poacher'. The reply was significant.

'I am sure that I speak for all ranks of the regiment when I say that there is no unit in the services which we would rather have associated with our regimental march.

'We all very fully appreciate the fact that there would be no Royal Lincolnshire Regiment but for the gallantry, devotion to duty and sacrifices of the officers of the Royal Air Force, who fought over Dunkirk and in the Battle of Britain, many of whom were trained at and were gained from the Royal Air Force College.

'Moreover, all infantrymen know the inestimable value of dose air support in the saving of casualties, and there is no more heartening sound when going into action on the ground than to hear the roar of the fighters and bombers of the Royal Air Force flying overhead ...'

From then on *The Lincolnshire Poacher* remained 'unpoached', for it became one of the official marches of the College. The band play it whenever the Queen's Colour is marched on parade, when officers rise after dinner on guest nights, and on other ceremonial and formal occasions.

There is also significance in the parodied version still sung by Royal Air Force Cadets.

'I joined the RAF as an Aircrafthand, as good as God can be;
But after a month my conduct sheet was one of the sights to see.
It was full of fines and days in quod that my Leader gave to me.
I was five times up to the Wing-Commander and twice to the AOC.
So I started again as an AC2 and now I'm an AC3.'

Since their formation, the Irish Guards have treasured for their mascot an Irish Wolfhound. The first was Leitrim Boy. When old dogs die, new dogs take over. One replacement did not conform to the norms of the Micks' law and order. Upon the officers' mess carpet he made an occasional mound; more often, puddles. The adjutant was infuriated and gave Jiggs instructions: 'If you can write music you should be able to write letters. Drop a line to the vet about this dirty dog'.

The vet's letter replied: 'If the dog persists in these performances, be firm. Each time he makes a mound, or even a puddle, seize him, rub his nose in it, then sling him out of the window'.

Weeks later, Jiggs and his band were giving a concert. Unknown to Jiggs, the vet was in the audience. One concert item was Elgar's *Nimrod*, the vet's pet piece. In the interval he thanked Jiggs for playing *Nimrod*.

'I played it for *you*,' said Jiggs, 'in appreciation of *your* help with our mascot.'

'How is the dog getting on?'

'You will be delighted to know that we now have the best trained mascot in the whole of the Guards Division. Mind you, he makes more mounds and puddles than he did before you gave your advice, but he rubs his own nose in them, and slings himself out of the bloody window!'

It was Jiggs who ordered me to write my book *The Band Rats*. Like the Micks' mascot, I obeyed. It was unfinished when he died, so I dedicated it to his widow. My instruction to write the book was delivered in the bar of the Students' Mess, Kneller Hall. Jiggs looked me in the eye. 'We will take you on the ration strength and clap you in our clink. You will start writing a book about Kneller Hall. You will be confined until you have written the book. You will then be released, and I will conduct the Kneller Hall Trumpeters to sound you two calls on their new Aida trumpets. The calls will be Last Post and Reveille ... *and*, as you were once a Donkey Walloper, we shall sound the cavalry calls. You will now fall out and get me a large Vera Lynn!'

Jiggs Jaeger was put to rest in the Guards Chapel. His military lullaby ... 'Nimrod'.

10

Make Much of Your Horses

'Never look a gift horse in the mouth!'

So runs the adage which horsy folk claim had its origin in the land of the camel and arch-necked desert Arab steed, where hook-nosed Bedouins and Tuaregs were wise enough to mount horses instead of Cadillacs, and gave horses to their friends – instead of a brace of oil wells. They considered it bad form to peer into horses' jaws to inspect their teeth and assess their age – far worse than Liz Taylor popping into a pawn-shop to value Dicky Burton's diamonds.

Today, far too few folk know about horses, but the vast majority are gift conscious. Not all the good gifts around us are sent from Heaven above, as the old harvest hymn tried to kid us. Daily and nightly they cascade from television gift shows, smack into the paws of persons with wit enough to answer brain-straining questions such as: 'Who made Stephenson's *Rocket*?' 'Who built the pyramids ... Wimpey, McAlpine or the Gippos?' and perhaps a real teaser: 'At what time is News at Ten telecast?'

Soon, someone will ask, 'What is a horse?' That will fox the lot. Our roly-poly Suffolk Punch is mighty thin on the ground. A few old Clydesdales and Shires still haul brewers' drays, but have now been given speaking parts on the 'telly' to advertise ale from Yorkshire. Pension them off! Let's have a choir of Suffolks singing anthems and operatic arias to Greene King's Abbot Ale!

Our Army, too, is horse-deprived. Apart from the blacks and greys of the Household Cavalry there remains but one Troop. Stabled at St John's Wood is the King's Troop, Royal Horse Artillery, used for musical rides and drives and for pulling their pop-guns into Hyde Park to fire salutes for old battles and royal birthday anniversaries. They then return to graze on Lord's cricket pitch – to keep the grass short so that our police can capture the unsteady as they emerge from The Tavern.

What a shame it is to lose our faithful friends! Horses are not merely solid-hoofed quadrupeds with liquid eyes, flowing manes and tails, and twitching telephonic ears to inform the rider what they intend to do with those slender legs grown from each of their four corners. Oh no! They are noble, faithful friends who have inspired warriors, kings, minstrels and bards to adulation. Take, for example, *The Arab's Farewell to his Steed*:

> My beautiful, my beautiful!
> Who standest meekly by,
> With thy proudly arched and glossy neck
> And dark and fiery eye,
> Fret not to rove the desert now
> With all thy winged speed;
> I may not mount on thee again,
> Thou'rt sold, my Arab steed.
>
> Fret not with that impatient hoof!
> Snuff not the breezy wind!
> The farthest that thou fli-est now
> So far am I behind.
> The Stranger hath thy bridle rein,
> Thy master hath his gold.
> Fleet-limbed and beautiful, farewell!
> Thou'rt sold, my steed ... Thou'rt sold!

On its peacetime establishment our Regiment had 481 horses. Thirty per Troop, four troops per squadron and four squadrons to the regiment. The odd number was the beautiful 'Coronet', our drum horse, the last of the fine Hanoverian creams. Today's cavalrymen, apart from the Household Cavalry, have never clapped eyes on a body brush or hoofpick, and I feel sorry for them, but give them full marks for being pretty slick with oil rags.

There was something majestic about our daily attendance at stables, although hard work was involved. Every trooper knew every note, and the jingle of 'Stables' was heard at its best when sounded by mass trumpets:

> 'Come to the stable
> All ye that are able,
> And give your fine horses
> Their water and corn'.

Many years ago some cavalry poet put in his tribute, which was published in our regimental journal, *The Eagle*, (No.8, 1928):

> There's a bustle and stir in the stables this morning,
> An additional zest to the work being done;
> With old Time, the weather-vane, gaily adorning
> Great flashings of harness and steel in the sun.
>
> All is keenest excitement and cheery commotion,
> With the stamping of hooves and the rattling of pails
> Where the grooms are outvying each other's devotion
> In the care of their charges – from muzzles to tails.
>
> The success of a Troop is the pride in its stables
> For by this a team's reputation is made;
> And a slip-shod establishment's never been able
> To compete with our old spit and polish brigade.

Tending horses twice daily was not all beer and skittles. They sometimes became quite ill, both in health and temper. Some developed 'thrush', which has no connection with mavises, missels, throstles and other thrushy song birds, but a painful disease which affects the frog of the hoof and emits a vile stench, midway between stale beer and Indian Army socks. It is believed to be a 17th century disease of unknown origin; once sniffed, never forgotten. We treated it with dustings of lime and Fuller's Earth. Colic is also a stench producer, causing griping pains in the belly with severe twitching and knotting of muscles. We kept affected horses up on their legs. If they got down and rolled, as they always tried, they ruptured their intestines and had to be destroyed.

'Windgalls' were soft tumours which attacked the fetlocks. Iodine jelly smarmed on leg-puttee bandages helped to relieve the pain. Other horses had their peculiar characteristics and vices. 'Windsuckers' drew in their breath with a rushing noise, a kind of gale warning. Great gulpings of air distended their bellies to such dimensions we sometimes had difficulty in girthing up – let alone win efforts to keep the saddle twixt mane and tail. 'Weavers' rocked and rolled like the denizens of discos, but were better looking – even when in pain. Perhaps the worst equine affliction was 'glanders', a highly contagious disease which produces swelling below the jaw, with thick discharges of mucus from the nostrils; a deadly disease which can be transmitted to humans by touch and through minor lacerations of the skin.

In the early 1930s at Trimulgherry, Secunderabad, Deccan, some troop horses incubated glanders and were returned to the old Remount Depot, Saugor, for destruction.

Before the horses left Trimulgherry, Lieutenant Anthony (Thunder) Gilliat had arrived, straight from Blighty, white of skin and guileless.

The whole regiment was put into isolation and all the horses in the squadron were ordered to be malleined. Malleining is the injection of a chemical into the horse's neck. It is not a cure or a prevention, like inoculation, but simply a test.

One morning at breakfast someone said to Anthony, 'As those horses were in your troop you'll have to be malleined as well.' At breakfast a couple of days later Anthony said, 'When do you think I shall have to be malleined?'

This was too good to be true. The officers vied in telling incredible stories about malleining. Some said it was done in the arm, others in the leg, but with equal risk as the patient usually lost the limb injected. They added that it would probably be done by a certain farrier corporal of the Veterinary Hospital notorious for his grave brutality and callousness. Anthony believed every word. He visited the Hospital and was told by the veterinary surgeon, who had been well briefed, that he could not be done that day as there was not enough stuff left to do all the horses.

Wintle and Brian Gore agreed with Anthony that things had come to a pretty pass when diseased horses received preferential treatment to a cavalry officer.

They then invented a special veterinary officer, one Major Wetham-Botham, VC, who had gained this award for malleining horses under shell-fire. The roof of his mouth had been shot away by German machine-gun bullets and his speech was seriously affected. All this because it had been decided that Wintle was to be the Major.

Gilliat was not enthusiastic. Next morning the mess waiter handed him a note from the letter box.

'Please report to the Outhouse at the end of HQ Squadron Lines at 1100 hours to receive your injection Malleini B2.

(Signed: J. Wetham-Botham, Major RAVC)'

A footnote in another hand suggested that to facilitate the operation the officer should change from riding breeches and boots into Trousers K. D., (slacks).

Gilliat showed the note to, and sought advice from, Wintle and Gore – who had concocted it. They warned him that the major's strange name should be pronounced 'Woofram'. That on no account should he be engaged in gossip as he was most sensitive about his speech impediment. Moreover, though normally of timorous and charming disposition, he was inclined to blow his top with 'yappers'.

Inside the Outhouse, preparation had already been made. A charpoy (Indian bed) had been installed, plus a screen and a sheet-draped table on which reposed sundry large flagons half-filled with tinted water. The pinky one bore a bold label: POISON – MALLEINI TINCT. (B2).

Major Woofram was on parade when Gilliat arrived. With a surgical mask hiding his dial, wearing bible-black sun glasses and a white smock, he was manipulating a syringe big enough to inoculate a herd of elephant or douse a fair-sized jungle conflagration. It was Captain A.D. Wintle, with a pebble in his mouth to disguise his voice.

He asked Gilliat to sign some form of receipt from which 'horse' had been deleted and 'officer' substituted – to prove to fellow officers that he had taken precautions.

He then asked Gilliat to take off his trousers, go behind the screen and wait. Wintle swiped the trousers and stole from the Outhouse.

Twenty minutes later the trousers were restored, in the mess. Gilliat joined in the laughter after Major Wetham-Botham, still in his veterinary ceremonial order, told Gilliat that it was not the form for a Royal Dragoon to go abroad in this wicked world being so bloody simple.

Gilliat was killed by a Bengal tiger. Brian Gore was killed in action and Wintle died at his home in Kent.

Wintle was a man of great determination and a rigid disciplinarian who held the view that no soldier could be fully intelligent unless fully physically fit to perform impossible tasks. To him the virtues of diligence, loyalty, fitness and punctuality had always been more than merely subjects for cynicism. Because he practised his precepts, he was a keen climber and a naturalist, forever contriving for us the most unorthodox forms of recreation, which gave us scope to see and learn far more about India than the Army Council stipulated. Although we feared him for his unremitting discipline, we respected him and held him in the highest esteem.

We were in the Nilgiri Hills when Wintle was put back a few horses' lengths at Wellington, without horses and away from the dusty hot plains. One Wednesday morning a notice appeared on the Order Board:

At 1355 hours today all Other Ranks –
including those Senior NCOs who normally retire
to their beds on recreational afternoons –
will parade on the main square, Wellington.
Dress: shorts, vests, ammunition boots.
(Sticks may be carried and dogs led)
Object: Exercise
(Physical and mental)

At 1150 hours disgruntled dragoons gathered in conversational groups off the main square.

'What the hell are we in for this time?' asked an apprehensive ancient who had not broken out of a slow walk since he became a cook.

'He'll probably turn up with a whip, a lunging-rein and a stop-watch,' I said Broadbent. 'He'll lash us round the square till we drop, then he'll piss off to his posh hill bungalow to write an article for *The Times of India* on human exhaustion.'

Across the square a monocle glinted.

'Parade ... fall in!'

At Captain Wintle's bark, and as if by magic, there appeared on the square two ranks of soldiers carrying sticks, some leading odd-looking dogs.

'I shall not inspect you, I might catch rabies from your dogs. You will all be delighted to learn that we are about to climb to Dodabetta, the highest point in the Nilgiris. From the top you will get a view which will improve your filthy minds. Getting to that point will remove fat from your vile, unfit bodies.'

We moved off at a very brisk pace, Captain Wintle leading. Only the dogs were delighted. Smiler Turnbull had put on his Lancashire thinking cap, as usual.

'Heh, listen ... to get to Dodabetta we've got to pass under a waterfall. We can hide in the water then scarper back to Wellington an' get old Wintle by the short an' curlies. Pass it back!'

This masterpiece of evasive strategy was passed back and

approved. After an hour of steady climbing, above the thumping of our near-bursting hearts we heard the roar of falling water.

'Nearly there, blokes,' said Smiler.

Ten yards ahead, the fall cascaded through great holes in the rock. Nine wily dragoons side-stepped into the falling water and held their breath until a gasping rearguard stumbled past. Sergeant Bill Ducker of the Signal Troop had been appointed to keep a sharp look-out for defaulters. This was a providential selection, for Bill liked a drop of jungle juice and would never look at neat water.

The schemers emerged undetected and ambled back to Wellington to sleep, perchance to dream, but not of Dodabetta.

Drenched in sweat, the remainder reached the summit and prostrated themselves. Still up on his hinds, Captain Wintle looked to the fallen.

'When you have recovered, take a look. Enjoy the majesty of this natural beauty. Notice particularly how primitive hill farmers conserve their water supply. Look at the terracing of their fields, and their ingenious system of irrigation.'

We took a long never-to-be-forgotten look. Mango and tamarind groves made a dark green irregular pattern on the lighter back-cloth of the more regularly cultivated sugar and paddy fields. We mentally compared this natural beauty with the drab tidiness and artificiality of our barrack rooms. But our reveries were interrupted by Wintle's barrack square parade voice:

'I am about to call the roll. Answer your names!'

Nine silences followed nine names. Bill Ducker could not account for the missing.

'Nobody fell out, sir ... I should have seen them!'

'You *should*, you did not, but you will. Bring them to squadron office tomorrow!'

The descent began. Apart from a dog fight, nothing untoward occurred until we reached the lake. It presented a cooling invitation which Wintle seemed to notice.

'If you have no moral scruples about human nakedness,

peel off and take a dip. You've got twenty minutes!'

In seconds, the placid surface was violated by stark naked dragoons and scruffy dogs.

Nine sheepish dragoons faced Wintle next morning, one at a time. Only Dixon from Leeds said, 'I've nowt to say, sir.' Only Dixon from Leeds received seven days CB. The remainder also received seven days CB but with pack-drill. For two hours each day, laden with military equipment, with sword in left hand and rifle in right, they marched in the heat of the sun, changing their direction every third pace to the raucous bark of the provost sergeant of the Lancashire Fusiliers – who loathed cavalrymen.

The last four days of torture were performed in greater heart than the first three. Dixon's 'news' was responsible. He approached Smiler Turnbull. Struggling to balance a bulging kit-bag over sore shoulders for the next two hours of torment, Smiler was in no need of trifling. He told Dixon to belt up and Foxtrot Oscar.

'It's about owd Wintle,' chortled Dixon. 'He's in t'mire hissen, pretty deep.'

'How come?' asked a most interested Smiler.

'Orderly Room clerk show me a letter from 'Mother Sufferior of the owd convent at Dodabetta. She's raisin' bloody hell about owd Wintle and her flocker virgins. Says she can do nowt wi' em since hairy-arsed troopers went swimmin' in t'drinkin' watter!'

> 'One was a Lancer, long of limb;
> And it took a good 'un to ride with him;
> The other a Guardsman, extra bold,
> He liked a horse that would take a hold.
> He liked a country strongly fenced
> And a solid pace when the play commenced;
> With a travelling fox and a serving scent
> There were few that would follow the way he went.
>
> Many a fun did these heroes see,
> Riding it jealously, knee to knee;

Many a fence did they cross together
With a touch of steel and a scrape of leather.
Many a time did the Lancer Land
With the Guardsman's whip on his bridle hand;
Many a time was the air turned blue
By the language flying between the two.'

11

Ashdon Waits and Ashdon Jack

My fellow author and friend for over sixty years, Christopher Ketteridge, and myself, have lived long in the village of Ashdon.

We knew Ashdon Jack. He was church-christened Raymond Smith, but posh Christian names were soon cut down to size in our village. Raymond soon became 'Ranier', and then 'Rainy-bug', arter that small black beetle which, if deliberately trodden on by a child's foot, would bring down a hull pourin' o' rain ... or so we were told by our elders.

Children had little chance of cultivating Rainy-bug's acquaintance. Parental warnings were rife. He dressed in shreds and patches and seldom washed or shaved. But the children knew he was a good man because of his questions. 'An' I'll give ye the right answers an' all!' he used to say.

And to every question he would give the same answer, garnished with cunning winks. 'The answer is "Jay Dee Kay", m'dear. An' that's short for Jack don't know!'

For long stretches before the Kaiser's War he worked at Street Farm, but as soon as he had saved enough from his puny wages he would go on a bender at The Rose and Crown, The Fox or The Lamb. Best beer was 2d a pint. Pubs were open all day.

Although wages were low, a minority of farmhands and travelling labourers added to their primary poverty and family distress by long and senseless bouts of drinking.

With the outbreak of World War One most of these improvidents were called up, including Rainy-bug, but he did not return to Ashdon on his demobilisation. He spent months in hospital recovering from a severe head wound. With a silver plate riveted to his skull to replace bone shredded from him by shrapnel, he returned with a surgeon's enjoinder: 'You must not drink to excess, it might be fatal.' Rainy-bug abstained.

William Bell & Sons, Saffron Walden, took him on as a builder's labourer, where he worked with my friend Christopher. Soon, Rainy-bug 'graduated' to improver, then Saffron Walden builders persisted in calling him Jack, after his father. Presently he became 'Ashdon Jack', and this made him mighty proud. He was named after his old village. 'It were better than a VC!'

Later the bricklayers mounted and marched to Wendover, Bucks, to reconstruct wartime Halton Camp into training quarters for the Royal Air Force. Ashdon Jack was fuming at being left behind, but within a week Christopher Ketteridge sent for him. They found him a job at Wendover, as scaffolder's mate, at double his previous wage.

Jack was elated. He celebrated right royally. Already several sheets to the wind the day before he joined Christopher, it was fortunate that he had bought some stamps at the Saffron Walden post office.

On arrival at Wendover he made a beeline to some old haunts where he had put down a few jars in his wartime service.

Starting at The Shoulder of Mutton, he worked a liquid path through the town until closing time in The Four Seasons. He arrived at the camp saying, 'There ain't a mite of thirst left in me', thus blazing a drunken trail that was simple enough for officers of the CID to follow after they had been alerted to keep a sharp look-out for a person of dubious appearance. A burglar had been at work the day before; the Rothschild mansion had been ransacked.

Next morning a squad car arrived at the site. Three plain-clothes officers interrogated Jack and accused him of the offence. He was about to be arrested when the Yorkshire manager intervened. 'Give t'lad chance to clear hissen... Y're not takin' t'lad til he's had chance t' speak up!'

To Jack's relief, he interposed his eighteen stone bulk to block the doorway. Further questions revealed Jack was in Saffron Walden at the time of the burglary. A telephone call to the post office verified that he had bought stamps. The law departed.

Jack heeded the warning of another doctor: 'If you over-indulge, you'll go mad, or die.'

He abstained, worked hard, saved money and slept in a disused hut with some of the building personnel, all to save paying lodging allowance. This communal sleeping soon revealed how deeply the war had left its mark. Jack used to shriek in his sleep, chatter throughout the night and challenge the whole German army. Next morning he would know nothing of it, not even as a dream.

Unfortunately, he was fortunate enough to win a sweep-stake, and for the whole of the week he celebrated. Late on Sunday he went to bed dead drunk, snoring horribly. Suddenly he leapt from his bed and charged down the centre of the hut. Beside the combustion stove – all cherry red with heat – lay a pile of coke.

Yelling challenges to, and obscenities about, the Germans, he began hurling coke hand-grenade fashion and kept up the fusillade until he staggered and clutched the red-hot stove pipe. At his scream of agony his madness left him.

He became stone cold sober and profoundly contrite, but lived in mortal dread of the police. He was convinced that they would gaol him, or send him to the 'grubby' (work-house).

About two years later he married an aged widow, whom he erroneously believed to be wealthy. When she died, Jack was left alone in the cottage. It was said that 'Owd Jack soon swallowed that cottage down in the pubs'.

Drink, his wounds, his fear of police, the 'grubby' and thunder and lightning were his downfall. In his cups he alternated between truculence and tomfoolery. During Hitler's

71

War he sometimes stayed in the old thatched cottage at Rickling Green, Newport, but he more often slept rough in ditches or the chalk quarry. He always slept in ditches during air raids for he was mortally scared of bangs and flashes. As Hitler's planes double-droned overhead, Jack would holler out what he believed to be their dread message: 'Where do you want 'em?... Where do you want 'em then? Oh, deary me. JAY DEE KAY ... JAY DEE KAY ... JACK DON'T KNOW!'

The last tiding came as a shock. From his chalk pit hovel, Jack was removed to become a patient in St James's Hospital, Saffron Walden, the 'grubby' he dreaded more than the police and thunderstorms. From there he would never run away, as he had protested he would if ever the police took him there. There was a reason for it ... both his legs were amputated.

Our age group remember him as a true eccentric, odd and whimsical and a mixture of many emotions; some, as a victim of the Kaiser's War. Others, of drink.

Chris and I like to remember him when he was mellow. Free from his many fears and filled with great happiness, he would bellow: *'I, owd Ashdon Jack, tha's me, bor! Owd Rainy-bug what's sorft in the head.' And then he would tap his forehead significantly, before repeating the name he loved...'Owd Ashdon Jack, d'ye hear? ... THA's ME!'

* * *

In July 1979 I received a telephone call from the Chairperson of Steeple Bumpstead's Women's Institute. 'Bring your saxophone when you come to the Waits!'

I had been living in Steeple Bumpstead for many years and had only made occasional visits to Ashdon since I joined the army in March 1924. I had never heard of the Ashdon Waits. The Blue Rinse Brigade of Steeple Bumpstead had hired the Waits for their annual shindig in our village hall.

'They are folk singers,' said the WI Chairperson. 'You lived in Ashdon and you might like to join in.'

I went, enjoyed their cheery part – and was deeply moved.

There were three men and a brace of mawthers, all with voices like spring larks and autumn linnets. They had a tidy mixture of guitars which they 'played', not 'strummed', aided and abetted by banjos, recorders, whistles, tambourines and a wonderful sense of music, fun and frolic.

A bearded policeman featured as baritone-cum-compère. A brace of silky tenors, one with thigh-revealing, ragged-edged shorts, sang duets, a solo apiece, and told earthy stories. I knew old ragged pants, for he used to live at Mill Cottage, next door to friend Christopher. The lovely lady who played the recorder so well, and bubbled with fun, was living in The Fox, one of Rainy-bug's favourites. The long, thinnish man, Peter Goodwin, reminded me of his parents, with whom I used to go to the village school. He got up on his hinds to sing a most moving song. 'It's the first time it has been sung in public,' said Peter.

He had composed both music and lyrics. A poignant and beautiful song about an unfortunate man. The title, *Ashdon Jack*.

Ashdon Waits have made some excellent records and have won awards. They deserve a double Oscar for bringing back memories of Rainy-bug!

12

Mawthers

> When one a giggling morther you
> And I a red-faced chubby boy
> Sly tricks you played me not a
> few
> For mischief was your greatest joy.
> (Bloomfield: *Richard and Kate*)

There are two spellings. The Fenmen of Norfolk call 'em 'Mor' or 'Morther'. In civilised Suffolk we call 'em 'Mawthers', but in both counties they mean the female of the species. A chuckling, bonny lass or a bed-worn gossip well past child-bearing, but with an agile tongue that never stops. These latter are also sources of wisdom; highly superstitious, they have added to East Anglia's folk lore.

When I was a lad, my friend Christopher used to tell me about his Aunty Sukie. 'Up to her eyes in superstition... Knew everyone's business and all the signs in the sky.'

Aunty Sukey merely gave vehement emphasis to be shared with most of the village wives.

'Doan't yew bring that there in here, 'cos I 'on't hev it. Tha's unlucky ter bring that into housen, laylock allus wor!'

White lilac was always considered to be unlucky if brought into the house. Elder blossom, May blossom – both red and white – bluebells, honeysuckle, ivy, maidenhair grass and the hydrangea were all harbingers of bad tidings.

Most treacherous was the elm tree, for without visible rot or disease its limbs could fall on folk taking shelter under its branches.

That twisted and distorted grain (warped by the Devil) of the wych elm was a magnet for witches, and cypresses were meeting places for evil spirits; doubly devilish if they were growing in churchyards and graveyards.

The elder was lucky and unlucky. It was the one and only tree to afford protection against lightning, evil spirits, drought and poor crops, but ill fortune would follow if its wood was cut, sawn, split or burnt after dark. If hung in the hall or porch, holly would ward off witches, but it should never be cut or burnt because, believed to be the tree on which Christ was crucified, Christ's blood would flow all over again, with the sap.

Willow should never be brought indoors if cut with saws. Bill-hooks, sickles and axes made clean cuts without making the willow weep. Ragged-edged saws brought tears, blood and sorrow.

Among the few symbols of good luck, two had prominence; the black cat and the chimney sweep. Blushing brides were encouraged to stroke the former and kiss the latter.

If hung where the family ate its meals, a spray of hops (in flower) would ensure prosperity and good health. If found in fields, woods or meadowland, but not in roads or lanes, a cast-off horseshoe was lucky, provided it was swiftly tossed over the left shoulder of the finder and no attempt was made to discover where it dropped. To fix it over a cottage door with the horns pointing heavenwards invited long-lasting fortune, but if the horns were pointed down towards Hell the luck would 'run down and out' and the Devil would trespass.

Life seemed to be one long search for better fortune. Even the young children knew a couple of verses:

> 'See a pin and pick it up
> Then all day I'll get good luck.
> See a pin and let it lie,
> Before the evening I shall cry.'

75

'If I find a four-leaf clover
All my troubles will be over.'

The monkey puzzle tree should not be disregarded. One prospered in the private precincts of the Parsonage. With dark green daggered leaves, it was spooky and frightening. Some elders had it that this particular tree was more of a puzzle to the parson than to some wandering ape. Devils and parsons abounded, but monkeys were very few on the ground and only a handful had heard of the little monkey brought back from India's sunny clime by old Bill Allgood who, with my father, had soldiered with Sepoys and became a lance-jack (unpaid) in the 12th Foot, The Suffolks, or 'Dutty Dozen'.

Children late for Sunday School, those lacking religious tuition through playing hookey, had but to climb the monkey puzzle and the Devil (if not parsons and parents) would never punish them. Yew trees were spookier, especially at night, when witches, ghosts and earthbound spirits lurked in the gloom, all trained to pounce upon the un-baptised and those who laughed in church ... usually choirboys!

The silvery moon figured largely in village beliefs. To ensure good luck through all its phases, females were exhorted to bow or curtsy 'towards the sickle' – when the first sliver of the new moon appeared.

If first seen through glass, windows or spectacles, misfortune would attend throughout the phases of the next brace of new moons, irrespective of the number and depth of curtsys made in its direction.

There were omens and portents about the new moon according to its 'position'. A coin in the pocket of a person first sighting the crescent should be turned over twice, 'tidy-sharpish' for luck.

If 'sleeping' on its back or halo-ringed, bad weather would follow as sure as God made little apples. If 'up on her tail', the harvest moon would make farmers 'whully delighted', for it meant good weather, a heavy crop and a quick harvest.

To sleep with undrawn curtains with the moon shining on one's face was an invitation for nightmares and ultimate lunacy.

Gardeners were convinced that seeds sown at new moon would germinate more quickly, and whatever weather prevailed at 'waxing' would persist to the 'waning'.

Butchers and pig owners allus kept a sharp lookout on the skies; not one of them would dream of slaughtering a pig after the moon had 'passed its full'. All fixed rigidly to the beliefs which had been handed down over the generations.

> A saddity moon an' Sunday full,
> Never wor no good, an' never wull.

In other words, pigs should be killed on the wax and not the wane.

Cock Robin was protected by superstition. Few would harm one, for it was well known that to kill a robin invited a broken leg. If a robin red-breast flew indoors, or even perched on a window-sill, we were in for a hard winter.

Ill fortune attended crossed knives, sickles, scythes and saws. Walking under ladders invited disaster. Children who picked dandelions would wet their beds. A stumbling upstairs meant that a wedding was imminent. To wear brown at a social function was 'daft as lights', for a funeral would follow. New clothes should first be worn on a Sunday, preferably in church, or sackcloth and ashes would follow.

Brides should not marry in green. No one should sit under oak trees during a thunderstorm. Never count between lightning's flash and thunder's clap to find out whether the storm is a-comin' or a-goin', you might get lightnin' struck.

You should never burn egg-shells, because thereafter the hens would lay only 'lush eggs' – without shells.

Christmas decorations should never be taken down afore Ephiphany. So they used to say in Suffolk, but just after Christmas 1988 I received a poetic message from Cornwall, indicating that the 'Tiddy Hoggie' devourers do not conform to Suffolk norms and old wives' orders. The poem was written by an octogenarian lady who later sent me two 'Tiddy Hoggies' (Cornish Pasties) and an instruction that I should read the poem aloud in a strong Cornish accent. As a Suffolker, I can't twist my tongue into Cornish, but I hope my typewriter will try. Here goes, with Mrs E. Watts's *Kind Thoughts for The Fairy.*

What do that little fairy do
A-top the Christmas tree?
Do she flutter tinselled wings
As she look down on me?
I bet she think, 'That silly twerp
Is made again this year,
Boilin' puds and bakin' cakes
For good old Christmas cheer.

Making mince pies by the score,
To scoff on Christmas day,
Her figure surely will expand!'
The little fairy say.

But when she sees the turkey
Without its little head,
It's bumsie spilling sausage meat,
A fairy tear she'll shed.
Then as she fold her tinselled wings
A fairy prayer she'll pray,
For all the lovely turkeys
That's devoured on Christmas Day.

I'm sure she can't stand Christmas
With all its rush and caper,
So I'll tuck her in her fairy box
Wrapped up in Christmas paper.
Next year I must remember
To tell her – if I'm able,
Of the little Christmas Baby
Born in a lowly stable.

I'll tell her the true meaning
Of the Carols we all sing
The cards we send to kin and friend,
The joy that Christmas bring.

Then she'll shout 'Allelluia!'
Shake tinselled wings with glee,
Join in the rush and caper
With silly twerps like me.

To open an umbrella inside the house was a positive indication that a black bordered letter would soon arrive giving news of the death of a near and dear one; but to put on a garment inside-out was good tidings unless it was done deliberately – but it should be worn all day.

Gifts of money or tops should be spat on for good luck. Presents of scissors, needles, pins, brooches or knives could cut the friendship unless paid for by the gift of one farthing.

Weathercocks had to be watched at noon on Saint Thomas' Day. Wherever the wind happened to be blowing from at that time, from that direction it would continue to blow for the following quarter. The 'lazy wind' was by far the worst. It blew straight from the Urals because there were no intervening mountains or features to impede the Siberian blasts. It was given the 'lazy' title because... 'It's too lazy ter blow round yet, metty, so the bugger blows straight through ye, makin' ye whully frawn.'

Although owls abounded and were common sights, if one heard the long drawn-out hooting of a Tawny and it was not repeated, one could be sure that a close relative had died at that precise moment.

Toads were regarded with some misgiving, and none would disturb them, for they were reputed to have the 'evil eye' and should not be provoked. Some species of caterpillar were dreaded, and no one ever touched one known as the 'Davel's Ring'. It was reputed that this furry one would coil itself round the toucher's finger and drag him down to hell.

There is one old tale, not talked about much these days,

belonging to the village of Ashdon, where I spent my boyhood.

The stagnant pond behind the Manse was overhung with weeping willows and is called 'Lady Well'. It is a sombre place and children were told not to venture there at night. The legend goes that many years ago a 'lady of quality' was driving in her carriage and pair along the carriageway when forked lightning flashed and frightened the horses.

The horses whinnied, bolted and the carriage overturned – hurling the lady into the pond, where she drowned. Only a footpath remains of the old carriage-way, but the ghosts of the frightened horses and the drowned lady still haunt Lady Well, the only Ashdon pond where moorhens are never seen...

13

Stick Orderly

Military historians of any consequence will know of a crack cavalry regiment once known as 'The Greys'. Their motto is proud, boastful and incorrect, 'Nulli Secundus' (second to none). Before their amalgamation they were the Second Dragoons, the Household Cavalry of Bonnie Scotland, The Royal Scots Greys.

As 'Second Dragoons' they were certainly second to the one that I served in, 1st The Royal Dragoons, now amalgamated with the Royal Horse Guards to form The Blues and Royals.

Each time we met, we of the 1st would remind those of the 2nd that they were second to the first. There were occasional punch-ups, but the status remained unchanged.

In desert-bound parts of the British Empire, the Second used to tart up stones with blanco and whitewash and spell out in large, lying lettering, around their second-class guard-room or tent, the words 'Second to None'.

And in the black watches of the tropical nights we of the 1st would steal out and swipe the letter 'N' from their tarted-up 'None', thus translating it to 'One' to put the blighters in their proper place.

They never forgave us. But we shrieked and hollered for mercy when they got their own back by reaching 'Top of the Pops'; just for blowing out *Amazing Grace* on their octopus-like bagpipes.

One of my best owd mets was a fellow trumpeter. He of the

Greys, I of the Royals. Steve Shadlock was his pukka moniker, but to add a mite of cavalry dash I switched Shadlock to Fetlock. It became his nickname.

Years after the Hitler War we met up again. Fetlock had become a PRO for the British Airways Corporation at Heathrow Airport and I a Press and Public Relations Officer at the Ministry of Aviation, also at Heathrow.

Fetlock and I trotted off one morning to welcome a swarm of Russian dancers who had just landed on Runway 28L from Moscow, later to delight London and the Provinces with their beauty and skill.

In No. 3 Passenger Building, the palace for long haul hops, stood a large notice in red lettering and a strange language: 'BOLSHOI'.

'*You* should know that word better than most,' sniped Fetlock, giving me a dig in the ribs. 'It's the Red Army word for spit and polish, commonly known to the Scots Greys as Royal Dragoon bullshit!'

Years before, in Cairo, I had bragged that I 'Got the stick' 42 times on guard mounting parades. I did not mind being reminded, and I am pleased today to hold a stick presented to me many years ago, of ebony, with an elk horn handle enscrolled in silver and bearing my name.

We had been dragooned into thinking and believing that cleanliness was next to cavalry godliness. That Dragoons should always be free from rust and dust, and brightly burnished, particularly on Guard Mounting.

Saddlery would be cleaned and inspected every day, with a stripped saddle inspection once a week. Much of the cleaning was superfluous and positively injurious to leatherwork. First, careful sponging to remove dust, dirt and horse sweat from the leathers – girths, surcingles, reins, stirrup-leathers, sweat-flaps and saddle-flaps – before they were treated with saddle soap to keep them soft and pliable. Polished surfaces had to be maintained (or surpassed) by an application of whatever brand and colour of polish was favoured by the Top Brass, who had shares in Propert's and other polish producing purveyors, or perhaps a regimental preference.

And while we were sweating and polishing away, the hellish steel of bits, curb-chains, stirrups, swords and scabbards was gathering a coat of rust which had to be removed with brickdust and water before drying and burnishing, in that order.

Steel was the bane of our never-ending polishing existence. 'Blue Burnish' was the polishing order of our day. Time seemed to pass so slowly and meaninglessly during the processes of reaching that blue and glittering state. We often wondered if there was any purpose behind this time-wasting polishing lunacy. But on parade, or on guard mounting, all tarted up, pipe-clayed, blancoed and Propert's-polished from nose to croupe, we felt that our labour had not been in vain.

In the Cavalry there seemed to be something almost sacramental about daily turnout and the wearing of uniform, and to us professional soldiers this became an end in itself; a strange combination of regimental and personal pride, an art, ritual or ceremony, almost a religion.

Each evening at six of the clock (1800 hours), six men would parade for guard mounting inspection: one trooper from each of the four squadrons, one corporal as NCO in charge of the guard, and one trumpeter to sound the routine calls for the next 24 hours.

Barrack-room verandahs would be packed with spectators, all highly critical of drill and turnout. Many would lay odds on who would get the 'Stick', a reward for the smartest man on parade. Years before, this man would be presented with a walking-out whip bearing the regimental crest; but in my time he was presented with extra work and became a kind of slave for those not excused guard duty. Taking their meals from cookhouse to guardroom, washing up dishes, sloshing Ronuk on linoleum-covered floors, then polishing the lot to the standard required by the RSM's instruction: 'I want to see my face in them floors. Make 'em shine like a shillin' up a chimney sweep's jaxy!'

The great honour for the stick orderly was that he had been chosen to be the Commanding Officer's personal orderly. One who once galloped on a fiery arch-necked steed from office to office with orders of mighty consequence, like the date of the next polo practice or officers' mess ball. But now this cavalry dash had dwindled and the pomp had petered out, although the dress had remained. To distinguish the stick orderly from other minor military mortals he wore no nine-pouched leather bandolier. Instead he boasted a white, pipe-clayed band pouch bearing 'The Monkey', a pseudonym for the silver Royal cipher, the Lion and Crown. He was fully breeched, putteed and spurred, wore well tailored tunic, and his Bedford cord breeches separated his bum from a soggy saddle – a bicycle saddle. He no longer galloped; he pedalled, and became a dashing dragoon on wheels!

On my very first guard mounting, two officers gave me the once-over. Humphrey William Lloyd, lieutenant, a fine regimental cricketer who once bowled for Essex, was learning the guard-mounting capers as supernumerary orderly officer under the tuition of Lieutenant Roger Bright Moseley. 'Babe Moseley' later became the famous 'Horse of the Year' Colonel until he handed over those reins to Colonel Mike Ansell, Colonel of 'The Skins', who was war blinded like me, and on the same day, near Bayeux, where Queen Mathilde stitched the Battle of Hastings.

This pair of lieutenants took an eternity to inspect me. Being the shortest dragoon on parade, I was on the left flank. They inspected my braces, which had to be blancoed and burnished, the nails and tips of my ammunition boots, which had to be blue burnished, and everything else in cavalry sight.

Humphrey Lloyd marched to the front and faced the guard.

'Guard ... Number!'

'One, two, three, four!'

Heads turned like lightning to bellow into the right ear of the man standing alongside. My head had not to turn, for on my left was nothing but space.

'NUMBER FOUR ... Stick Orderly!' bellowed Humphrey.

My heart thumped. The barrack square seemed to turn cartwheels, but I remembered the drill, took two swift paces to the rear, returned my sword to its scabbard and stood to attention.

'Stick orderly ... Dismiss!'

I turned to my right, saluted, and marched off to the 3rd Troop of C Squadron. Across the square I heard clapping. 'Well done, C Squadron. Well done, Tich ... Up the band rats!'

Bill Titchener, my troop sergeant, patted my shoulder and grinned. Simpson, my troop corporal, grinned and said: 'Bloody smart return swords, lad. I'll buy you a pint!'

I was much agitated and had to bite my lip and try to remember that I had not been awarded the Victoria Cross, although I felt that I had.

Next morning was a different kettle of fish. After I had waited upon the guard and tarted up the orderly room, Captain and Adjutant Campbell Sutherland Dumbreck galloped up to me: 'What the hell are you doing in my office, Mays?'

'I am the stick orderly, sir!'

'Stick orderly! For the love of God go and take a bath, you look like a bloody chimney sweep.'

'Sorry, sir. I got dirty lighting your fire.'

'What bloody fire?' said Jim Crow (that was his nickname). The fire had gone out. From then on the glory began to fade, and I was glad to wash and dress up in stick orderly gear and take a boastful ride round Beaumont Barracks. As I was pedalling past the Forge a brace of farriers beckoned me. 'Are you stick orderly?'

'Yes ... on my first guard mounting too.'

'Well, this is your very first job. Go to the QM Stores and get me half a dozen horses' toothbrushes. Six remounts just arrived from the depot at Weedon an' they've got to be smartened up for the veterinary officer's inspection. Write it down in your notebook,' said Shoey Corporal Dempster. Then, turning to Farrier Albin: 'Didn't you want something from the quarterbloke's, Bill?'

'Write this down as well,' said Bill to me. 'Ask the storeman for mess-tin spots. Seven pounds of 'em in separate sizes and in separate bags and tell Darky I want 'em in a hurry.

I knew the QM storeman, Darky Dawes. He was the oldest

soldier in the regiment and had been in the band until wounded, and not able to play his instrument any more. He was given a staff job and a special corner bed space. He had 'dodgers' (good conduct stripes) on his left sleeve from wrist to elbow for 30 years' undetected crime, and it was reputed that he had worn a hole in the brick wall where he used to strike his matches.

'What the hell do you want here?' growled Darky.

I handed over my writing tablet, with the orders in my best handwriting.

'Wicked bastards!' said Darky. 'They are pullin' your bloody leg, boy. Horses don't have toothbrushes. If they gets the jaw-ache we put them in the stocks and trim up their bleedin' molars with a farrier's rasp. Know what mess-tin spots are, boy?'

'No ... but Bill Albin wants 'em quick, and will you put 'em in separate bags?'

'Bollocks!' said Darky, then disappeared behind his bulging shelves. Presently he returned with a new mess-tin and a cake of brickdust.

'Watch out, boy ... here comes a bloody mess-tin spot!'

He moistened a forefinger with his tongue, then rubbed the wet finger on the brickdust. He pressed his dusty finger hard on the polished surface of the mess-tin and turned it round until there was worn on to the surface a little burnished circle which reflected light from all angles and seemed to sparkle. That was a mess-tin spot.

'We used to make 'em like that, in different patterns for kit and strip saddle inspections years 'n' years ago. And when the old Indian sun shone on 'em they'd light up, an' dance an' sparkle like the Nizam's bleedin' diamonds. Them were the days!'

Darky looked a bit wistful, as though he was sickened by the gloom of the dingy store rooms, and longed to be back in the warm sunlight again – in the land of mess-tin spots.

'Now, don't you let on to them wicked sods what I've told you about tooth brushes and mess-tin spots. You're a smart young lad and I'm glad you got the stick. Keep it up, boy!'

86

He patted my shoulder, leaned forward and in a mirthful husky whisper gave out first a warning, then an instruction.

'Before your first day of Stick Order is over, somebody will ask you to go to the stores of the 10th Hussars to fetch striped paint for the barber's pole and a gallon of whitewash to paint the Last Post. Got it? Now then, go back to our forge and tell them wicked sods that Darky is very sorry, he's run out of toothbrushes and mess-tin spots, but he's expecting a new consignment from Woolwich Arsenal in about three years' time. If they can't wait, they can fetch 'em their bleedin' selves!'

14

Toe-Rag Smith

Although absent when required for international functions like bashing soft balls over bits of pig net in washed-out Wimbledon, the kindly sun helped Mother Nature to do more useful things in the summer of 1988. The kindly light and warmth beamed upon the fertile fields of East Anglia, and all that wealth-producing Rape that had canaried the landscape for a month was raped by the combine harvester, already flexing its iron muscles for an assault on the battleground of barley.

As usual, we had swarmed into church, chapel and the village pubs for thanksgiving services and Horkey Suppers and belted out the old hymns: 'Come, ye thankful people, come...' and I was reminded of the choirboys' version.

> 'All is safely gathered in
> And if it ain't it oughter bin.
> All upon the barn-yard floor,
> For the rats an' meece to gnaw'

Then I thought of another hymn: 'There is a green hill far away...'

There used to be a green hill *not* far away. About two cricket pitch lengths behind my bungalow. Bulldozers made it flatter than an international snooker table. On it, a swarm of tractors and combine harvesters, whose clanking, thumping dawn chorus has banished our beautiful song birds. The sight of a combine harvester takes me back to gingery-whiskered Toe-Rag Smith, horsekeeper of Place Farm. I was the 'shrieker an' hollerer', the boy who led the horses at harvest time.

Toe-Rag was our Lord of the Harvest. He led the hymn singing in The Bonnett Inn for the Horkey Festival, and in the fields of harvest his mellow tenor would ring across the golden wheat stubbles; sometimes hymns, more often songs about lovesick sailors who had gone off to the ocean waves. Too-Rag had never seen the sea, but his favourite sea shanty was 'When the fields are white with daisies, I'll return.'

He lived in a tied cottage at the foot of Overhall Lane, with his daughter Laura. His constant chewing on oat straws – to hide the horny wart on his lower lip – only drew attention to this minor blemish which had embarrassed him for nigh on seventy years.

Younger children of the Hamlet addressed him as Mister Toe-Rag, for they did not know that long before they were born a careless scythe-sweep had all but severed his left great toe, or that his real name was Mr G. Smith.

He stanched his blood flow with moss and grass, tidied up the wound with dock leaves, then bound dandelion leaves over his toe with the tail of his grey flannel shirt and resumed his mowing of the headlands barley – in the field named 'Woodshot'. Fellow farm labourers christened him Toe-Rag, the name he loved and kept until he died.

Most of us had nicknames. The four brothers of the 'Free' family were never addressed by surname or by Christian name, but their nicknames were household (and tap-room) words:

> 'Pipper an' Pie,
> Nickett an' Ninn,
> Can allus be found
> In the owd Poplar Inn.'

As a family, we were five. Four boys and one girl. All

beautifully church christened: Cedric Wesley, Leslie Gordon, Audrey Phyllis, Jack Aubrey and Frank Percival. No one knows us by those lovely monikers, not unless the nicknames are bunged in: Spike, Peddler, Pops, Tanky and Chaffy.

Horses are never subjected to such indignities. Once named, the name stuck, even for one common or garden cavalry troop horse in Cairo, whose name was once that of an Egyptian god, but more of him anon.

Toe-Rag loved horses and loathed mechanisation: 'The sight o' that owd tractor make me want ter spew. That'll put a lotter good men out o' wuk. Yew mark my wuds!'

My father held the same view and penned an odd ode:

> Mechanical contrivances
> Have superseded steam;
> The old style saily vessel
> Is an antiquated dream.
> We now have horseless carriages
> That run without a hitch.
> Our women wear silk stockings
> That have never seen a stitch.
> 'Progress is our motto.'
> That's what the bright boys say!
> But thank God we still make babies,
> In the good old-fashioned way.'

Of the sixteen- to seventeen-hand Shires, Clydesdales, Percherons and Suffolk Punches, he loved the Suffolks most and called them his 'Roly-Polies'. Sometimes after grooming he would make them 'stand' and then show us and describe their points from nose to croupe; saying how they had been bred from ancient strains, from countries remote, down all the years, for heavy work on fields, log-pulling in the woods.

'They're a bit of a mixture, lad, like some of they varmints down the village who ain't married. Same mares, but all kindser stallions: Brierley Turks, Darley Arabs an' Godolphines. Mind ye, that's gooin' back hund'eds o' years; but not much more'n a hund'ed years agoo the Suffolk farmers set out t'breed the roly-poly Punch. Can't be bet on heavy soil. Short, tidy legs, no feathers and can wuk all day with no more bait arter breakfast till orf-collarin' at fower. Easy to drive by just talkin' to 'em. Not a mossel o' vice in 'em, an' willin' as milkmaids!'

George had special horse-brasses for his Punches, one lot for each side of the head-collars. When he braided their manes and tails he used the split plait process with the fine straw of rye.

I learned a lot about horses from George, but when I was eleven I was with them all day in the harvest fields as 'hoss leader'. Leading the wagon team from one shock to the next and hollering louder than boys on other farms: 'Howd yew hard!' when leaving a shock, and 'Whoa, there!' when reaching the next, so that the wagon loader would not fall off the load.

Life was marvellously healthy and exciting in the clean air and sun-drenched golden stubbles, and I felt stronger than old Jack Dempsey, Joe Beckett, Georges Carpentier or those other boxers and athletes Tom Webster used to caricature in the *Daily Mail*.

I was in secret training for the boxing championship of the whole world and was developing my secret punch, and felt that I was bound to win because I had three real live punchbags – those bulging muscles on the near-fores of three Suffolks: Jockey, Boxer and old Punch.

I used to spar up a bit, clench my mighty fists, grit my teeth, get my full weight behind each knock-out punch, and lash out double-handed with devastating combination punches, whilst the horse was standing still by the corn shock and the men pitched the sheaves to the loader.

But my hairy, mighty-muscled punch bags never once fell for the count. Sometimes, as if a gnat or midge-fly had landed, the muscles gave a bit of a twitch. I told Toe-Rag about my training. His reply was not encouraging. 'Punch, boy! You couldn't punch the skin orf a rice pudden'!

After I left school I drove those same horses from the seat of a horse rake, on foot behind drills, shims, rollers and from the ridges of haywains and tumbril carts. They always worked hard without any urging, never kicked or bit and they were my best friends. There is a sadness in me now that they have gone and I well recall that day when I went to the old stables, where I had to stand on an inverted feed tin to collar 'em up. Not a mite of chaff or oats in the feed trough, nor hay, clover, sanfoin, but a great emptiness covered with oil-stained tarpaulins – the bedding for tractors and such.

Just over fifty years later, I walked the roads and lanes and met an old farmhand who had been in my class at school.

'Damn an' blast!' said Albert. 'What the hell are you a-doin' on owd Shanks's Pony?' I told him I was walking, hoping to see men and horses on the fields I knew so well.

'That's all my eye and Peggy Martin!' said Albert. 'I reckon you were going shopping, to the Three Horse Shoes for a pint. Cum yew on, they're open. Hev one alonger me!'

There were other changes. A pint of best bitter was nearly one pound. Years before, with only a tanner (6d), we could get a half of bitter, five woodbines, the top off a cottage loaf, cheese and a few spring onions. I started my pint, and Albert, his philosophising:

'The young 'uns of today know bugger all about the land. They've never walked a stretch with one foot in the furrow and one on the brew. Jest plonk their arses down in a tractor-drawn greenhouse on wheels. That owd perspex stuff. Never get a drop o'rain fall on 'em. We uster git soaked. Ten bob for a seventy-two hour week. They don't hear the birds an' they've killed orf a helluver lot on 'em with they owd sprays; they get music all day long from they blasted transister wirelesses. Got posh motors an' all – Land Rovers and Jaguars. But good luck to 'em. They ain't farmers' slaves no more!'

'What would old Toe-Rag think to it?' said I. 'Would he sing?'

'He'd tell about the Agricultural Rising in 1913, when you an' me useter march along of the strikers. Remember that strike started right here on Copy and Helions Farms... We was schoolboys then, under owd Shaw the head master. I'm a gooin' now.... Pudden time! Do yew take care, my owd met, there ain't many on us left!'

The sun still shone on the combine harvesters as they thundered along in dust clouds of their own making. I wondered if there would be farmhands left to sing the old Horkey song. There would be no Toe-Rag tenor to lead them – he is long gone – but the words remain:

Here's a health unto our master,
The founder of the feast!
I wish with all my heart and soul,
In heaven he may find rest.
I hope all things may prosper –
That ever he takes in hand;
For we are all his servants,
And drink at his command.

Drink, boys, drink, and mind you do not spill,
For if you do, you must drink two –
It is your master's will.

Now our harvest is ended, and our supper is past,
Here's our Mistress's good health,
In a good flowing glass!
She is a good woman,
She prepares us good cheer;
Come, all my brave boys,
And drink off your beer.

Drink, my boys, drink till you come unto me;
The longer we sit, my boys, the merrier
Shall we be!

(Horkey song. Anon (n.d.))

15

Stop Swerking

On Christmas Eve 1972 I was delighted to receive a letter from Thorpe, Surrey, part of the stockbroker belt inhabited by refugees from the BBC.

> Dear Mr Spike Mays,
>
> I am so sorry not to have returned your copy of *Call My Bluff* sooner but I had to wait until the next recording session which was only a few days ago. I quite agree with you shuddering on seeing my picture in the *Daily Mirror*. I am sure one should be able to sue under the Trades Description Act or something. With best wishes and strength to your pen.
>
> Yours ever, Frank Muir.

Had it not been for Frank Muir and that overgrown leprechaun Patrick Campbell, I might never have come across the word 'Swerk' and be threatened with expulsion from the Steeple Bumpstead Scrabble Society, who maintained there was no such word, and that I had won the last game by cheating. I cheered up when Frank sent me the book, duly signed by the joint writers. In short, I had stopped being swerk because there *is* such a word and it means becoming wretched and mournful, 'coming over swerk'.

We worn't a mite swerk at Ashdon Bonnett Inn a couple of years back when four unlikely lads met again after many a long year. All East Anglians, all ex-servicemen, all 'brown jobs' (soldiers, not matelots or Brylcreem boys), we compared notes on how we managed to get over the perils of 'swerk' when we were young and pure.

Barney started the ball rolling by comparing the newly launched, new-fangled Bonnet with the old (the one with two Ts).

Barney had pottered about East and West of Suez trying to dodge his comrades. He had been some kind of cook in the Catering Corps and took offence at two of their queries. 'Who called the cook a bastard?' and 'Who called the bastard a cook?' Barney used to sit next to me in Ashdon Elementary School and blamed me for his not passing one examination because he had copied my answers. As usual; but *I* managed to pass.

Gordon Greig, a proper owd Suffolker from Stoke-by-Clare was with my brother Chaffy in the pair of sieges of Tobruk before they beetled off to the Chindwin to save Orde Wingate from the Aussies, who didn't go much on 'Top Brass Poms'. He had joined 'The Pompadours' (a battalion of that Essex lot), instead of The Dutty Dozen (The Suffolks – 12th of Foot). We told him he should have known better!

Arthur Chapman, Barney's brother, had been a Grenadier and still looked like a Guardsman of the 1st of Footguards. When I was a bandboy in The Royals in 1924 I used to creep to Barosa Barrack, Aldershot to see brother Leslie and Arthur blancoing their belts and measuring their capes (by millimetres). If the rolled cape was only half a millimetre too long, the guard commander would not let 'em out of barracks. I used to wonder how the hell these foot guards (who only proceeded to a place on foot) would manage cavalry capes and a horse!

We had all soldiered in Egypt, India, Burma and places in Europe too numerous to mention. We had escaped with our lives and a few wounds and returned to conform to the norms of an East Anglian hamlet. After church, to assuage 'the thirst after righteousness' – usually from twelve noon till 'pudden time.'

Few of the old farmhands were left alive, but Barney's voice brought them back to life. 'Remember the games we used to play? People of today could never believe how we enjoyed ourselves. We didn't want TV or wireless. Come to think on it, there worn't TV then, it worn't in the villages!'

My mind flashed back to Wuddy Smith, the farm labourer I worked with on Place Farm. He had two claims to fame. During the First World War he served as a Gunner in the Royal Horse Artillery. His horse bucked and tipped Wuddy out of the saddle. Everyone laughed, except the Riding Instructor, who galloped up to Wuddy and touched him on the shoulder with a bunching-up stick and yelled, 'Who the hell gave you permission to dismount, Smith?'

Everyone laughed, except Wuddy, who yanked the instructor from his horse and tanned his backside with his own bunching-up stick. Everyone laughed except the Instructor and Wuddy, but Wuddy laughed a bit later, after he emerged from Aldershot's infamous clink, 'The Glasshouse'. 'By rights I should hev bin shot, seein' it were wartime,' chuckled Wuddy. 'All I got were fourteen days' rest and my sore arse got a rest from the saddle!'

His other claim to fame was featured in my book *Reuben's Corner*. Wuddy had been tutoring me in the highly important art of spreading dung with a four-tined fork.

'Flick yer wrist more, boy,' said Wuddy. 'A tidy owd twist an' yer don't hev ter tramp abowt spreadin' it more even-like.' He croaked out his Chinese dung-spreading song:

> 'Sling-shit hi,
> Sling-shit lo;
> The quicker yer flicks
> The further it go.'

Wuddy lived in a cottage opposite the Bonnet (it is still called 'Wuddies'). He shuffled into the taproom one evening and glowered hard at gamekeeper-cum-landlord Fred Threadgold.

'Git the cards, Fred. Me an' Jack'll see 'em twice round the board for a couple o' quarts!'

'Cards' were dominoes. The pubs kept several boxes with cribbage boards and coloured bone pegs to mark the scores. 'Laying Out' was the simplest and most popular. Each player had only to match the first card with a similar number, or to give a knock on the table if he could not follow. For this, Threadgold would fetch us the 'old cards', those ranging from double-nought to double-nine. The object was for two partners to rid themselves of all their cards before their opponents.

'Windmill' began with the laying down of the double-six. From this centre, all other cards had to be laid in the form of an 'X', to represent the sweeps of a windmill. 'Honest John' varied from district to district and from pub to pub, and many were the accusations and arguments about a player not conforming. 'Hellabit! I ain't hevin' that bor. He were a-playin' Cambridge fashion!'

'Fives and threes' required a bit of arithmetic; simple calculations were sometimes beyond labourers who had taken to the fields at the age of ten to twelve years. Each player was required to match up a numbered card in such a fashion that the total of the two ends was divisible by three or five. If, for example, there was a five at each end of the laid cards and the last player had matched up one end with a double-five, he could score the maximum of fifteen points. Fifteen being divisible by five threes and three fives, he could then peg eight – five threes and three fives – on the cribbage board.

Apart from nap, banker and cribbage, few card games were played in the taproom, but in the bar parlours, farmers, travelling salesmen and tradesmen of superior wealth, if not education, would play pontoon, brag and poker for quite high stakes.

Labourers preferred games calling for a sure eye, steady hand and low stakes. Thus shove ha'penny and skittle boards were in great demand.

'Ringing the Bull' was a great favourite of the elders.

Suspended by a cord from the taproom ceiling was a heavy metal ring, the cord being just long enough to allow the ring to swing, reach and engage over a wall hook. Originally the hook was the horn of a bull, and from it derived the name of the game. The object was to swing the ring onto the hook and score valuable points. Much practice attained the right momentum and uncanny accuracy by the elders. Some could ring the bull time and time again, with greater facility if beer and bets were involved.

'Pitch and Toss' and 'Pitch Penny' were also beer winners for the ancients, but could be expensive – mostly for the young who took them on.

'Nix and Bricks' was less expensive but more popular for all ages. The taproom floors were paved with bricks or square pamments (paving stones liberally sand sprinkled.) First the players would clear sand within the areas of one pamment or a number of bricks. Each of the players in one team, and in turn, would toss a handful of coins to the cleared section. Coins falling within the cleared areas were retained by the thrower. Those falling outside or straddling the intersecting joints, would be gleefully collected by the opponent, who added them to the next throw.

Craft and cunning were the order of the night for spectators, and some would persuade farmers and others who were returning from market a few sheets in the wind, to take part in the game. If they were a mite far gone they could not discriminate between silver and copper and when the coins rolled out of the cleared area, feet would be clamped down hard on 'mites o' silver'. The old ones excelled at 'Pitch Penny', a good source for cheap beer. A hole slightly bigger than a penny had been bored in the seating boards of the old oak settle. Below the hole had been fixed a box to catch the coins. The throwing point was at the far side of the room, about twelve feet away. All coins failing to get into the box were forfeit. A successful thrower would take all in the box.

Dart boards did not enter our village pubs until after the Kaiser's War. The elders objected to them because throwers kept marching up and down, cluttering up the room and wasting a lot of drinking time. But one game was appreciated by all. Bunk Take versus Wilkes, Captain Chapmen, Barney's father. 'Captain' was a nickname, not a rank.

Bunk had a bad night. Captain had licked him five times and white-washed him twice. 'Let's hev one more game, Bunk. This'll be the last!'

'Can't play agin, Captain. Nearly skint me. Only got a shillun left now!'

'Never mind. Never let yer mother know she bred a jibber! Tell yer what, I'll play the next game left-handed and give you a better chance.'

Bunk played. Bunk lost. Another white-wash. He turned to the maestro of scoring.

'Dew you know tergither, owd Captain plays *better* left-handed!'

'Yew oughter know, Bunk. He's bin a-playin' left all night and all his life. Owd Captain is left-handed!'

Usually played on holidays in taprooms of local village pubs, sometimes in the home at family gatherings, 'Tip It' was a game enjoyed by both sexes. Half a dozen a side was the usual team. Two teams would face each other across the table and could be reinforced if seating permitted and was heartily encouraged by the mawthers. But if the women played they were banned from sitting at the ends of the forms or settles.

Only 'The Bit', a threepenny piece, was needed for the play. Each team appointed its 'caller', whose job it was to toss for the start and pass the 'bit' to his team mates. At the caller's shout, 'down then', his team would drop their hands and hide them under the table. With a great show of passing, fumbling and re-passing, they would attempt to baffle their opponents as to the precise location of the 'bit'. At the call, 'up then, bring 'em up clean', they would withdraw their hands from under the table and plonk them fully clenched on the table top. The other team had to point to the hand they thought was clutching the bit. If successful, the team would take over the bit and the procedure would be reversed. The game was played mainly for fun, especially when the women took part, and it could be quite hilarious. Shrieks of mirth came from the women when men groped and fumbled below the table top searching for 'The Bit'!

Fred Rawson, a retired ID officer, brought his wife and son to The Bonnet, where he became landlord. He also brought a new game or practice known as the 'Cork Club'. He spoke of the fun (and funds) it had brought to his Derbyshire village when he was young. The object was to make money for refreshment, liquid and solid, to be taken as required throughout the year, but with a share-out at Christmas.

My father was appointed Recruiting Officer and swiftly shanghaied a willing battalion whose membership was confined to regular patrons. There were no membership cards, no secret handshakes or mason-like nods, winks, blinks and gestures. Not even a cap badge or colour. But there was a membership fee of 6d, on receipt of which the fully paid-up new member was given an identity disc, specially known to members as a Crown Stopper, from a mineral water bottle. Funds were raised by challenges. First of all the challenge should be made within the premises of The Bonnet, then extended to the whole of the universe within challenge reach.

The rules were simple. Any member of the Bonnet Cork Club – on production of his own cork – had to challenge other known members by commanding, 'Where's your cork?'

If the cork was not produced, the defaulter was fined 6d, but if the challenger challenged without producing his own cork first, he was fined 6d. It became a club of much merriment. Challenges were made in church choir-stalls, chapel vestries, the Labour Hall and the Conservative Club. Sometimes when people were dancing and courting.

One example of club spirit and craft became village gossip for days. A dozen Cork Club members arrived at The Bonnet in time for a final drink. They had returned from the seaside, one of those 'mystery' charabanc tour jobs where everybody knows where they were going. Seeing them all tarted up in their Sunday best blue serge suits, Landlord Rawson challenged the lot to produce their corks – and quickly increased club finances by six needed shillings. 'The cunnin owd varmint knew we worn't likely to cart corks to Clacton!'

Bunk Take was another victim. Now seventeen and, like many others just after the Kaiser's War with no regular employment, now and again he found seasonal jobs and was once threshing wheat at Place Farm. His colleagues persuaded Bunk to go The Bonnet for a gallon of beer. One of them pinched Bunk's cork, and showed it to Jim Marsh, who challenged straight away. 'Got yet cork, Bunk? Owd Rawson's bound to ask you for it!'

Bunk searched, failed to find it and was fined 6d.

'Never mind. Take mine to show him,' then, to the others, 'You'd better give him yours as well, lads.'

Bunk (Arthur) Take departed, with a gallon jar bumping in the sack across his shoulders and eight crown stoppers jingling in his pocket.

'Mornin', Fred! I wanter gallon o'bitter for me mets.'

'Morning, Arthur! Here's my cork, where's yours?'

Bunk chuckled. 'I gotter hull handful. Look!' He slapped down eight crown stoppers and was promptly fined for being in illegal possession of other members' corks. It cost him eight shillin, plus another sixpence for failing to produce his own.

Being a true blue club member, he paid up straight away from the money given to him to buy the beers, and had nothing left.

'Carn't let me owd mets down,' said Bunk. 'Fill the jar, but give the buggers one gallon o' water!'

Despite the usual penalties of deprivation, our village children were far from 'swerk' and had a great capacity for happiness. There were few 'shop toys', not even a shop in our hamlet. The children played most of the games their forefathers had played a century before. They made their own toys. Girls had wooden hoops and rag dolls, boys had iron hoops and shut-knives.

We cut our own bows and arrows, catapults, water-pistols, hooks and whistles. Nature supplied all the materials in woods and hedgerows. When early autumn winds blew down the first green husks of the horse-chestnut trees, the glistening brown nuts were carefully extracted and inspected.

Only the finest were drilled and strung for the ritual contests of the conker campaign held at any time on any road. The roads were our playing fields and were safe. Just one motor car in the village!

Toy making was time absorbing, full of new tricks to learn for each change of the seasons. There was no better implement for conker drilling than the stiletto-pointed horseshoe nail, begged, borrowed or swiped from one of the two farriers' forges. The conker was then threaded on stout string about eighteen inches long. The bigger the better, for like atomic bombs, it was intended for destruction. A boy would hold out his conker for an opponent's strike. The object was to shatter the nut, and many more nuts until he had many wins, thus classifying hit nut battle honours. Young Donald Pettit had the village record – a fortyniner – but he had cheated, they said.

Baking the nut, soaking it in brine, vinegar and egg-pickle, with the object of toughening it up as athletes toughen up themselves with drugs and such for the Olympic Games – to make them virtually indestructible – was definitely cheating and considered unsportsmanlike.

'It ain't fair! He's got an owd baked-un!' Few would play with one who resorted to such base tactics.

Except for those little black ones on grandma's high boots, buttons were valuable currency for schoolboys. 'Buttons', as a game, was even more popular than marbles, and had many staunch adherents in the teams and sides. To be left out of one's playing team by a lack of buttons was embarrassing and degrading.

White mice, Albino rats with pink eyes, Belgian hares, pet rabbits, ferrets, frogs and toads in jars and goldfish in bowls, as well as shutknives, whistles, pop-guns and pea-shooters (all home made) were often swapped or temporarily pawned, for a few bits of bone with holes in them. Just to play 'Buttons'.

Variations of the game were legion. The oldest, much played in Bartlow, Cambridgeshire, was a throwing game. But Ashdon boys preferred the 'wall pitcher'.

To begin 'Bartler Fashion', a boy would throw a number of buttons a distance of twelve to fourteen feet, with the object of landing them in a hole about four inches in diameter. All buttons landing in the hole would score 'one'. Those failing to hole could be flicked in by finger tip, each flick counting 'one'. The player who holed all his buttons with the fewest flicks was the winner, and confiscated his opponent's buttons.

For 'Ashdon Fashion Wall Pitching', a boy would pitch a button against the school wall. All eyes would be on the button as it bounced off the wall and fell to the ground. A good pitcher could make a button bounce a tidy way. The next player would try to bounce his button close to the first one. If by spreading his fingers he could span the two, he would take both.

When a player had exhausted his stock of buttons he was compelled to drop out of the game. But this poignant state of affairs was not reached so long as buttons were still on his clothes.

Many a boy has returned home from school with his baggy home-made breeches held up with binder string, but within a week, he would go off home from school with pockets stuffed with buttons and arms filled with pets. He had won enough of the former to redeem the latter. Fortune was forever fickle in the good old game of Buttons.

There were many variations of 'marbles' and games with cigarette cards. We played 'fivestones', 'Hare and Hounds' (a kind of paper chase), and pick-a-back wrestling, but most games were seasonal, according to the state of nature's utensils.

When hazel and willow were pliable, sappy and springy it needed only one boy to arrive at school with a new bow and arrows to start off the annual urge for archery. A boy might trundle to school a new iron hoop, and in no time the smithies were pestered for hoops, tantalised into making iron hoop-guides with wooden handles. Others would flog along the hoops with blows from a stout stick, but a forked stick was ideal for trundling and guiding the clanking ring of steel. Hoops, catapults and slings seemed always to be in vogue at the same time and one was considered to be inferior if one had not extracted the digit and made all three.

Catapults were expensive to buy, but cheap and easy to make. The only financial outlay was for a two-foot length of square gutta-percha, greyish-black rubber from Malaysia. This, carefully bound to the upper ends of a forked stick cut from some hedge, and the other ends secured to a piece of soft leather – usually the tongue of an old boot – was a lethal weapon. Many a pheasant, hare and rabbit met its end at the hand of our catapult marksman.

Spinning tops made their appearance in sunny days of springtime. The flint-capped village street became alive with boys and girls, all busy flogging away at home-made tops with home-made whips. Tops were made gay with bright paint or coloured crayon.

Home-made toys were legion, effective and ingenious: whistles, from the tenderest wands of willow, pop-guns from the hollow-stemmed elder, with oak or ash for the pop-rod. Pea-shooters were also made from the elder stems, plus a steel spring 'busk', stolen from mother's corsets.

From stems of sheep and cow-parsley we made water pistols and syringes and intriguing wind instruments. By making incisions in a six-inch length of cow parsley stalk, and bending it in a certain way while blowing down one end, simple tunes could be played (if one could stand the rank taste of the mouthpiece).

Girls kept mostly to spinning tops, walking on stilts, parading and dressing dolls, teddy bears, hop-scotch, 'touch' and rounders. Much of their activities centred upon skipping to tunes and nursery rhymes. 'Tinker, tailor, ploughboy, sailor, rich man, poor man, beggarman, thief'. Then at a furious increase in skipping speed, transportation and dress would be brought into the act.

'Horse and carriage for my marriage. Wheelbarrow, tumbril, brougham, pony-cart, silk, satin, cotton, rags', and so on before they lined up, out of puff and beetroot-red for turns on the short rope, the real test for speed and accuracy. 'Salt, mustard, vinegar, pepper, BUMP.'

Both boys and girls gathered to collect wild flowers to press between the pages of perhaps the only two books then in most tied cottages, *The Bible* and *Pilgrim's Progress*. Some had their own little garden plots and grew favourite flowers to take to teacher.

Well, that's how it used to be, and it is grand to think of the beauty and tranquillity, then to compare it with today.

Last evening, the village clock had not pushed out crotchets to announce it was eight of the evening hour. I passed three cottages with undrawn blinds. Children's eyes were glued to the goggle-box, their ears to shrieks and moans of 'group singers'. And in the grass, about a table-cloth sized lawn, were the toys of young swerks. Plastic machine guns, tanks, rocket launchers, and a garden gnome wearing a space helmet. And do you know? They can't tell the difference between two eggs, robin's and ostrich.

> Will you take a sprig of hornbeam?
> Will you try a twig of pine?
> Or a beam of dusky cedar,
> That the ivy dare not twine?
>
> My larch is slim and winsome,
> There's blossom on the sloe...
> Timber, tell you,
> Tell you, timber,
> How my trees do grow!

16

Kitchen Cunning

A good housewife provides, ere sickness do come,
Of sundry good things in her house to have some,
Good aqua composita, vinegar tart,
Rose water and treacles, to comfort thine heart.
Cold herbs in her garden, for agues that burn,
That over-strong heat to good temper may turn.
White endive and succorym spinach enow;
All, with good pot herbs, should follow the plough.
Conserves of barbary, quinces and such,
With sirops that easeth the sickly so much.
Good broth and good keeping do much now and then;
With diet with wisdom, best comforteth man.
In health, to be stirring should profit thee best,
In sickness, hate trouble; seek quiet and rest.
Remember thy soul, let no fancy prevail;
Make ready for God-ward, let faith never quail.
The sooner thyself thou submittest to God,
The sooner He ceaseth to scourge with his rod.

(Thomas Tesser, 1523-80)

Be-whiskered, weather-worn and nigh on sixty, grandfather
Reuben Ford tethered his Suffolk Punch plough team to a
five-barred gate to eat his mid-morning dockey (elevenses).
His sharp shutknife conveyed to his mouth a sliver of cheese
topped with raw onion. He pointed to the bottom half of a

cottage loaf made the day before by Granny Ford in the bakus behind our twin cottages, Brick and Stone Villa: 'With half a quartern o' that, a mite o' cheese an' onion I can larst the day!'

He washed some down with a gulp of two of home-brewed ale, made by himself in the same bakus.

Bread was our staple diet. Every cottage housewife was taught by her mother the arts of mixing, kneading, firing and watching, to make bread and bakestones in brick and clay ovens.

One received an immediate restoration of energy from a slice or two, with or without butter, cheese or the butcher's hard dripping, but as Granny said, 'That's gotter be done proper.' For the once-a-fortnight ritual she prepared the dough overnight, placing careful measures of white wheat flour in her kneading trough, the keeler. Secret measures of salt and water were added, plus a little mysterious 'some-thing' to the yeast – a family secret.

When the dough was thoroughly mixed, the wooden lid of the keeler was pressed down and covered with warm sacking to assist the fermentation. By morning the rising dough would have forced off the lid. Pressing firmly and gently over the sacking with the flat of her hands, a trick to expel the gases, Susannah would then get busy shaping and moulding on the up-turned, well-floured lid. 'A tidy owd lump for the base, a small one for the top, and the shape of the cottage loaf was formed.'

Meanwhile Reuben, after feeding Overhall Farm's horses, brought the oven to baking heat. The correct temperature was of paramount importance. Deep inside the clay-plastered oven was placed an ignited faggot of dead or well-dried blackthorn or whitethorn. Carefully directed jets of air from hand bellows drew the fire to an even white head on which more branches of whitethorn were continually thrust until they became white hot.

The right time for putting the dough in the oven was determined by a glance at the 'watch and tell-tale', a small pebble specially selected from the fields, which changed colour with variations of temperature. This was built into the oven. When it became fiery red, embers were raked into the recess below the oven which was then cleaned with a mop made of sacking tied to a pole and saturated with water.

One at a time, each loaf was placed in the oven with a peel, a long spoon of circular board mounted on a wooden handle, and left to bake. Granny then scrubbed down the keeler (a much prized wedding gift from the wheelwright on her wedding day) and would stand sniffing that truly wonderful smell of baking bread. By her sense of sniff she could tell when the bread was properly baked. Then, sliding a steel-bladed peel under the loaves, she removed them one at a time to the deal table to cool. Her fortnightly baking was over, and we would get hot bread to sample, smelling of wheat and heat-softened cheese.

Now was the time for Reuben to creep into the act. 'Sue allus looks arter the solids, but I take care o' the moisture.' It was also a time for brewing. Not a bit of the oven's heat could be wasted. Faggots were cut and made by hand, carried from hedgerow and woods, or were sixpence a-piece to buy. Therefore King Teddy potatoes were placed in the glowing embers before Reuben really got down to business. Never before have spuds tasted so good; smarmed with home-made butter the colour of marigolds, a pinch of black pepper and salt. Pots and pans filled with clear spring water were poured into the still hot oven. It was ale day. Licking his lips as though in gleeful anticipation, Reuben would be surrounded by odd-sized sacks of berries, hops, malt and yeast. He brooked no disturbance as he brought twenty gallons of Adam's Ale to the boil. He poured it over the malt in the keeler, gave furious stirrings, then added sugar and hops. When cool, it was sampled by adults and children alike, at the stage of 'sweat wat'. We children were only allowed one 'taster', for the beer was intended for the men working so hard on the fields, but if the 'taster' proved good enough, it could be entered for judgement at the Flower Show.

But now, the pale, weak, sugary liquid was brought back to the boil and yeast was added. For four or five hours it was left to 'gather itself'. When gathered, the weak pale ale had transformed itself into strong brown and was strained into casks, enough to help down many a hunk of home-made bread from seedtime to harvest. Other than the zinc and copper containers, every article used for 'Reuben's Brew' was hand made: keelers, stirring paddles, ladles, casks and taps.

Few utensils were required for Granny Susannah's wine distillery. She was a dab hand at making heart-cheering wine. Tubs, already to hand, had been bought from a publican for one shilling; sawn in half they produced two 'mashers'. Jars, too, had been filled and emptied over many a year. Mostly of stone, they ranged from half a gallon to four gallons. There were also in the secret place of the bakus some sweet-smelling wooden casks, and when they were unveiled we knew that glasses of lovely belly-warming wine were coming our way.

Granny first went to the little brook running behind Walt's Cottage, with all kinds of roots, herbs, flowers and fruit. She would sort and carefully clean them in the running water, then immerse them in cold spring water, sometimes for weeks. From time to time, the scum forming on the water was skimmed. When ready, the juice was strained through fine muslin into the stone jars; demerara sugar was added, and the juice was put into an iron boiler and heated, but not brought to the boil, and poured into a cask, stirred and left to ferment. Some folk used brewer's yeast to aid fermentation, either by dissolving it in the liquid, or by spreading yeast on a slice of toast and letting it float on the surface for a few days. After standing for several days, according to the variety of fruit, the wine was poured into broaching casks and corked loosely – to allow it to breathe. After fermentation, corks and bungs were driven home and final instructions given. 'That marn't be meddled o'er fer a year or more. Wine ain't wine till it's seen a couple o' buthdays!'

Although elderberries were profuse and easily gathered, they were not much used for wine making in the 1920s. Our bread was spread with elderberry jam during the Kaiser's War, and we were sick of it. But our folk in Bartlow Hamlet were expert in making six favourites from field, allotments, hedgerows and meadows. Parsnip, rhubarb, wheat, dandelion, barley and cowslip. There were many others, including bee, potato and carrot. My favourite was Granny Ford's hip wine, just like a fine liqueur. Old Joslin, the master thatcher, didn't think much of the last three. 'Don't seem to tickle the owd gizzard like Sue's hip wine, my brethren!'

Granny had a little book. Once white, it is years-stained sepia. Concertina creased and furrowed like Granny's brow, it was given to my mother.

COWSLIP

2 peck cowslips
Lay to dry in sun a few days
18 quarts spring water
To each gallon water add 3 pound raw sugar.
Put on fire.
When nearly boiling put in beaten white 2 eggs
Boil 1 hour
Allow to cool
When lukewarm put in cowslips, juice and peel of 3 lemons
Add 2 tablespoons yeast.
Stir twice a day for 3 or 4 days
When gathered strain into barrel and bung
Stand for 1 month
If bottling add 1 lump sugar each bottle.

If warmed and served with a pinch of ginger, just before bedtime, this most delicate distil was guaranteed to banish warts, colds, fevers and put ingrowing toenails into reverse. But 'top of the pops', easiest and cheapest to make, was the oldest.

DANDELION

4 dandelion heads, 1 orange
gathered in sun 3 pound loaf sugar
3 quarts spring water 1 lemon

Granny did not limit her kitchen cunning to wine making. From the bounteous fruits of trees, hedges, allotments, fields and meadows she made jams, pickles and other preserves. Her jellies were as clear as a Girl Guide's conscience. Her chutneys were as hot as Hades. One little taster of her cauliflower chutney would bring one out in a muck sweat. She specialised in pickling walnuts, Reuben's favourite with cold roast pork, but Granny preferred salted beechnuts – to fetch the phlegm off her chest.

Bottles and jars of all these wonderfully tasty provisions stood in serried ranks on her home-made kitchen shelves, all topped and sealed with waxed paper, each labelled with the date of manufacture. But Granny put a foot wrong with one batch of raspberry jam. Perhaps she had mislaid her *Old Moore's Almanack*, perhaps she wished to keep up to date: 'Raspberry' (this year's).

There is no doubt in my mind that Granny Ford turned me into a greedy glutton. In those hard years just before Kaiser Bill's War, when skilled farm workers earned only ten shillings a week and decided to strike, our tied cottage larders did not bulge with fodder, and I can recall Granny's words. 'There's no need to fret. There's plenty of food about if you look for it, and enough t'keep yer belly-button a long way from yer backbone!'

Grandfather Reuben Ford was partly responsible. I used to watch him preparing his favourite meal – toasted Yarmouth bloaters. Now and again a man would come to our village in a pony cart. He said he had walked all the way from Gorleston, just to bring old Reuben his favourite grub, on sticks. He had many sticks in his cart on which were threaded by the gills a dozen beautiful bloaters. A stick of twelve cost only 9d.

Grandad would draw his armchair close to the fire. After he had cut two thick slices from a cottage loaf and placed them on a dish in the hearth, he went to the bakus for his special toasting fork, one he had made from buckshee fencing wire. When the bloater began to sizzle, Grandfather sizzled. For, like old Pavlov's pups, he would salivate in gleeful anticipation and little dribblings of spit ran down his ginger whiskers.

The sight of it always made me hungry. Sometimes old Reuben would give me a whole bloater for myself. One day he gave me very good advice which has served me well over many years and in many lands.

> Allus eat when you get hungry.
> Allus drink when you get dry.
> Close yar eyes when you get sleepy,
> But don't stop breathin', bor, you'll die.

According to my *Old Moore's Almanack* this advice was given to me over seventy years ago. From that important day in my life, until fairly recently, I have never refused food, but am now paying the penalty for over-indulgence. It is now my turn to dish out advice.

You may stuff your Yarmouth bloaters, Norfolk turkeys, Aylesbury ducks, geese and chickens – any old way you wish, for in the 1990s I shall stick to 'the fruit of the fowl' as my staple diet.

For this chicken, the plain and simple omelette, with no heavings of spur-shaped breast bones to have wishes and desires fulfilled. I shall jettison my bicarbonate of soda, pull the ejection-seat lever to hurl into space that Maclean's concoction that transformed grumpy, liverish Gilbert Harding into riches and fame, almost overnight.

Over-eating, too much 'gravy' and not enough shut-eye nigh on stopped my breathing and left me with scarce enough strength to carry a verbal message. I dizzied, gasped, belched, then groped toward tomes on dietary and kitchen cunning.

Lo and behold, I discovered the panacea; that the simple omelette had been invented and perfected by a chap named Marcus Gavius Apicius, who lived in Rome way back in AD 25. He did not confine himself to omelettes, but wrote about cookery and its reward in the heyday of Roman gluttony.

You know that old pig's fry we used to buy as offal? Over sixty years ago, when you could buy a whole 'pluck' for a tanner and fry the lot with onions – liver and lights and 'curtains' – well, old Apicius even improved that good old East Anglian dish.

The cunning varmint used to fatten his pigs with dried figs. He gave them choice wine sweetened with honey and, what pleased me most to read, he crept up on his porkers when they worn't looking and killed 'em by surprise. He reckoned that if they knew death was shortly coming up the straight they'd get such a shock that it would spoil the flavour of their livers.

Having spent enormous sums (his whole fortune) on eating and drinking, he found that life had lost its favour (or flavour), so he committed suicide. But before he went he had the wit to put us properly in the picture about the omelette.

It didn't matter a mite whether we used the eggs of partridges, plovers, pheasants and peewits, or any size from wren's to ostrich's, so long as they were fresh. Like a Suffolk spring-morning day.

Granny taught me to discover freshness. 'Howd it to the sun with yer eye at the little end an' look through. If that's fresh you'll see a bright light like a star.'

Like children peering through smoked glass to watch an eclipse, we peered through eggs and the starless ones were handed over for pickling in brine.

Most hen-keepers knew that a new-laid egg was at its best about 24 hours after the 'drop'. Mrs Expensive Beeton held to this view, but added that a dozen-egg omelette was a fairish meal, although it might be preferable in terms of economy and ease of cooking to settle for half-a-dozen, just a snack.

The ancient Roman postulated that the frying pan should be proportionate to the number of eggs, to the size of the omelette. He would not look at the fancy pans of today, tarted up tine, pretty-picture aluminiums, cracky enamel and that non-stick muck that gives fried eggs black bums.

Old Marcus swore by his good solid iron pans. They should never be washed with water but rubbed hard, when good and hot, with palm leaves and salt – the best way to stop the hen-fruit sticking.

Swarms and hordes of TV cooks of every channel have

produced their recipes, but their cooking ain't a patch on the methods of Marcus. For three non-gluttons, one should seize a dozen eggs by the point of balance, break them into a glazed basin, season them with salt and ground spices and add a drop or two of cold water. This should then be bashed about with a bamboo whisk until large bubbles build up on the top – for half a minute. It is disastrous to bash them longer.

As the iron pan is now stoking up – not too hot, mind you – we bung in an ounce and a half of olive oil or butter and let it ride in the pan until it stops frothing and turns poetically to summer gold. Now pour the eggs into the pan.

Take a deep breath, drink a large Scotch and seize a fork or palette knife. Turn down the heat a bit. Loosen the edges of the omelette all round one or twice, but quickly and in the middle, letting the liquid smarm itself to fill the middle gaps. Have another large Scotch, for here cometh the great moment. Like folding a saddle-blanket at night in the Sahara in a sandstorm, with all the composure one can muster, fold over the omelette and peg it down like a Bedouin bell-tent, sabre-like with the fork along one side. Roll it into the shape required. Whip it from the pan, all golden brown outside, wet and sloppy inside. Slide it onto a hot plate and leave it so that it can cook its own sloppy innards. More Scotch!

Make its golden face slippery and shiny by dabbing on flicks of butter. These last dabs make all the difference, and the job is done. Not quite! Omelettes should always be cooked whilst the guests are seated at table, all salivating like pricked water blisters in anticipatory relish, for guests should allus wait for the omelette – never the omelette for the guests.

If perchance your bank balance is well in the black, have a stab at this refinement. This 'royale' omelette was made for HM King Edward II by a French chef of international repute, one Nignon, who has put his recipe in the permanence of the written word in his book *Les Plaisirs de la Table*.

OMELETTE RICHMONDS

Mince 300 grammes of fresh parish mushrooms. Fry

them golden brown in butter and add a liqueur-glass of excellent port wine.

Cover it with double cream and two spoonfuls of meat-glaze veal. Simmer slowly. When the mushrooms are enrobed with a thin veil of cream, you will dispose them in the centre, along the whole length of an omelette.

Slide this omelette on a dish and cover it entirely with a sauce Mornay. Sprinkle with Parmesan, moisten with melted butter. Finish off with the salamander to give a fine golden glaze.

Who wants turkey after that? Or Christmas Pud. I remember what we used to sing about Christmas Pud in the army, that stuff made by farriers in the NAAFI!

> Up spoke the workhouse-master
> His face as bold as brass...
> 'We don't want your Christmas Pud,
> Stick it on your wall!'

17

Smoke Signals

Early in autumn 1978, when Cardinals calculated, poppies
bloomed and there was huffing and puffing in Rome, I
received a letter from a total stranger; an ex-reed thatcher
from Swaffham, Norfolk. He thanked me for writing books
and articles that had given him pleasure and said he thought
of popping down to Steeple Bumpstead before Christmas. His
postscript was interesting.

'You have written about every facet of our lives except
religion. Why don't you write about the new Pope?'

I replied and thanked him for his generous words, stating
there was no reason why he should not pop in to Steeple
Bumpstead, the natives were friendly, even to Norfolk Dump-
lings, but as Popes were thin on the ground in this neck of the
East Anglian undergrowth I had not clapped eyes on one. I
continued that if Dave Allen could get away with saying
extremely disobliging things about Their Holinesses each
time he goggle-boxed, there was no reason why an East
Anglian ex-choirboy of the Anglican tribe should not put in
his two-pennorth. Particularly when this choirboy, on his last
trip to sunny Italy, had been blessed by the Pope in the Square
of Saint Peter (himself).

Two days later the Norfolk Dumpling sat opposite me in
the Red Lion. He had popped over to Steeple Bumpstead to
make me sign one of my books. I introduced him to other 'old
sweats'. Our natives and the Norfolk Dumpling got on like

housen afire, and it turned out to be a week of great
importance, what with attending the centenary parade of my
elementary school at Ashdon, gathering with other ancient
warriors of the Royal British Legion (some had served in Italy
and Burma, and there were a couple who used to either freeze
in the icy barrack-rooms of Catterick Camp, or get smoked
out). Then, at the end of the week, seeing more smoke, ancient
smokings from former Papal elections, for BBC TV were
transmitting flash-backs of white smoke and black smoke
with not a Dave Allen in sight at all.

Before the Norfolk Dumpling left the village, we managed
to lubricate the larynx and croak out the barrack-room song:

> We pushed the damper in
> And we pulled the damper out;
> But the smoke went up the chimney
> Just the same.
> Just the same, as before;
> Never less, always more.
> So we pulled the damper out
> Instead of pushing in.
> And the smoke went up our chimney nevermore.

A brace of foreigners are to blame for my being blessed in
Rome. Dottore Ettore Carinelli really started the papal ball
a-rolling in Newbattle Abbey College, Dalkeith. Ettore and I
were students, learning the perils of English Lit. from Doctor
Edwin Muir. For two years we swotted with another friend,
George Mackay Brown, the Orkney author, poet and play-
wright. Ettore was also indulging himself in the study of that
bastard art of science generally known as 'economics'. After a
couple of months he got up on his hinds at a seminar and for
half an hour gave a faultless report on the Division of Labour.
We, his fellow students, were unaware he was a millionaire
who owned large lumps of Wopland. He told us he had
fought against us in Hitler's War, but had helped to string up
Mussolini by his heels on a kind of lamp-post in Milan,
Ettore's home town.

'One day, Spiko, you will come and stay with me. I can offer you only blue skies, sunshine, lovely wine and beautiful women. Will you come?'

The college boiler had gone up the creek. There was no hot water. Outside the sky was sad and lowering, the lawns under two feet of snow.

'Let us mount and march right now!' said I.

'Some day soon!'

I waited only two years before I was bound for Milan by Alitalia Caravelle. Ettore had nowt to do with my flight. Foreigner two had crept into my act in the form of Yavar Abbas, BBC TV cameraman. I was then engaged as Press and Public Relations Officer at Heathrow Airport. Yavar had been sent down from Auntie Beeb to take pictures for BBC News. This was a highly important newsworthy job. The inaugural flight of Uganda Airways was due to leave mother earth that morning from Runway 28/Left. There were not many about. If one had strong field-glasses and trained them on the fuselage of the Boeing 707, one could make out the word 'Uganda' on a kind of postage stamp. There were only passengers, ten of whom were to dismount at Manchester.

'Typical of the bloody BBC!' said disgruntled Yavar.

'I know,' said I. 'Wasting our licence lolly. They probably thought there would be thousands of Zulus prancing about with banners stuck in their navels!'

'You are not very helpful,' said Yavar. 'Let's go for a drink!'

We sat in the scruff of the smelly Green Dragon, a corrugated horror of a hut owned by the Ministry of Aviation. The coffee was cold and looked like mud from the Nile. 'What's your next job?'

'Number ten, Downing Street. I'm going to complain to the Prime Minister!'

Yavar had been a news-cameraman for the British Army and for Claude Auchinleck. Although of Muslim faith, he had served as an officer in a Sikh regiment. We swapped yarns about India, where I had served for five years and left in 1933, before the deplorable partition. We shared a love of India and he said he would like to jack in his BBC job and make films

118

about India. In a few months we had formed a film company, 'Current Affairs Productions Limited'. Sir Claude Auchinleck became our President. Our first film, *India! My India!'* had been telecast by BBC TV before someone discovered that a film festival was coming up the straight in Milan. Our application for entry was too late, but wires were pulled and seats booked on Alitalia. Dottore Ettore Carinelli met us on arrival, and through meeting these two foreigners I was able to meet yet another foreigner, and was blessed, in more ways than one.

I returned to Italy in the springtime to collect the award. Our film, *India! My India!* had won the award for the best documentary. Almost every day at the Fair, we lunched and dined with Ettore. I remained in Italy for three weeks, often the guest of Ettore's lovely wife Lydia and their children, less frequently with his artist and architect friend Sergio Coccito, not forgetting Sergio's lovely Australian wife, who taught English to Italian children. Everyone was kindness incarnate. It was instant 'open house', for in my pocket were the keys to five homes in Milan. They took me on tours of that lovely, kindly land.

On one sightseeing tour we started off in Milan for a five-day jaunt of sheer splendour and delight, and took in many churches. Ettore's eyes seemed to sadden as he pointed out where Benito Mussolini had swung from his heels. We kissed the infant Christ on the bronze door of Milan's magnificent cathedral, which boasts a spire for every day in the year. The bronze head of the child Christ had worn shiny from the lips of worshippers.

'Have you a cold?' asked Sergio with concern.

'No ... I am trying to smell your violets. What a pity they don't smell as strong as your cheese! In East Anglia we can smell the violets. The sweet scent of the English violet is wonderful!'

'For you, yes! God and the Archbishop of Canterbury did arrange it. To hide the stink of the English!'

Next day we drove off the main Volterra road, through the medieval Giovanni gate to wonderful San Gimignano and

119

wandered through narrow streets all a-bustle with poor country folk, before we climbed the 170ft tower of the town hall, Palazzo del Popolo.

We stood in the council hall where Dante once had stood, and looked from a wooden platform onto the enchanting vista before and below. The twin towers of Salvucci, the Piazza del Erbe, the square Pesciolini tower and, far beyond, the Tuscan hills, across light greens studded with tall dark green sombre cypresses and a smoky-blue hazy light which transformed human beings and cattle into misty fairies.

Ettore touched my shoulder: 'What are you thinking, Spiko?'

'I am thinking what a lucky man you are. You can look on this beauty and say "This is my own, my native land".' We stayed silent.

Into the Citroën and away to Rome, where we stayed one night in the Motel AGIP, Via Aurelia. Next morning we were up and about with our own impromptu dawn chorus. There is something about Italy and Wales that lubricates the laggard larynx. We warbled willy-nilly, three different songs, each in a different language, 'Con spirito'.

Soon the trio was reduced to a duet. Ettore had to meet Dottore r.f. Santagati, who would be travelling with us to Bari. Sergio and I had a more important appointment.

I have telephoned His Holiness on his "hot number" (VAT 69) and we shall go quickly now to the Vatican City.'

'I am familiar with the number!' said I. Sergio winked and replied, 'I have arranged with His Holiness that he must come this morning to bless just you. Already he has blessed me, but you need it more!'

To my surprise, and as sure as God made little apples, His Holiness blessed the pair of us. A bit of a long-distance blessing, for he was chairborne on the shoulders of strong Italians through Saint Peter's Square. Women abounded and lifted up their children for blessing and kisses.

'Now you are blessed, I will show you great treasures, Spiko. The rich Catholic baubles of Christianity. Do not look at the big pots, the vases and sculptures, which are useless.

Do not look at the paintings of Leonardo da Vinci. They are "comic cuts", Walt Disneys compared with my favourite masterpiece, except two, "It Cenacoli" in the church of S. Maria delle Grazie, Milano. "The Last Supper", I will show you that when we return, and the other is in the Louvre, Paris – "La Giaconda" or "Mona Lisa". Come!'

He bought tickets for the Sistine Chapel, at 500 lire apiece, and crossed himself and cried at the very sight of the fresco painting, Michelangelo's immortal 'The Last Judgment'.

What moved me most I shall never know. The glory of the painting or friend Sergio's tears.

'I cry, Spiko, for commercialised Christ and for the poor who cannot afford to look at 500 lire per ticket.'

We motored off to Naples and drove slowly past Cassino, where sun-washed walls were dazzling white and the green earth thick with soldiers' graves, and dark cypresses stand Grenadier-like; so still, like sentinel mourners, and the new Monte Cassino shines from its hilltop like a marbled jewel – as a memorial to those Polish infantrymen and Johnny Gurkhas with naked kukris who had stormed the shell-blasted original and wrested it from the Germans, in bitter, blood-pouring, hand-to-hand combat.

'Our earth is rich with blood!' said Ettore.

At Bari, a kindly gentleman conducted me on a tour of honour. I had been nominated for life membership of the Bari Yachting Club for services rendered to Italy. Not very much to write home about, but at dinner the previous evening one of the guests asked me a leading question. 'What is it, those three fruits you see in streets of the market? One is red, one is yellow and one is green.'

The room seemed to explode when I gave my reply. 'Traffic lights!'

We walked slowly through the old Bari to the Norman castle, since enlarged by Frederick II. 'Come, Spiko,' said Sergio, 'to see the relics of Father Christmas.' I thought he was joking but he led me into the church of Saint Nicholas of Myra, the original Santa Claus, and related how his bones had been stolen by seamen, but were returned in 1087, placed in a silver casket, and were now heavily protected by iron bars in the crypt shrine.

We went to the shrine and knelt, elbows touching. Sergio prayed for me aloud. I was deeply moved.

Later, we sat in the sunshine, separated by a table top and a brace of bottles, some kind of liqueur made in Foggio from the husks of the walnut. So soothing and mellow, a benedictory drink that made one feel the same towards all of mankind, that one could trust and love the cunning, scheming lot. Sergio wrapped it up very neatly. 'I am not, as you would say, a devout or devoted Catholic, Spiko. I pray only when I am in emotion and moved, and for my close friends, but most for all the poor people of southern Italy. They pay much to our church. They receive only blessings and blessings, words and more words, but the church is rich and gets more rich!'

His eyes lit up as he leaned toward me.

'I think I will put you on the list for to become our next Pope, old Spiko. Only the poor know how to look after the poor, and remember, you owe me lire for your ticket to see "The Last Judgment".'

'What colour smoke will come out of the Vatican chimney if I am chosen as Pope?'

'Because I am an artist I will choose for you, my friend. We will have bloodshot smoke to match your eyes, followed with puffs of red, white and blue because you are English!'

Many friends came to Linate Airport to see the back of me. I can still feel the bear-hugs of Ettore and Sergio and hear the direct order Sergio gave to the Customs and Immigration Officers. 'If he comes back, send him back, please!'

When I arrived at Heathrow a package was handed to me. A mystery package. On the Alitalia label, two words. 'Papa Spiko.'

Gifts galore, from sunny, sunny Italy.

Parmesan cheese, Parma violets and silks for my wife, Vera. Bottles of Ettore's best wine for me. For us both, gramophone records, made at La Scala, Milano – *Aida*, *La Forza del destino* and *La Traviata*. There was also a large envelope containing the menu we had enjoyed at Ginnaninos, and Sergio's note:

'You must go to church and pray for the Pope, but most for our poor people.'

Well, now... They've pushed the damper in and out several times since then. The smoke goes up the chimney just the same!

18

Andrew Marshall

Trimulgherry had long been a main garrison for British Cavalry and we, the Royal Dragoons, arrived there at Allenby Barracks in October 1929 to form part of a garrison comprising a division of infantry and two Indian cavalry regiments. Our cavalry brigade was under the command of Brigadier Campbell Ross, an old campaigner and one of the few survivors of the Indian Sillidar system, when cavalrymen had to buy their own horses and grow their own forage, a system which had been adopted in England at the beginning of the eighteenth century.

Trimulgherry was in the territory of His Exalted Highness the Nizam of Hyderabad, whose forebears had helped Clive to defeat the Mahrattas. Reputed to be the richest man in the world, possessed of hordes of jewels and gold, his own coinage, banks and narrow-gauge railway, he was a self-confessed miser, said to enjoy ill health because he was too miserly to buy himself food. What he wanted most he was unable to get – a commission in the British Army. Barrack room gossip had it that he had tried to bribe our Colonel-in-Chief, HM King George V, by offering half of Secunderabad, Deccan, for one little pip. But the offer was declined. His next bid was to supply the whole of the British Army in India with a set of solid gold buttons, for free, gratis and nowt. This too, received regal rejection.

'Know what happened then?' asked Andy Marshall. 'He

wrote to our King and said Hyderabad was being put "out of bounds" to all cavalrymen, and if a Royal Dragoon tried to get in, he would be returned to Allenby Barracks, Trimulgherry, with his throat cut from armpits to breakfast-time, and no goolies! Wicked old sod! All those riches, and if he was a ghost he'd be too mean to give you a bloody fright!'

His Exalted Highness's wide domain did not impress me overmuch. It was ill-cultivated and boulder-strewn with rocks as big as East Anglian barns, and spiteful shrubs whose dirk-like thorns played havoc with our horses' fet-locks. There was a scarcity of water, scantily supplied to arable areas from reservoirs called tanks. They were like lakes, on which cavalry officers of the garrison temporarily forsook their spurs and learned sailing, under hazardous conditions. Without even a whisper of warning, great squalls would rend the sails and capsize craft. On one occasion all the sailing craft in one tank capsized and a young officer was drowned.

At most of the main garrison towns of India on 1st January each year the Proclamation Parade was held, when the pomp and ceremony and circumstance was to be seen at its precise and colourful best. The Proclamation Parade of January 1930 was held on Secunderabad Race Course. As always, the cavalry stole the limelight, mostly because of the gay plumage of the Indian cavalry who paraded in full ceremonial dress.

Like ourselves, the Indian soldiers took pride in a good turn-out. They loved soldiering, King and country; and on this important day the pride could be seen on their faces and ram-rod stiff backs as they sat in their saddles like non-breathing statues.

First the proclamation was read by the senior officer, then followed a march past of troops. A magnificent sight, the cavalry in brigade order and the infantry in battalions as the bands played the regimental marches. After came the *feu de joie*. This was a ceremonial firing of blank rifle shots which began with a thundering salute by the gunners of the Royal Artillery. Then the rifles were aimed at the sky, the firers' heads statue-still and eyes looking straight to their front. On the command 'fire', the right marker, the rifleman on the extreme right of the front rank, fired one round, then in rapid succession each man along the whole of the front rank fired one round. This produced a great rippling of rifle shots along the whole of the front rank; without pause it was taken up by the rear rank, starting with the left marker. The effect was startling. First, one saw little puffs of smoke spurting from the muzzles along the lengths of the ranks, and then came the sounds, single shots like a prolonged burst of machine-gun fire. Indian spectators clapped and yelled, for of all the goings-on, they preferred the *feu de joie*. I preferred the sight of the Indian cavalry in full dress.

Each regiment wore different jackets and facings. All wore the lungi (turban), red or blue kurtas with shoulder chains, and long regimentally coloured cummerbunds tied tightly round the waist. The officers were mostly British and wore the same dress except for white Melton breeches. Their black, glistening thigh boots had screwed into their heels silver spurs two inches in length from the 'U' of the spur to the rowel. One could hear the spurs all a-jingle! A sure sign that the proud rider has loosened the rowels to make cavalry music. Lances were 'couched', butts resting in the stirrup beds on the off-side stirrup irons; they were held vertically with their two-colour pennants all a-flutter in the light breeze. They were the petals of military flowers in Secunderabad's annual show, their burnished barbs shooting off reflected flashing of India's sunlight. A sight for future reflections ... maybe!

We were on excellent terms with our Indian comrades. At one time they were over 40 regiments strong, but after the Kaiser's War their numbers were reduced (like the British) by disbandment and amalgamation. Some Indian cavalry regiments' names are still music to the ears of surviving English ex-cavalrymen.

Senior was the Governor-General's Body Guard, raised in 1774. There were others of equal fame. Central Indian Horse, Skinner's Horse, Probyn's Horse, Sam Browne's Cavalry, Poona Horse, Hariana Lancers, Cureton's Mooltanis, Balach Horse and the Deccan Horse.

We were reminded of those famous names in the evening of Proclamation Day 1930.

* * *

Fifty years later I received another reminder. I am not sure whether I was plussed or non-plussed when Andy poked his haggis-bashing nose into my kitchen. I was blue-and-white aproned and busy at my culinary capers. Our Steeple Bumpstead copper had challenged me to make a curry superior to the one I had made (and he had eaten) about a year before.

Modesty compels me to state that, as curries go, that one worn't at all bad. It certainly 'went'! Copper Ken Marks had popped in on a previous curry bash, one I was making for wifie Vera's lunch. I asked Kenneth if he would like to try some. He tried the lot and Vera had mutton broth.

Andy entered the kitchen door and sniffed.

'To hell with the curry, get cracking with the teapot, I'm as dry as a bishop's throat and could use a drop of "gunfire" (strong hot tea served at reveille by Indian servants).' He and I had ridden, lived, hunted and danced with our comrades of the Indian cavalry, before words like racial discrimination were invented by desk-bound social anthropologists and pompous politicians who had never seen an angry man.

'We are not in India now!' said Andy after a few more sniffs. 'If you keep stinking out this lovely village, Maggie Thatcher or Enoch Powell will get you repatriated to Rawalpindi!'

* * *

During the open season, special invitations were given to us to accompany Indian soldiers to their homes for game-shooting expeditions and sometimes to the vast estates and preserves of maharajahs, for the Indian soldier was not socially ostracized like his British counterpart. He belonged to the warrior caste, the second highest in the Indian caste hierarchy.

Our friends would make arrangements for transportation and conduct planning for the shoots. We supplied guns and ammunition, but there were conditions. We could not proceed unless one of us was reasonably fluent in Urdu or Hindi, or one of their party in English. We had to take rifles that would not accommodate the military 0.303 ammunition, specially manufactured to kill human beings with our short Lee Enfield Rifles.

Going deep into the jungle and bush, to live upon the products of our guns and knives, was a tremendous experience. We were taught to stalk cheetle stag, chinkari buck and blue boar; to creep so close upon them that not a shot was wasted and death was quick, without suffering.

After a good day's sport in indescribably natural glory we would assemble at the arranged meeting point for the 'big meal', to roast buck over a scented wood fire. The spit would be turned by some self-appointed chef, while others would pluck, then supervise, the cooking of sand grouse and snipe. There would be curry galore and snowy rice spiced with succulent herbs.

What an unforgettable aroma as the air was filled with the fragrance of roasting venison; the effluvium of taste-bud tormenting grouse to the sizzling of gossamer-like chappatis, as we sat in circles round the crackling perfumed fires!

When all was ready, the toast would be drunk, in toddy or arak – both soldier-like brews and aperitifs – then we would get busy on the solids with our fingers.

Unlike lots of poor Indians and Pakistanis now in Britain, we were given first choice to off cut off the most succulent steaks and tit-bits from the crispiest or tenderest grouse. Then, filled with good food, we would make our individual contributions to the singing and dancing. Andy was popular, if not intelligible. He rolled his R's in a true Glaswegian accent, a kind of happy growling, and he could dance an Eightsome Reel, after a few araks, all on his own.

When the Royal Dragoons left Trimulgherry for Meerut, about 40 miles from Delhi, I lost touch with Andrew Marshall, and the next time I was back there, on what should have been Proclamation Day, 1st January 1933, I left India on my repatriation to the United Kingdom, having served my stint of five years' overseas service. Although the United Kingdom appeared still to be 'united', India was not. Mahatma Gandhi and the Congress Party were beaver-busy in their efforts to rid India of the hated British rule. In 1947 they succeeded, and Proclamation Parades were to be no more.

Andy next surfaced, so far as I was concerned, in June 1975 at Windsor, for a regimental birthday parade of consequence. Way back on 10th June 1925 I had paraded with the regiment on Rushmoor Arena for the presentation of a new Guidon by His Majesty King George V. Because the War Office, Ministry of Defence, or some other body, had decided that Guidons should be replaced every half century, worn out or not, we were due for a replacement in 1975. Everybody turned up for this birthday party, including serving soldiers, in and out of uniform, in tanks, armoured cars, and just a few on horses to demonstrate a pukka cavalry charge. There were hordes of Old Comrades, among whom there were just one dozen survivors from that first presentation in 1925. Andy was one, I another. I did not recognize him, partly because of my defective vision – I had been temporarily war-blinded at Falaise in Hitler's War – but more so because Andrew had altered. He looked almost human; the Glaswegian growl had mellowed. What was more important, this once poverty-stricken bairn from the Gorbals had managed to get something the old Nizam, His Exalted Highness of Secunderabad, had failed to purchase with all his ill-gotten gains. Not one pip to indicate that he held the Queen's Commission, but three of 'em! He was now Captain Andrew Marshall, with a breastful of campaign gongs and TD decorations, plus the 'Rooty Gong', correctly described as the LSG medal – long service and bad stations – or 21 years' undetected crime.

We had to parade in a line to be presented to the Queen. In turn we were presented to Her Majesty and Prince Philip and some big-wigs and brass-hats of the Household Cavalry. You could have knocked me down with a guided missile when Andy told Her Majesty that he was living at Glemsford, Suffolk (Little Egypt), my village of birth on 5th August 1907! Like myself, Andy was very much a soldier. Our wives insist that we have never left the army. Maybe they are right. Up to his last minute on earth, Andy was doing the most positive things for 'old sweats'. Now and again he would quote from Burns.

> For the merchant ploughs the main,
> The farmer ploughs the manor;
> But glory is the sodger's pride;
> The brave poor sodger ne'er despise,
> Nor count him as a stranger,
> Remember he's the country's stay,
> In hope and hour of danger.

This was his battle cry, his trumpet call to charge into action and endeavour to raise funds for The Army Benevolent Fund, whose address is (donors please note) The Duke of York's Headquarters, Chelsea, London SW3.

Lovely and charming Dorothy, Andy's nursing sister wife, did her bit, when not too busy delivering more cannon fodder in Suffolk's maternity hospitals. Entries from their precisely maintained case book are indicative of the paucity of politicians' promises, like that bit about the land fit for heroes to live in.

a) An ex-soldier and his wife, both in their eighties, have been struggling to exist on £30 a week. The husband is very lame, his wife blind. An allowance should be made to help them obtain bedding and clothing they badly need.

b) A 70-year-old soldier's widow is a chronic arthritic, has badly ulcerated legs and is diabetic. An allowance will help her to have the warmth and special diet she badly needs.

c) A 64-year-old war-wounded ex-soldier, now disabled with arthritis and rheumatism, has been sharing a total income of £15.20 a week with his 64-year-old wife. She is herself an invalid and periodically has to enter hospital.

I persuaded Andy to write his memoirs. We read through them together, sometimes licking old wounds, fighting old battles, then off to the old warriors' local for a pint!

I often wonder what has happened to all those carefully

typed pages and to dear Dorothy. She has gone from Glemsford, alas! Perhaps she and the pages got blown away on that sorrowful day when those two trumpeters of The Blues and Royals came down to Glemsford at our request to sound *Last Post* and *Cavalry Reveille*. Captain Andrew had been struck off the ration strength, for good.

Kenneth Marks, my curry-stealing policeman friend, drove us to Glemsford Churchyard. Major Spud Lewis, who enlisted with me in March 1924, was there with Burma-starred veterans of the Royal Anglian Regiment, ex-Chindits who had helped Orde Wingate to ginger up the Japs in their own jungles. Four of us had survived the 1930 Proclamation Parade of Secunderabad. Two of us had been present for the presentation of the Guidon at Aldershot in 1925 and at Windsor in 1975.

The first trumpet notes of *Last Post* scared rooks from the trees and they ca-caw-ed in protest.

We were silent! Our thumbs were well behind the seams of our 'civvy suits' as the Standard Bearer of the Royal British Legion gave the exhortation.

> They shall grow not old
> As we that are left grow old;
> Age shall not weary them
> Nor the years condemn.
> At the going down of the sun
> And in the morning...
> We will remember them.

Thoughts and memories were not silent, and imagination had its own truths. As I stood in that green Glemsford vale, below the church where I had been christened, I saw Andy. He was not in that box. Oh no! He was up on his hinds, in an Indian jungle, dancing, with our comrades of the Indian cavalry.

19

Vocational Training

Way back in the tail of 1935, long before the advent of Youth Employment Schemes and similar stunts for obtaining a labour force on the cheap, I was stationed at Mons Barracks, Aldershot, flexing my ex-military muscles for tuition in toil.

According to Part II Orders, within six months of my termination of 12 years' undistinguished service with the Colours, I was about to be hurled into the secrets of Electric Wiring. I had already qualified as a GPO Telegraphist in Morse and Teleprinter at Cardiff Post Office, but was concerned about getting a job in 'civvy street' and thought it might be wise to have another string to my unemployed bow.

At that time (as it is today) no one seemed to be worrying overmuch about finding people real jobs, except (perhaps) the Army Council. They (or it) had drawn attention to the prevailing civilian mass unemployment and made arrangements for soldiers nearing the end of their service to be discharged prematurely, if civilian employment could be guaranteed.

I applied for two jobs from Bulford Camp, near Salisbury. While waiting for one, or both, to come up the straight, I learned to drive motor cars, ride motor cycles (a retrograde step for a cavalryman) and to operate the first radio telephony wireless set in British military communication history, the famous No. 1 set.

This was a different kettle of fish from operating wireless sets in India, which were conveyed on mules and pack-horses and had bright emitter triode valves as big as street lamps. They lit up like sex symbols in Soho, and hissed.

My No. 1 was compactly packed with sorbo into a two-seater Austin Seven. Still in the stages of test and trial from the Creed laboratories, it was designed to operate on telegraphy (morse key punching) and telephony (speech) over hitherto undetermined and untried distances.

To my good fortune, a special wireless exercise was begun to test No. 1's performance. Four sets were employed and three were sent off to various points within a 12-mile radius of Stonehenge. I was selected to remain static as operator of the Control Group, and parked my brand new Austin about eight inches from the stone circular shrine of the ancient Druids' stone dominoes. On the last night of the four-day exercise came a lull in the storm of wireless communication. Rumour had it that we had broken some kind of communication record by radio telephony. We were bound to. No one had ever tried it before! As the Law Lords have it, we had created a precedent.

Life began to improve. The officers were so pleased, they lubricated themselves lavishly before creeping into their fleece-lined sleeping bags to snore away through what was left of a bitterly cold night.

As a common or garden signaller, who had done all the work and established a record in military communication, I was not allowed the luxury of sleep, let alone a fleece-lined bag. It was most important, they said, that I should remain awake to maintain non-existent communications.

Because not one dot of military morse, or one syllable of speech, was polluting the ether at 0300 hours, I idly tuned the receiver to 5 megacycles to a station belting out morse at about twenty-five words a minute. The transmission was automatic and consisted of enciphered groups of five figures. Excellent practice for figure reading!

I had filled the blank backs of several pink message forms before the stream of figures halted. I heard the call sign of the

New York Stock Exchange, followed by a series of V's and the commencing sign for a new item: 'QTC'. Then, into my ear'oles poured the news:

'MAN MOUNTAIN BATTERED AND BLASTED BY BATTLING BAER'

I knew I was on to a good thing, and took down a round-by-round description of Primo Carnera's humiliating defeat by the 'Clown Prince of Boxing', Max Baer.

I also knew that the Bulford Camp paperboy (a long-haired lad of 71 years) would not deliver this news for a couple of days. There were no wireless sets in our tin shacks, not even in the officers' mess and (fortunately) transistors had not been invented. But every soldier in Bulford Camp that I knew was convinced that Baer's block would be bashed off, and his clowning in the ring would be stopped by Italy's 'Man Mountain – The Ambling Alp'.

My favourite signals officer was a pleasant young one-pipper. I told him the news and gave him the pink sheets when the officers emerged from their sleeping bags long after reveille, and swore him to secrecy. On our return to camp we each made rewarding wagers. He, with fellow officers; I, with anyone in verbal distance sufficiently stupid to place pennies on Primo Carnera. This was the most beneficial of my many morse readings. Not only did the receipts cover my expenditure for each day of my two-month course in Electric Wiring, but my ego became inflated because I was regarded with high esteem by the top brass of the Royal Corps of Signals, who asked my opinion on the new No. 1 set. I lauded it beyond the stratosphere, stating that morse could be received loud and clear through great atmospheric interference, from stations very remote. Even from New York!

Our Electric Wiring wizard instructor was a straight-talking Lancastrian.

'You'll be lucky, you lot! The last folk proper businessmen take on are old soldiers. Most of you have picked this course because you think there's no hard graft puttin' in lightin'. You think all you have to do is to snip about with a pair of side-cuttin' pliers, like virgins cuttin' roses in convent gardens. You're wrong. Bloody great holes have to be dug to put in cable ducts. You'll climb roofs, poles, lofts an' trees far better than the apes you all resemble, an' by the time you've done you'll have blisters from finger-tips to arm-pits. Got it? This is where we start. Get on them benches!'

We signed for boxes of tools, overalls, belts and climbing irons, and were handed pamphlets from the Vocational Guidance Library, drawn up in baffling English by unspecified Industrial Psychologists, and an interesting list of occupational hazards, ranging from muscular strain to risk of falls. 'Lanky' gave us one short lecture before we filed out to work.

'This course would not have been started but for me. It's because light is needed. Folks down here didn't know what light were until we came down from Rochdale to clean your bloody windows!'

We enjoyed it all, even more so when 'practicality' entered the training act. At Aldershot lurked many high-ranking officers, mostly chairborne, married, and living in rent-subsidised houses.

'Why not have your trainees do the electrical repairs to our homes? This would give them opportunities to tackle "real" problems!'

Now this appeared to be good sense, considering the origin, but not a word was mentioned on the major advantage – the saving of costs for material and labour. Some of us volunteered for these 'outside jobs'. Some were lucky enough to be rewarded. As much as half-a-crown between two, for two days' work. More often we got a thimbleful of tea to wash down a socially esteemed sandwich, too small to stuff a dental cavity.

At one house on the Farnham–Farnborough Road where rooms had been rewired, switched and plugged at the tax-payers' expense, two trainees worked for a week without a thank-you. Only one thing of consequence came out of that house. A telephone call, made by the officer's lady.

'Are you the wiring instructah? Good! Those two chappies,

your electricians? Could you send them back? No, not this afternoon, I'm playing bridge at the Club. Ectually, I would prefer this evening, it's urgent!'

'What's up, then?' asked Lanky.

'Well, it's all very tahrsome and embarrassing. You see, every time we pull the toilet chain the lights come on – all ovah the house, and we carn't switch them orf. They all go orf when the toilet cistern fills up, then we carn't switch them on again until we pull the toilet chain. The colonel is furious and says something must be done!'

Nothing was done. The 'electrician chappies' refused to go there again, but next evening they enlightened Lanky on their cunning capers with an insulated busch and some crafty wiring of a master switch to the cistern plug – all carefully concealed from human view because they really did not require vocational training; they were both A1 Instrument Mechanics.

Lanky laughed so long and heartily that he blacked out. We restored him by whisking him down to the 'Ratpit', better known to Aldershot's civvies as The Trafalgar. We put him outside with several very large whiskies. We all passed out (at Electric Wiring).

I became 'employed'. The GPO at Woking, Surrey, started me off, not as a telegraphist, or electrician, but as an 'Opener'. Opening mail bags from 0200 hours to 1000 hours, seven days a week, for fifty bob a week. Rum old world, ain't it!

20

Cackle!

A mild heart attack inspired advice from my village doctor. 'Take it easy. Mount a comfortable armchair, put your trotters into your brothel-creeping slippers and watch the goggle-box.'

Ever obedient, I did my best to watch (but not to hear) a brace of Test Matches telecast from Lord's and Leeds. To see (but not to hear) countless tennis tussles from watery Wimbledon, and guff-free golf from Troon. I shall never forgive my doctor.

It should be understood that I have represented my old squadron at cricket and tennis, but golf was never my cup of tea. Not that I wish to be disobliging to peculiar persons who proceed to places on foot to clout a defenceless little rubber-packed ball with hunks of wood and steel. In the pukka cavalry, particularly in the Punjab, it was our custom to clout a big swiftly moving ball with an overgrown mallet – from the back of a galloping horse, cavalry dash. We seldom uttered the word 'golf' and dubbed this procedure 'hockey at the halt'. Poets have ranted and raved about the game, but I will deal with them after I have dealt with decibels.

From a physical point of view, my enforced squatting proved fairly beneficial, but mentally and morally most disquieting, because I was thrust into abstract thought. I recalled my earlier introduction to a brace of experts, albeit by

lecture. The first was Frank Gilbreth, a New Englander born
of Scottish parents in the USA way back in 1868. The second
was Robert Owen who, a century earlier, started to in-
vestigate and measure all movements involved in human
activities. His primary object was to eliminate superfluous
movements and thus increase human pleasure and industrial
production. Had they survived to watch the 'box' with
me, they would have enjoyed a beanfeast in the field of 'per-
petual motion', the incessant clacking of jaws by sports
commentators.

Long-dead economist Adam Smith would have loved to
have been present to 'hear' cricket and to analyse certain
staffing problems. Although universally acclaimed as an
expert on the division of labour, he would have been baffled
by the division of labour between never fewer than five
commentators, whose diatribes are broadcast in separate,
personal half-hour stints punctuated by cheery 'introductions' and loud hand-overs before their probably frequent
migrations to the Lord's Taverners' watering hole. Doubtless
Adam Smith would have dubbed it 'shift work'.

Their postulation would have been more tolerable had they
but stuck to cricket, but one felt inclined to overlook some of
their literary misdemeanours because they all looked pretty.
In their sartorial splendour, bristling with club blazers and
badges, all sporting the red and gold neckwear of the Taverners,
which is identical to the regimental tie of the 12th Royal
Lancers, they reminded me of an apt quotation from the Holy
Bible, taken from old King Solomon himself. 'They toil not,
neither do they spin. Yet Solomon in all his glory was not
arrayed like one of these.'

Instead of commenting on the cricket in progress, they
resorted to the past, resuscitating ancient records, pitches and
players. They gave weather reports, horticultural hints about
the conservation of grass and groundsmen, before drumming
into our earholes the optically obvious.

'Snow is about to start his run-up.' 'The umpire is looking
at the clock.' 'Drinks have arrived.' 'The batsmen are walking
out from the pavilion.' And then, possibly because cricket

spectators by goggle-box lack the intellectual equipment to hazard a climatic guess, when hordes of scantily clad spectators appear within inches of their eyes in all-revealing close-ups, oozing sweat globules and fanning themselves like fury, they let us into a secret. 'It's a warm, sunny day. Don't you think so, Denis?'

An ex-cricketer sufficiently patriotic to aid our financial inflationary problems, I hereby proclaim that I am available in a dual capacity, scorer and commentator, for half the salary dished out to one commentator today. I need no accomplices!

Many overs and matches ago, I learned tricks of both trades from Jasper, my grandfather's uncle. He didn't talk a lot. It was said he could neither read nor write. He had no books, pencils or electronic scoreboard, but for the matches in Park Mede he kept children and bullock at bay, swept away cow-pats, filled in outfield rabbit holes and mole hills, and kept the cricket scores – with his sharp shutknife, on a little stick of nut hazel or willow. He was 'the man of the match'.

Once upon Test times, there was a scorer named Ross Salmon who used to produce masterpieces of Gothic calligraphy on costly vellum. Jasper did the job in the bark of little sticks. He recorded every run, bye, leg-bye, wide and no-ball. He nicked into the plain bark an impeccable bowling analysis. All with the point of his knife. All for free, and no nattering. He was precise, silent and content, earning ten whole shillings and sixpence for his 60-hour week, as a ploughman.

There was little indication of impending lockjaw at Wimbledon, but Dan (the yap) was licked into comparative silence by a newcomer who seldom paused to take breath. He specialised in probing into the personal characteristics of stars of the past and the future and had no time to say a word about those before our eyes. He prattled on. We could not hear line-calls, scores, but only the cackle.

Life worsened when the women crashed into the tennis racket. My rest room volleyed and thundered with the strangest expressions as 'Ginnie' and 'Anne' monopolised the microphone. 'Very, very vital.' 'Very, very essential in keeping one's composure.' Then, 'I think that Ginnie is thinking what I think I am thinking' and so on, *ad nauseam*.

My protesting heart jumped. I swallowed my pill, then forgave them. It occurred to me that they were all paid by 'wordage'. They were working for the BBC who, if they were ghosts, would be too mean to give listeners a fright. I had discovered what had happened at Lord's from the newspaper. Golf was the next ordeal.

Troon, like the environs of most British international airports, and only a willow-tit's flight from Prestwick Airport, was rainswept, fog and mist-shrouded for the British Open.

There was noise. Not all from Jumbo jets. Commentators' verbals were over-long, inconsequential, but 'very, very' clear. Those clever cameramen did a first-class job, keeping us up to date shot by shot, as they zoomed skilfully from green to green, and with clear pictures of the ball in the clouded sky, tracking the ball from strike to bounce. But, to ensure that we, the imperceptive, were kept climatically up to date, the 'talkers' invited our attention to the fact that it was raining. We might never have known! Not even from excellent pictures of that multitudinous array of multi-coloured gamps and all that Adam's ale cascading down everything in sight! Let us not be unfair. If one is paid to yap, one should give good measure. But is yapping a national affliction?

A Welsh hooker from Sospan Fach (Llanelli), told me at Arms Park, Cardiff, that the English are the most loquacious of the tribes of Great Britain. 'You see, Spike, boyo, the Welsh, Irish and Scots all have their old tongues stitched down at the back, down by the tonsils. But not the English. Have to be different, don't they? Can't sing, but they can yap all aright. Their tongues are stitched down in the middle, so they can clack at both ends!'

I decided not to blame my doctor for my neurosis. Had not my Welsh wife, Vera, entered my room of rest the moment that an American 'Hockey-at-the-Halt' merchant appeared on the screen to tap a small defenceless ball a few inches into the final hole, to win the British Open, I might well have become psychotic.

Vera spoke to me, well below the sound level of the cackling commentators. I could not hear. I wound back the volume wick to give her a sporting chance and heard an unfamiliar sound. Of silence. I am cured!

The only Patrick I know who spells Patrick without a 'k' is Patric Dickinson, a very good poet who began to play golf at the ripe age of four years, and became such a dab hand at it that he won a Blue for Cambridge against that dark blue Oxford lot.

In July 1953 his words about golf were broadcast on the radio, and those words are worth remembering. He did not 'cackle' but used his poetic skill and love for our wonderful language. He said that the two greatest external influences on his life so far had been Henry Cotton and W. B. Yeats. This is how he began.

'A true influence confirms you in your own way. It is the soil you plant your own seed in, and out of which you may grow with luck to be yourself. I shall never swing a golf club like Harry Cotton. I shall never write a poem like W. B. Yeats. I don't want to do either of those things *like* them. I should love to do them as well, in my own way. I never shall, but that does not prevent me from trying, and from saluting these two great masters of rhythm, and it does not prevent me from saying that I am better at golf than I otherwise would have been because of the influence of Yeats. And better at writing poems because of Henry Cotton.'

'Some of my old cavalry comrades consider that golf ain't much cop. A good walk ruined and a total waste of time, etc. Patric had other opinions:

'Golf is a great game and an art. Like a kind of marvellous moving outdoor chess. It is a combat with the elements of nature. The rhythm of golf is slow. You play it at man's basic speed, at his walking pace. In the course of a round you walk five good miles, and the round will take you close on three hours.

'Three hours is a long time to concentrate upon anything.

141

This inescapable tempo of golf is one of its delights and tortures. There is time for reflection, yet the mind must not dwell on the good shot, or fluke, once it is over. Nor upon the disaster. To put disaster completely and resolutely out of one's head is very difficult, far more so than in a game of speed as rugger, cricket or squash. And one's emotions become more deeply involved. Rugger forwards can lose their temper and play the game of their lives. Golfers, never.

'Golf is magical and elementary, like poetry. You must get the rhythm right and set it right in your heart.'

It was Hugh Neilson who asked Patric if he would play against Oxford. When they returned victorious to Cambridge, Patric did not celebrate with the others. All alone, he went to his own room and got drunk, very drunk, on the poetry of Yeats.

Patric considered himself to be luckier than Yeats, for the snows always melted for him. He could release himself in an enthralling form of physical exercise.

I prefer to watch folk shortening their lives by physical strain, but in silence, and I cannot recall when I last broke out of an unhurried walk. I once hit a golf ball at St Andrews. The ball hit a dog. The dog yelped and the mistress shrieked about people not shouting 'fore'.

Like Patric, I am dotty about poetry and once dotted down a dose of doggerel about commentatory cackle. Published in the *East Anglian Daily Times* this masterpiece generated telephone calls from football fanatics and scurrilous denunciation from frenetic fans.

A secret someone sent me a cutting from an equally secret newspaper which, in part, supports my denigration of the 'waffle merchants'.

OVER TO THEM

Is there too much inexcusable chatter coming from our sports commentators?

Soccer, by common agreement, is particularly ill-served while Rugby Union is blessed. To some of us lawn tennis, an extremely tedious and deplorable intrusion, seems to find a suitable reflection in its commentators, summarisers and sages. Athletics is served with much of the tedium of lawn tennis commentaries and with an hysteria all of its own.

Golf is simply a dawdle.

Cricket commentators and seers are a lustrous body, however, and are as much part of the game as marl, the shifting of sight screens and a profile of Brian Close's jaw.

Unfortunately this simple truth is not understood by everyone and the odd criticism of the commentator's art has been detected near the boundary fence. We feel obliged to defend this fine body of men.

More than a Contest

Where these unfortunate heretics err is in the supposition that cricket is simply a contest between bat and ball and that the commentator who deviates into such matters as the condition of the grass, or level of the gas holder and the significance of some record or other is guilty of extraneous chatter. He is nothing of the kind. *These things matter.*

Cricket is more than a game. It is a rich mosaic of memory and reflection, inducing good humour, companionship and a predeliction for philosophising. The actual contest is the blade of the bat, but not the handle. This explains why a love of cricket can surmount even the dreariest of negative matches. Only golf, a sound but inferior game, can approach cricket on this score. Soccer and lawn tennis, by comparison, are simply dramatic acts without music or poetry.

The art of the groundsman – art, be it noted, for in other sports it would be a mere function – the movement of the winds, the comportment of a fielder, a shared memory, all the reflections of benevolence are part of cricket and consequently the trade of the cricket writer and commentator.

In its highest form it is to be heard on the radio to the solace and elucidation of which all *bona fide* seekers after truth, light and charm are urged to repair.

I am pleased indeed that the anonymous author of the cutting
had the civility to associate cricket with poetry and music.
Music is held in scant regard by commentators of sports
programmes, even at rugger and soccer international matches.
Even the regimental bands of the Guards Division are
shouted down, muffled, muzzled and suppressed. It drives
one to doggerel, like this:

Peace, Perfect Peace
In This Daft World of Din
Cut out his blether, we would prefer a dearth
Of yap – from Raymond Illingworth.
Eliminate each triple-trite-tirade
From ever-psycho-spouting, Virginia Wade,
But first, we plead, IMPLORE – in fervent tones,
Sack 'very, very' Anne (yap-happy) Jones,
Together with old King Incessant Yap
Dan Maskell (constant tennis-tittering-chap.)
For Bowls and Snooker, most of us opine,
A gag be thrust deep down long-winded Vine.
And Dickie, with his touched-up tuft snow-white,
Hurled far from earshot and well out of sight.
Gruff Greaves and smirking Saint, treat them the
same
Lest their crude cackle impairs another soccer game.

But worst of all this cackle-happy lot
Is one who very shortly should be shot
On Horseguards, for the birthday of our Queen
The Trooping of a Colour should be 'seen',
But scarce one note of national music 'heard';
Some clip-board cretin muffled all – by *word*.

Useful hints for Clip-board Editors
Soldiers are not commanded 'Order Arms' when standing at
ease.
Soldiers do not 'sheath swords', they 'return swords'.
Clarinet players of the mounted band of the Household

Cackle!

Cavalry do *not* 'always ride on white horses.' There are no white horses. It is the Trumpeters of the Household Cavalry who are mounted on greys. Unlike the ill-informed aforementions, the Trumpeters have something worth blowing about. Take, for example, a motto apiece for The Blues and Royals:

Honi Soit Qui Mal y Pense
Spectemur Agendo.

Roughly translated: 'Evil be to him who evil thinks', and

'By our deeds are we known'. (Not words!)

Come to think of it, an old East Anglian hit the nail right on the head. 'As a bird is known by its note, so is man by his conversation!'

21

Spectemur Agendo

At Twickenham there is a tidy acreage of blood-soaked grassland on which barbaric international rugger rascals bite off each others' ears. Some say it is to stop the row coming from next door, the Royal Military School of Music, Kneller Hall. Old Father Thames keeps rolling on past both places. I wished to roll towards K.H. but my rolling came to an abrupt halt in October 1988.

The windows of my soul were the first to crack up. This I discovered the day I mounted and marched to Addenbrooke's Hospital, Cambridge, where specialist Jo Scott locked my head in an iron mask and squirted laser lights into me.

'You are cracking. You are 81. Your left eye is useless, the other is not much better. We cannot help medically or surgically, but a good optician might help!'

An optician did help. Not me, but himself – to £70 for half a lens for one eye. It was useless, and I am soldiering on with a magnifying glass the size of a Chinese frying pan. The rot really began at the local dental torture chamber a month earlier. Liquids hot and cold played puck with my moaning molars.

He puggled about in my mouth with what looked like a farrier's rasp, making more molars moan, and said gleefully: 'Oh, yes ... Extractions! Come Tuesday, same time. Good morning!'

Tuesday's hypodermic needles pierced my inflamed gums,

but not without pain. He reached for his torture tongs and began. I felt crunchings and agony, splinterings and agony, and a voice: 'It's difficult to get a purchase!'

Three crowns had snapped off. He dug deeply to yank and prise out the roots. The pains of childbirth are but flea-bites compared with what I endured before staggering off, to survive for three weeks on a diet of hash, mash, mince, slops and stiff shots of antibiotics. A friendly chemist smarmed my infected gums with a salve tasting of fish glue.

Enough of this petty carping. My real torture was mental. Due to this abomination of pain and misery I was unable to travel and unable to accept an invitation that meant so very much to me. My old friends in the Band of The Blues and Royals had galloped back into my life, but I could not meet them.

On Friday, 13th May, 1988, the regimental bands of The Blues and Royals and the 9th/12th Lancers were due to 'Beat Retreat' on Angel Hill, Bury St Edmunds. Bill Donovan and his wife Eileen, former neighbours banished to Honington, Suffolk, picked us up and the four of us watched and listened to the wonderful music of the band in which I once played as a Band Rat in 1924. After the event we were plodding towards Bill's car.

'Come and join us, Spike,' said one of the bandsmen. I told him that I was under martial escort and was not permitted to join them at the watering hole to which they were proceeding.

'Bring the lot. Tell them to make for the Guildhall. We're going there for a snifter.'

Bill went for his car, with the two ladies. I clambered into the band wagon and found myself sitting next to the extremely smart Director, Major Roger Tomlinson. Some of the band began to talk about my book *The Band Rats*. Major Tomlinson turned to me: 'Did you ever meet the man who wrote that book?'

'I see him every day,' said I. 'I'm fed up with the sight of him!'

'Don't say that,' I said the DOM. 'I would very much like to meet him!'

'You have met him. I'll let you into a secret. You are sitting next to him at this very minute!' You could have knocked him down with a Crusader tank. I helped him undress and dress for the snifter at the Guildhall and we walked there together, where we were welcomed by big-grin Jeffrey Archer. I soon recovered from that, and the DOM said he would write to me with a special invitation, saying I would meet up with George Evans and other old friends who had served in the Band. The letter came and here it is:

BAND OF THE BLUES AND ROYALS
(Royal Horse Guards and 1st Dragoons)
By permission of Colonel A. H. Parker Bowles OBE
Director of Music – Major R. G. Tomlinson BA, FTCL, ARCM, LGSM, PSM

Hyde Park Barracks
Knightsbridge
London SW7 1SE
7th June, 1988

Mr Spike Mays
Bow Lodge
Steeple Bumpstead
Suffolk
CB9 7DS
Dear Spike,

Thank you for your interesting letter. I must say it was a great delight to meet up with you at Bury St Edmunds, and I am pleased to have met 'the man who wrote the book'.

I mentioned our 'Open Day' at Knightsbridge, when we will be hosting the International Military Music Society. The date is Friday, 23rd September, and the programme for the day is as follows:

1000 – 1020 Coffee
1020 – 1040 Watch the Queen's Life Guard prepare for Guard Mounting
1100 – 1230 Band Concert
1245 – 1345 Lunch

148

1400 – 1415 Band Marching Displays
1415 – 1515 Tour of Knightsbridge Barracks
1515 – 1530 Tea and biscuits

Guest conductors will include Sir Vivian Dunne and George Evans. We expect a turnout of 40 to 50 members.

I would be thrilled if you and your wife could come along too, and of course you must bring a couple of dozen copies of *The Band Rats* to sell and autograph. It would be tremendous if you could play your saxophone, but I won't press you on that. Do look out for me on Trooping the Colour on June 11th. It is my year this year, and my first Trooping to boot. I hope my nerves don't show!

With very best wishes
Yours sincerely
Roger Tomlinson

Due to the trials and tribulations of optical and dental deterioration, and to my everlasting regret, I was unfit to travel for I lacked the strength to carry a verbal message. There were present at this congregation of military music maestros many old friends who had spread their musician's aptitude all over the world. Sir Vivian Dunne had written to me in most generous terms, but took me to task for misnaming his colleague at the Kneller Hall School of Music, Twickenham as 'Ted Ricketts' – the man who wrote 'Colonel Bogey'.

Major Spud Lewis was too poorly to attend. His ticker went on the blink, possibly because he became part-worn like me, for we had both enlisted in The Royals in March, 1924. Even after we had both retired and The Blues and Royals had amalgamated, he kept gingering me up and said that Colonel S. C. Cooper, Commanding Household Cavalry, had insisted that I should write an Appreciation for the jacket of a recording made by the Band and Trumpeters of The Blues and Royals when they played the music for the Combined Cavalry Memorial Service in Hyde Park in May, 1981.

After I wrote the piece and sent it off, they wished to know my fee. I said I would settle for a copy of the recording endorsed with the 'dhobi-marks' (an Indian form of identification on one's laundry (sic) signature) of the Director of Music. Major Spud Lewis said they were pleased with my effort and a copy of the record would be sent eventually.

It was *not* sent! It was delivered in person by a new Director of Music, one who had his civvy habitat in Woodbridge, Suffolk. Major Brian I. Keeling, LRAM, ARCM, PSM, himself, no less.

'I have brought your record, complete with dhobi-marks!' said Brian. 'We are very pleased with your Appreciation.' We nattered, mostly about cavalry musicians. His beady eye lit upon my old saxophone case.

'You keep your case in good nick. I wish our lot would keep theirs like yours. Play something!'

'The case is clean, so is the saxophone, but it is up the creek and is silent. I washed the pads; they have shrunk and I cannot get new ones.'

'Let's have a shufti,' said the Director of Music. I yanked it out and placed it in his cavalry mitts. He made a peculiar whistling noise of surprise, after looking at the bell of my silver 'C Melody', which today are very thin on the ground.

'This is a genuine Adolphe Sax instrument. Actually made in Paris in 1909 by Adolphe Sax, who first introduced the saxophone to orchestras and bands. It is worth a bomb as a museum piece. Give it to me. I'll take it to Windsor and see if our instrument mechanics can fix it!'

Months later, after I had suffered music deprivation so acutely that I lashed out on a Boosey & Hawkes B-flat clarinet, I telephoned the Director of Music at Combermere Barracks, Windsor, and asked him how much he had made on the saxophone. 'You said it was worth a bomb, so I presume you have flogged it, and it's only fair that I should share!'

'Haven't you got it back?' He promised to look into the problem. Within a few days my priceless instrument was returned as good as new from Boosey & Hawkes, the instrument makers at Aldershot. They did not charge the Regiment for repairs, neither did they charge me, and it sang like a mavis in full Suffolk throat. Later, the band used to pick me up and whip me off in their posh coach to schools in East Anglia where they gave concerts and taught children the various instruments. I had hoped to meet Brian again, possibly at the International Military Music gathering at Hyde Park Barracks. I had also hoped to meet Colonel George Evans, who had helped me considerably with my book on military music. But, as Rabbie had it, 'The best laid schemes o' mice an' men gang aft aglae'. But I did write about friend George in one of my articles for the *East Anglian Daily Times*, in which I much enjoyed writing a column for nearly a dozen years.

George did not join the band of The Royal Dragoons until October 1957, but he was largely responsible for a number of innovations during his eight years' stay, particularly in the introduction of outside jobs where bandsmen could make pin money in concerts and dance bands.

During the regiment's tour of duty in Germany with the BAOR, they provided an increasing number of concerts at such non-military events as police shows, the Queen's Birthday cocktail party and a long tour of Denmark, for the twentieth anniversary of the Liberation.

This engagement was a tremendous success and the band's only regret was that they could not end it with a concert in Copenhagen, which, as the regiment had wrested it from the Germans, had been a keenly anticipated highlight of the tour. Lightning sometimes strikes in the same place twice. The tour was cancelled, due to a strike in the Carlsberg brewery.

Throughout this period of tours, the band did not neglect the regiment, not even when they were engaged in the field for tank manoeuvres. One exercise was aptly christened 'Treble Clef', when wireless and signal instructions were given as follows: 'The Band will net in on A440 VPM at 1930 hours ... and will remain on net for approximately one and a half hours.'

When George Evans left the band in January 1966, Bandmaster Douglas Mackay took over. Formerly Bandmaster of The Tangier Foot (the Royal Scots, First of Foot and/or Pontius Pilate's Bodyguard), he had to earn his spurs and learn cavalry capers with the Royal Dragoons (the Tangier Horse). He was the only Bandmaster to have charge of the two first regiments of Britain's standing army, both formed in 1661, believed to be a dowry, or defence, of Catherine of Braganza against the Moors.

Duggie was sometimes taken to task. As a person used to proceeding to places on foot, he could not refrain from addressing Squadrons as 'Companies' and SQMSs as 'Colour Sergeants'.

David Shearn, the last Trumpet Major of The Royal Dragoons, who put my first book *Reuben's Corner* to music when he taught composition at Kneller Hall, told me that Duggie eventually lost his lust for the bagpipes of the Royal Scots, but not until he began to train the trumpeters in the art of Alpine Horn playing.

Nevertheless, Duggie perpetuated the practice of outside concerts begun by George Evans in Germany, and a total of 102 performances were given by the band in under six months. Lovers of music, the Germans were swift to show their appreciation.

The band played at the Gutersloh Schutzenfest for the third year. At the Detmoldfest they played almost continuously for the three-day event, supplying beat group and dance band in addition to the marching band.

At the Horn Schutzenfest they had to march round the town hall at least six times before they could find their way out of the packed square. At Bad Meinberg they had an audience of over 3000, and at the four-day show at Kikssijde, Belgium, they gave marching displays. The audience joined in with *Tipperary* and *Pack up your troubles*.

At a concert given to a packed house in Lage, the band received an unusual compliment. The local choir went on strike for their scheduled performance in the second half of the programme.

'We are not going to sing!' said the leader. 'Everyone wants to go on listening to the band!'

In the previous year, the herald trumpeters had returned to France for the British Trade Fair, to sound those rousing fanfares composed by my good friend Trumpet Major 'Taffy' David Shearn, and later, at the Opera House in the presence of Their Royal Highnesses, the Duke and Duchess of Kent.

The fanfares were sounded on their new trumpets, specially made by a German firm at a cost of Deutschmark 4,7000, then about £5,000.

Late in 1968 the band formed part of the Guard of Honour to escort the Colonel of the Regiment on his arrival at HQ, BAOR, and were gratified when General Fitzpatrick complimented them on their turnout and performance.

But for the band of The Royal Dragoons, in which I once played, this was the beginning of the end. A sorrowful occasion after all the hard work that had gone into restoring their strength to 35.

The Royal Dragoons had their band for over 150 years. Except for short periods, it had always been with the regiment, at home and abroad, and the regiment held it in the highest possible regard, though some wisecrackers pulled our legs when we formed up mounted, and guided our fine horses with stirrup-reins to keep our hands free to play our musical instruments. *'Fall out the Band ... The Regiment is going to trot.'*

About this time rumours were rife of an impending amalgamation with The Blues (Royal Horse Guards). Early in January 1969, the rumour was confirmed in the press and in the two Regimental Journals, *The Eagle* of The Royal Dragoons and *The Blue* of the Royal Horse Guards. The two were to amalgamate and form a new Household Cavalry Regiment, The Blues and Royals.

Our farewell party was partly in a German aviation hangar at Detmold. The Colonel of The Blues and Royals gave the Loyal Address to Her Majesty the Queen, and he read to us The Queen's reply. He then addressed the new regiment, shortly and to the point. We managed to keep our chins firm and Dragoon-like until that last command came.

'Blues and Royals ... by the right, Quick March!' And the young serving soldiers of Britain stepped smartly off, in a once Lufthansa hangar.

The chins of the many Old Comrades present were wobbly, the eyes moist, as the new band struck up with an old and apt march: *The Old Grey Mare She Ain't What She Used To Be.'*

Although The Old Grey Mare has changed, and most of her riders are now sardined into tanks and other armoured atrocities, as far as her music is concerned she is still a frisky filly. George Evans had much to do with her preservation.

When I popped down to Combermere Barracks, Windsor, George had successfully completed his first 'Troop' as Director of Music, Blues and Royals. They had Trooped the Colour of 'The Micks' (Irish Guards) on Her Majesty's Birthday, 16th June, 1974. I had heard a tribute paid to him by BBC TV for his remarkable capacity for composition.

He had written a new march for The Blues (Royal Horse Guards) and the regiment marched past to the old one, *Tangier* which George had scored for 1st B-flat cornet as part of his training at Kneller Hall.

He had already helped me with my book. I remember him diving into his archives as I asked if he had any 'gen' on the original composition of the band of The Blues.

With a blink and brow-furrow he replied: 'When Charles Godfrey conducted them at the Edinburgh Exhibition in 1886, they were 40 strong. Mind you, Spike, I was not present on that occasion.'

Although dodgy dentistry and dicey vision prevented me from meeting the international military musicians in person, in a way I was with them all on that important day. Imagination and music have their own truths, and they marked me 'Present and Correct'.

The Royal Dragoons are rich in regimental music and probably possess the oldest British cavalry march in *Dragoons of Tangier*, composed in 1696 and arranged for modern instruments by Bandmaster Mackay. The Royals at one time used Gounod's *Soldiers' Chorus* as their march and they have two more, *Spectemur Agendo* and *The Royals*, both by Trythall.

Finally, as both a slow and a quick march, Blackenburg's *The Royal Dragoons* was composed during the colonelcy-in-chief of Kaiser Wilhelm II and is now used in conjunction with the marches of the Royal Horse Guards. Trumpeters were mounted on greys, as they are today. But the great pride of all cavalry regiments was always the Drum Horse. There was 'Danny', who served in the Royals up to 1889, and 'Jack', a piebald of later years. But the most famous was the one I used to groom in Beaumont Barracks, Aldershot, in 1925–26. 'Coronet' was presented to us by King George V. He was a Hanoverian cream, who joined from the 2nd Life Guards (The Tins) in 1922 and soldiered on until he died in drum harness, on 'foreign service'.

22

From 'The Scrubs' to 'The Lords'

Wormwood Scrubs is reputed to be a completely serious prison for moderately serious offenders. It never expected to receive a non-paying guest like my old friend and former Troop Officer, Lieutenant Colonel A. D. Wintle, MC, the Royal Dragoon who was properly dressed when he entered the grim gates and waved to many of us who had turned up to see him off and in. As usual, he wore a red carnation. In his one good eye, a monocle; around his neck the tie of the Royal Military Academy, Woolwich, where he had begun his career as a professional soldier.

We, the onlookers, knew that he was about to serve a six-month sentence for de-bagging a solicitor after his many legal attempts to right a grievous wrong. A Brighton solicitor had drawn up a Will, in his own office, witnessed only by his own clerks, thereby enriching himself with a client's money, and he also made himself the residual legatee by inserting a codicil: 'This gift shall not lapse.' This meant that if he predeceased a rather simple old lady who signed the Will, his own successors would benefit.

Wintle had complained to the Public Prosecutor, the Law Society and national newspapers.

In the saloon bar at Wrotham Bell one sunny morning, when the Kentish Weald was garbed in apple blossom, Wintle whispered wily words into my nearside ear.

'Mays, there comes a time when a man's conscience makes

him mount and march into action. In the next 24 hours I shall be taking that action, which may result in my spending a holiday at the national expense. Maybe you would be good enough to attend to some of my affairs for a bit.'

'Consider it done!' said I, and for several excellent reasons. Way back in 1925 he had saved my life when I was desperately ill in the Cambridge Military Hospital, Aldershot. A telegram was sent to my parents. 'If you wish to see your son alive, come at once.'

Because Dragoons never do things by halves, I had contracted diphtheria and then underwent an operation for mastoiditis. I was bedded down in a small individual ward known as 'The Stiff's Retreat', one from which few occupants emerged alive. Lieutenant A. D. Wintle, MC, was a distant but fellow patient. He was in the officers' ward. His horse had fallen and broken Wintle's leg. Learning that I was in dire straits, he hobbled to my ward to inspect me, at 0300 hours. When I told him that I was dying, he waxed very frosty. 'It is an offence for a Royal Dragoon to die in bed. You will get better at once, that's an order. Then you will get a haircut!'

Although scared of death, I was terrified of disobeying the command of a fire-eating cavalry officer. I survived, got my mane clipped and soldiered on, thus beginning an unusual friendship which lasted for over 40 years. Ten years my senior, Wintle was born on 30th September, 1897, of 'rich but honest parents', he insisted, in Mariopol, Russia, where his father was a diplomat, who gave his son good advice which proved useful in his military career. 'Never be rude to anyone below the rank of full colonel.' In the Kaiser's War he lost an eye, some fingers from his left hand, and some bits off his left knee, and was awarded the Military Cross with a citation 'for marked gallantry and initiative of a very high order'.

Between the wars we served together in India, Ireland, Egypt and at home; sometimes Wintle served in Military Intelligence, which he described as a contradiction in terms and was performed by remaining seated for long periods in the presence of writing materials. As befitted a cavalry officer, he kept horses. 'Always one more than I could afford.'

157

He spoke French better than he spoke German and spent four years in Paris lecturing at the French Staff College.

He had once lived in Dunkirk, and during those dreadful days of June 1940 he was restive in London, aching to get to France and to put into effect the secret plans he had helped to arrange with French generals, to save some of their forces from surrender. Under a superior officer's name he telephoned Heston Airport with an instruction: 'Have a plane made ready to take a Colonel Wintle to Bordeaux tonight.'

Someone at Heston telephoned the War Office for details. Wintle's plot was discovered and he was made to confront the man whose name he had used.

'Blood is flowing in France,' he said. 'You have seen nothing flow but ink. I am deadly serious. If you don't believe me, I will convince you by blowing off the remains of my left hand.' He whipped out his revolver.

Placed under close arrest for threatening to shoot a superior officer, he was imprisoned in that place usually reserved for discarded royal wives and persons accused of high treason. He occupied a comfortable suite in the Tower of London, guarded by the Scots Guards whose officers, when they learned why he was there, regaled him with whisky, cigars and duck in aspic. 'A most comfortable hotel,' asserted Wintle. 'But the music was atrocious. You see, all the routine calls for those haggis-bashers were played on bagpipes.'

Colonel Wintle was tried by court-martial. The first of the nine charges against him, 'stating that certain of His Majesty's ministers ought to be shot,' was quickly dropped when Wintle began to call the roll of those he considered to have earned a firing squad. Hore-Belisha, then Secretary of State for War, was 'top of the pops'. Wintle suffered only a severe reprimand.

Later he was on his way from Syria to Marseilles, disguised as a French schoolteacher, with a revolver and a bag of gold sovereigns, but was betrayed, caught and imprisoned. For 13 months he endured solitary confinement in Fort Sainte-Catherine, a Vichy military prison near Toulon, from which he escaped twice and was recaptured. Before his final escape, accomplished by sawing through a window bar and jumping into a passing dung-cart, he decided to ginger up his guards by going on hunger strike for two weeks. He felt that such a filthy, unshaven shower were unworthy of the custody of a British officer, but chiefly 'To challenge their manhood – and make them ashamed of serving Vichy.'

After the war, Wintle retired with a 100 per cent disability pension. Still sporting his red carnation, monocle and silver snuff box, he was regarded by certain gentlemen of the press as a midget Colonel Blimp. They changed their song when it was revealed that soon after his escape from Fort Sainte-Catherine, the prison commandant, one Maurice Molia (inspired by Wintle's example and goading) had himself escaped from the grim prison, taking with him 250 of the staff to fight the Germans.

I wrote and congratulated Wintle, informing him that I was getting my ex-cavalry head down and was reading Psychology and Economics at the University of Edinburgh. His reply was *not* congratulatory:

'Dear Mays,

I am surprised that you are reading Economics. I thought you to be intelligent. I am not sure whether it is a bastard art or a misguided science. Ancient professors of this subject are content to eke out a meagre existence in dingy garrets, content to earn 9d a time for lectures couched in a special language to make the obvious appear difficult. Among its many peculiar definitions one is attributed to the London School of Economics: "The Science of Wealth." If I were lecturing on The Science of Wealth, I should do so from my diamond-encrusted yacht – moored off Monte Carlo.

As for Psychology. It simply means telling people to stop dying and get their hair cut.'

Shortly afterwards I passed a civil service examination to work at Heathrow Airport. *The Times* did not mention the fact, but they did manage to publish an unusual advertisement: 'Ex-cavalry officer wishes to purchase wardrobe of out-of-work piano tuner with view to getting position of responsibility with international organisation.' The applicant's address – 'The Cavalry Club'. The Club was not amused!

Wintle had applied and been interviewed for a post with NATO but had been told, unofficially, that his appearance was against him. 'I had been too well dressed for the job.' But he was already engaged on a task that took ten years. He had an elderly second cousin named Kitty Wells, the testatrix of the Will formerly mentioned. Over many years this old lady had received care and love from Wintle's sister, Marjorie. Kitty was not overstocked with grey matter, but she owned real estate from which she derived a considerable income. She divided her time between her houses, and no matter in which house she was, she wrote a letter every day to herself at the other, enclosing tram tickets, timetables and pointless paragraphs she had copied from seed catalogues. She had promised to 'look after Marjorie when the time comes'. But in the Will drawn up by Brighton solicitor Frederick Harry Nye, the original bequest had been amended to a measly annuity of £40.

Colonel Wintle was outraged and leapt into the saddle. Marjorie's love and care of the dotty old lady had been disregarded, and solicitor Frederick Nye was due to receive, even after death duties had been deducted, an estimated £65,000. The Public Prosecutor and his various minions, press and police, all agreed that something should be done, but not by them. The trouble was to get Nye into court, but the Will had been probated and so appeared to be legally correct. On an April afternoon, the trembling Nye stood trouserless, with shirt raised fore and aft, before Colonel Wintle's camera which clicked and revealed. Wintle had lured him to the Brighton flat, purporting to be a Lord and former colleague in Cambridge University.

'You are now dealing with a man, not defenceless old ladies!' said Wintle. He ejected Nye from the flat, and his pants, and took the trousers to his home in Wrotham, Kent, intending to hoist them on his flagpole next morning. But the police arrived before he could troop this colour and Wintle was charged with assault. At Lewes Assizes he was given a six months' sentence, to be served in Wormwood Scrubs.

The preliminary skirmish had succeeded. Nye had been flushed from his Brighton burrow. The main offensive was to attack the Will in a Court of Law. The first fence was the Probate, Divorce and Admiralty Division of the High Court of Justice. Wintle's counsel, Phillimore, contended that Kitty was too dim of wit to unravel the intricacies of the Will she had signed and was unaware of the sum that would go to the pocket of her lawyer. When the verdict was announced, Wintle was defeated. The Will was to stand.

'You see, Mays, we shall conform to our norms. If a cavalryman is knocked from his saddle, he remounts!'

Five months later we were again in the saddle, unsupported by counsel, for we had jettisoned Mr Justice Phillimore. Just a half section of Donkey Wallopers against the hordes of the law.

Wintle argued his case for four days, a difficult one for even an accomplished barrister. We were in the Court of Appeal before three judges, and Wintle's case revolved about a subtle and intangible point; had the learned judge, on his summing up in the previous hearing, been guilty of misdirecting the jury? One judge said yes, the other two said no, so Kitty's will stood and Wintle was unhorsed.

I was deeply disappointed and said to Wintle, 'Let's go to the Wig and Pen for a stirrup cup.'

'NO!' said Wintle. 'We will go to the Embankment and spit in the Thames for luck!' – and we did.

Because the verdict was not unanimous, Wintle was granted leave to re-appeal his case to the highest court in the land, the House of Lords. Once again he decided to appear in person, with me instead of counsel.

We did not lack for ammunition. Between us we had made 42 copies of a 253-page compendium of previous testimony. At last came the day of truth and final judgment.

Seated before us, in mufti, were the best legal brains in

England; Viscount Simmons (Lord Chancellor), Lord Tucker, Lord Birkett, Lord Reid and Lord Keith of Avonholme. Frederick Harry Nye was represented by a Welsh barrister, Mr Ifor Lloyd, and I sat in counsel's seat next to Colonel Wintle. We sat for six days.

'I see that you are not represented by counsel, Colonel Wintle,' said Viscount Simmons.

'No, my Lord. I have jettisoned them, they do not understand!'

'You do not always say the thing that endears you most,' replied his lordship, and I felt so pleased that he smiled when he said it.

Wintle presented his case for three days and was almost continuously on his feet. The Lord Chancellor complimented him on the clarity of his exposition. Others, taking no part in the proceedings, were curious. During a break outside the Chamber, Wintle was approached by three smart ones who knew Wintle almost as well as he knew them, and their professions.

'Why is Mr Mays sitting in counsel's seat, Colonel Wintle?'

'A good question, gentlemen, but there is a better answer. You see, gentlemen, Mays served with me in our regiment, a very good one, The Royal Dragoons. Now, if I had said to my RSM, "Mr Marryatt, get me a Law Lord, a QC and a Fleet Street hack," do you know what he would have done?'

'Pray tell us!'

'He would have clicked his heels, rattled his spurs, saluted and replied, "Sir! One man or three men?" You see, gentlemen, any soldier of the Royal Dragoons can do the lot.'

The grounds for appeal were that the judge in his summing-up in the Probate Court had misdirected the jury, and was too lenient to Mr Nye and hostile to Wintle, who put the complicated case in a nutshell.

'My Lords, Miss Wells came into this world with nothing. During the interval she amassed a considerable fortune which, according to the terms of a Will drawn up by her solicitor, in his own office, witnessed only by his own clerks, was left in the main to that solicitor. Did she know he was going to get it? If so, did she have full knowledge of the amount?'

As his carefully considered words continued, I sat beside him making occasional notes. Then came that wonderful moment when I knew Wintle had won. He had just made his personal explanation of a complicated clause in the codicil.

Viscount Simmons intervened.

'It is quite dear, Colonel Wintle, that no one in any of the courts has understood this Will and its complications.'

Wintle jumped to his feet with a ready answer.

'My Lord, would it be presumptuous of me to suggest that Miss Wells, described here as a feeble-minded old lady, might not have understood it?'

The five Law Lords withdrew and returned in six minutes. Nye's QC approached me in that interval. His client wished to talk terms, possibly to settle out of court. Then Wintle did his piece of informing, telling the QC that the case should go through the 'proper channels'. As *he* had been so informed after he had de-bagged Mr Nye, and went to prison for six months.

When they returned to the Chamber, their lordships announced their unanimous decision. They had granted the appeal, reserving their reasons to be stated later; and this they did at a further hearing in the House of Lords on 18th December, 1958. Viscount Simmons said that when the trial was heard at the High Court, the judge's summing up was so gravely at fault as to amount to misdirection: 'It would be difficult to pack more mis-statements into two short paragraphs.' The Colonel was granted his costs out of the estate. An order was agreed that Frederick Harry Nye set aside any benefits to himself under the Will.

We left the Chamber, hotly pursued. I felt very proud that I had been at my old Troop Officer's side for the last charge in the long battle. We were tired, but on the following Sunday morning I stood in a room at Coldharbour, Wintle's home, fetlock deep in letters and telegrams of congratulation, many from distant lands in which we had served. This was the first successful appeal in the House of Lords by a commoner this century, and the one and only to receive a unanimous verdict.

The 'gentlemen' of the gutter press, who had branded him as 'Colonel Blimp' and 'Colonel Bogey' now hailed him as a national hero: 'The Dashing Dragoon', 'The man who stood up and fought'.

At a dinner held by the barristers of Lincoln's Inn, at which HRH Princess Margaret was their guest of honour, a toast was drunk to Wintle's success. A signed menu card was sent to him, together with a jeroboam of champagne. 'For the successful amateur to drink the health of losing professionals.'

Wintle was impressed by the bottle's dimensions.

'Take my Bible and look up a precedent, Mays. You should be used to that now you have graduated in the Lords. Look up I Kings xi,28,xiv.16,' said he. I did, and this is what the old book said: 'A mighty man of valour, who made Israel to sin.' His name was Jeroboam.

I, too, was impressed and suggested that he might let me have the bottle, whip it to my workshop and make a table lamp from it as a souvenir for him.

'That is not a bad idea, Mays, but I have a better one. We shall now proceed to the more important task of draining it.'

No less rewarding for Wintle and me, was the receipt from the Commanding Officer of the Royal Dragoons of the regimental sports tie, dark blue, embellished with golden eagles, to commemorate the capture of the Colour of the 105 Regiment of the Line, from the French in 1815 at Waterloo. This tie is only awarded to Royal Dragoons who have represented their regiment in a sporting event. But in the *Sporting Life* of 7th February, 1974, journalist John Bliss had this to say:

'A man whose chivalry ought to be rewarded with a knighthood is Lieutenant Colonel A. D. Wintle, MC. His victory was celebrated by a dinner in Lincoln's Inn, attended by Princess Margaret. His residence in one of HM institutions was made respectable. On such narrow margins, a reputation for virtue depends; but an honour for Wintle and his faithful

164

friend – from the State – would be received among sportsmen everywhere with great delight.'

Wintle did not stick to his precepts. In 1925 he told me it was an offence for a Royal Dragoon to die in bed. In May 1966 he died ... in bed, on the morning we had arranged to take a stirrup cup in the Wig and Pen Club, opposite the Law Courts, which he often described as his Town House.

Not long before he died, we were both in that place to celebrate his appearance on the television programme *This Is Your Life*, which I had arranged with the BBC and also rounded up the cast.

The following conversation took place:

WINTLE: Mays, I think I shall go home. I feel unwell.

MAYS: Well, off you go. I shall stay, but please remember me in your will.

WINTLE: Do you think that I'm going to die, Mays?

MAYS: Of course.

WINTLE: That is a most sobering statement. We shall now have some very large whiskies. (We did).

Much later I walked with him to Charing Cross Station.

WINTLE: Apropos of your earlier statement in the Wig and Pen, I now charge you with a most solemn undertaking. Should I predecease you, you will arrange for the band of the Royal Dragoons to play over my grave. Tell them it must be *Standchen*, Schubert's Serenade.

MAYS: Consider it done.

WINTLE: It has just occurred to me that the band might be engaged elsewhere. In that event I will settle for two Royal Dragoon trumpeters – one at the head, one at the foot – to sound cavalry *Last Post* and cavalry *Reveille*.

MAYS: Consider it done.

WINTLE: It has just occurred to me that if neither the band nor the trumpeters can be present, you, Mays, will have to sing the lot.

MAYS: Consider it done.

So, as soon as I learned of his death, I tried to get the band, but they were in Germany. So, too, were the trumpeters. I attended the Maidstone Crematorium where they put him down. I then went to a pub where I put down one bottle of Glenfiddich.

Next, I motored to Canterbury Cathedral, the Chapel of the Cavalry of Britain. Much to the consternation of sundry worshippers, I sang bits of the lot. Not too badly, I think ... It's a bit dicey standing to attention in a cathedral, singing through a mist of whisky and tears.

But it was done!

23

Gwylad Y Gan

It has happened to us all. Some snatch of melody brings back
half-forgotten incidents, places, people. I never thought that a
brawny bunch of Taffies hailing from a village which, when
written in English lettering, resembles a Chinese meteoro-
logical report in cipher, would remind me of war. But they
did!

A coachload of our Steeple Bumpstead villagers sallied
forth one fine night, to listen to nightingales. On our £2-apiece
ticket was printed:

> GUILDHALL ... CAMBRIDGE
> Cambridge and District
> Multiple Sclerosis Society
> YNYSYBWL
> MALE VOICE CHOIR
> 22nd April, 1978
> 7.30p.m.
> (Bar opens at 8.45 p.m.)

Our good friend, Kenneth Marks, who shares my birth
date, waxed wary. He inspected the ticket with care. As our
village policeman he probably suspected illegal immigration.
His brow wrinkled. He spoke:

'Do you know, some people reckon Steeple Bumpstead is a
rum owd name for a village. Some thought it was comic opera

like Much Binding in the Marsh, but this bloody YNYSYBWL! How the hell do you pronounce it?'

Vera, my Welsh-speaking wife, did her best to help, slowly and distinctly.

'Thanks, Vera! I can't wrap my tongue round that lot. I'll settle for "Aniseed balls".'

The Cambridge and District Branch of the MS Society was formed in 1967 by a small band of sufferers and willing helpers. Quickly established, it raised very considerable funds for research and the welfare of 96 victims of the disease. There are 280 branches in all, doing wonderful work caring for the 50,000 people in this country who have contracted MS. Perhaps more distressing is the fact that the cause of the disease remains a mystery. Help is needed. Donations, however small, may be sent to any of the branch treasurers. The Taffies found their own method for raising the good wind. On that Saturday the Guildhall was packed.

To my surprise and pleasure, the gentleman who first addressed us was once the late Sir Mortimer Wheeler's goggle-box quiz mate. I began to suspect that he had been occupationally maladjusted in digging out old bones and ancient rock. Glyn Daniel was superb. An 'intellectual' comedian. Far funnier than flat, fat Secombe from Swansea!

It worn't all 'male'. Three charming, talented ladies added to the lustre of the male choir. Marjorie Harris, a brilliant pianist, was the accompanist; Ann Hill from Cardiff, the lark-like soprano; and Betty Jones Reeves from Ynysybwl, the mellow contralto.

David Arnold wielded no stick or baton. Throughout the choir singing, not one chorister's eyes strayed from his sensitive, expressive hands. He conducted superbly, but methinks he might once have been a drill and PT instructor in the Welsh Guards and had inspected and instructed his music squad every five minutes.

His choir boys, some 60-plus in age, were sartorially splendid in evening dress. They stood stiffly to attention whilst singing, and sat statue-still when the soloists were regaling us. What a treat to hear good singing from the throats of dedicated, disciplined men!

What a welcome change from that unshorn, unwashed, non-musical riff-raff who can barely twang over-amplified electrical guitar strings, but writhe like contortionists and Burmese belly dancers to wear out their over-tight tattered jeans from the inside, as those unintelligible noises blast out in monotonous repetition from the gaping holes in their heads!

'I've seen Welsh choirs on the box,' said my friend Harold, no mean blower of the cornet. 'But never in the flesh. They are marvellous!'

Geoffrey Westrope, competent singer in our Steeple Bump-stead Players, was overjoyed. 'That's the best show I've seen and heard in years. I could listen to their programme every night for a week!'

The programme had an international flavour. Rodgers and Hammerstein burst into the act with *Nothing like a Dame*, Wagner was on musical parade with 'The Pilgrim's Chorus' from *Tannhauser*, and one Joe Tanti from Malta represented the George Cross Island with a catchy little piece entitled *Il Karozzin* which the versatile Taffies sang in Maltese. Ann Hill charmed us with her beautiful rendering of *Resulka's Song to the Moon* (Dvorak), the waltz song from *Tom Jones* (Edward German), followed by three enforced encores. Betty started her solos with *What is Life Without Thee* (Gluck), then *O Love Thy Power* from Samson and Delilah (Saint Saens), then the lovely ladies coupled up their vocal cords and sang duets.

Welsh male choirs are at their best when singing in their own tongue, and it was entrancing to listen, to feel the joy that music brings. They continued with two magnificent render-ings: *Nant y Mynydd* (Mountain Stream) by Silcher and *Bugellio'r Gwenith Gwyn* (Watching the Wheat); but my heart was gladdened when I saw on the programme my favourite, *Calon Lan* (Pure Heart), because it once gave me hope when I was in the depths and shoals of despair.

I was in Normandy. Two days before the Allies' main

169

attack began on 14th August, 1944, we had established a new radio link and communication with a new HQ. We left the cover of the forest and operated on the move during a slow advance by the River Laize.

Heavy bombers roared overhead, there followed nerve-shattering bomb blasts and the thunder of gunfire. Lightning-like flashes stained the night sky clouds with incessant bursts of coloured lights, ranging from saffron yellow to deep carmine. From the bombs came Mars orange sulphur flashes and electric blue flarings from cobalt. The earth heaved and quaked, dancing a fiery protest. The Germans were receiving a very strong dose of their own medicine – in the Falaise Gap.

Leaning against a nearby tree was a motorcycle. It coughed into life at my kick. I aimed it in the direction of higher ground, where I hoped to get a grandstand seat for the firework display being dished out to Jerry. I never made it. Had I not been so inquisitive I would not now be drawing a disability pension for defective vision.

I shall never know what hit me, but well remember regaining consciousness. Bed-bound, bandaged and blinded, I was in the field hospital below Bayeux. I did not know this for a long time. Under the impression that I had got my deserts for being a good choirboy, I thought I was in Heaven. It was not the voice of angels singing round a throne. Merely a bunch of wounded Welsh Guardsmen singing *Calon Lan*. How it all rushed back at the Cambridge Guildhall!

By that time I had learned smatterings of Welsh and words of songs and hymns. Alwyn Jenkins, my wife's nephew, a glider pilot who held distance and altitude records for the South Wales Gliding Club, helped me by taking me to Pontardulais to hear that wonderful choir at singing practice. 'We must leave at a quarter to nine,' said Alwyn. 'Otherwise we'll not get a seat at The Fountain, the pub the choir goes to after practice at the Technical College.' We beetled off to The Fountain, which was packed with miners and steelworkers, knocking back pints of Felinfoel and Buckley ale, all on music

170

parade for the post-practice concert in which they would join. The bar was a long one. Barmaids were filling glasses in readiness for the singers, for they could be heard long before being seen, singing, on their way from singing, to singing.

As usual, they were merely conforming to the national norm; just obeying the musical command of the last line of the chorus of *Calon Lan*: 'Canu'r dydd a chanu'r nos'. Roughly translated by an owd Suffolker, it means 'keep you on a-singing, by day and night.'

The Ynysybwl Choir came to Cambridge by coach and spent a couple of nights in digs provided by friends living in nearby villages. Some stayed with us. Our bungalow rocked with song well into the small hours. There came a telephone call. 'We are meeting to board the coach at Cambridge, as was arranged. Meet us at Duxford. Some of the lads want to go to the War Museum.'

I went with them and spotted an old comrade, some kind of arranger. In about five seconds flat he arranged that we should enter that first faster-than-sound exhibition Concorde, now shackled down in concrete. Drinks came up and song poured out for a good hour. My arranger was delighted ... 'Bring 'em again, Spike, bring 'em again!'

Later, glider pilot Alwyn whisked me to Carmarthenshire. Just outside Haverford West was an old aerodrome once used by the RAF, not a Spitfire or Hurricane in sight. Quite a few gliders and some gnat-like Cessnas, but hordes of derelict, played-out Tiger Moths used to yank the gliders into the sky. The control tower was a wreck, similar to an old shooting lodge-cum-Japanese Army toilet, but it boasted a bar from which one had a choice – whisky or milk. Most took both and called it a Scotch Shake. Concerts were given in it after the Scotch Shakes! Songs were plentiful. A mixty-maxty of Wesleyan hymns and rugby ballads (Sacred and Profane). They had a gramophone with a horn, like that relic for advertising His Master's Voice, and just one record which sounded like an air raid warning but was some Yankee dame shrilling out *Hello Dolly*.

All tarted up with leeks and daffodil button-holes, we set

off for singing to the Royal Albert Hall. Welsh invaders were congregating. This was a kind of anniversary of old David of the White Rock, and we were four, Vera, two of her Welsh lady friends, and this old (foreign) Anglo-Saxon. At Door 9 we queued, a long time, in bucketing rain. I looked to Door 4. Its entrance was roofed. We switched our queue location. A many-medalled Commissionaire disregarded our tickets. He sniffed, then was terse: 'Tenor or bass?' he said.

Trying to be friendly to the natives, I replied 'How about a Worthington!'

'Singing, it is, boyo, *not* drinking. Up the front, by there! Women to the left, gentlemen to the right!' said he.

'There's rude!' said Vera.

I left the ladies and 'up by there' I found myself midway planted between the bass and baritone warblers of Treorchy and Pontardulais. There's clever for you!

Seated that night at the organ was maestro Cyril Anthony. His fingers ran not idly over the keys, for he knew he had much to play. No less than 38 hymns! There before me in the booklet *A Nation Sings* (Cymanfa Ganu – 1965), every word in Welsh and every note in tonic sol-fah. To a soft purring of the mighty organ, introductions were made, to receive thunderous ovations from throats and crescendo clapping of hands.

Emrys Jones was presented as The Reader, who would, and did, read the opening lines of each hymn like a stone cold sober Dylan Thomas. There's lovely! Dr Terry James, a fiery-headed and bearded slave driver, had a stick, just a bit of a twig. He was not a doctor of medicine, nor a water diviner, but a Doctor of Music and his stick was a baton. He was ruthless. If we were half a tone out, a bit too quick or slow, he would take us back to sing it all over again.

We were singing for a good four hours, although I thoroughly enjoyed it all and learned a bit more Welsh. But I did not appreciate the full significance of personal participation until I read bits in the newspaper and on the record label of the *Delyse*. 'The biggest selling record of its kind ever made. Five thousand Welsh voices singing in the Royal Albert Hall

... *Tremendous success* for *A Nation Sings* at the Cymanfa Ganu (singing festival).'

Vera was delighted, until I wrote to Welsh Wales a simple letter stating that their claim was a bit economical with the truth. It should have read 4,999 Welsh voices. And just one East Anglian, without which the vaunted Cymanfa Ganu might well have been a flop.

No one answered my letter ... There's rude for you!

I had expected letters almost by return of post, but had overlooked the fact that Welshmen are always determined to retaliate, even though time is required for them to act, unless for playing Rugby and singing. After a couple of months I was quizzed, interrogated, probed and pestered by phone and post.

'You don't know the words, you're English!' 'Why don't they sing all the words?' 'Is it really a love song?' 'Is it the Treorchy Male Voice Choir?'

Last came a hiccup-punctuated statement from the mouth of a horse-riding spalpeen from the Emerald Isle who works in a stud at Newmarket, who could recite W. B. Yeats' *Lake Isle of Innisfree* backwards.

'It is the best commercial in the whole of world TV, it is. 'Tis a psalm and an anthem combined, taken from the first chapter of Guinness. Who the hell wants to hear about old cocoa and Tetley tea bags? Listen to the Dubliners! It looks and sounds better in colour!'

Eureka! Rejoice with me. That which was lost is found. Words and verses in English and Welsh. Music in tonic sol-fah, in the key of D flat, by Joseph Parry. I have dug out the bare bones of *Myfanwy*, that moving Welsh love song so beautifully sung by a handful of Welsh choristers to boost the sales of pints of Liffey Water from Dublin's fair city.

My mole, or informer, hailed from Ynysybwl, once famed for its coal and choristers. For many a year this microscopic village, about eight miles from Cardiff, on the way to Rhondda Fach and Rhondda Mawr had produced the highest quality coal for ships. The choir has produced music, money and love to help the Cambridge and District Multiple Sclerosis Society

173

in research. From one of their nightingales, I gleaned the secrets of *Myfanwy*. There are three verses. 'Myfanwy' is Welsh for our English Arabella.

> Why shoots wrath's lightning, Arabella
> From those jet eyes? What clouds thy brow?
> Those cheeks that once with love blushed on me.
> Why are they pale and bloodless now?
> Why bite those lips that bore my kisses?
> Where lurks the smile that won my heart?
> Why will be thy, oh Arabella?
> Speak love, once more before we part.
>
> What have I done, oh cruel fair one
> To merit e'en a frown from thee?
> Am I too fond, or thou too fickle?
> Or play'st thou but to humble me?
> Thou art my own, by word and honour,
> And wilt thou not thy word fulfil?
> Thou need'st not frown, oh Arabella,
> I would not have thee against thy will.
> Full be thy heart with joy forever.
>
> May time ne'er cypher on thy brow.
> Though life may beauty's rose and lily
> Dance on thy healthy cheeks as now.
> Forget thy broken vows and never
> Allow thy wakeful conscience tell,
> That thou didst e'er mislead or wrong me;
> Oh, Arabella, fare, fare thee well!

Myfanwy did not appear on the printed programme for the Cambridge concert, but I had a crafty whisper into the lugs of an ex-Welsh Guards chorister that this lovely song should become top of the pops should special items be requested and, as sure as God made little apples, leeks and daffodils, the choir sang it for me.

Diolch yn fawr, Howard! I will never forget!

174

Gwylad Y Gan

* * *

Next day the Duxford Aviation Society allowed us to sit in the driver's seat of the world's most up-to-date aircraft.

Five years earlier, at Tangier, this Concorde 001 managed to creep through the skies at a speed of mach 2.23, to create a record. By cruising at twice the speed of sound, Concorde can nip smartly across the Atlantic Ocean in three hours, fifty minutes.

'Frighteningly impressive!' said one ancient choirboy. 'I've been looking round the other hangars here. Lots of stuff from the Imperial War Museum. Thousands of tons of iron and steel, possibly from Wales. All turned into machines to destroy human life. When will they ever learn?'

The evening before, he had been singing about real values. The 23rd Psalm (Franz Schubert), *Cast thy burden upon the Lord* (Mendelssohn Bartoldy), *Prayer from 'Under Milk Wood'* (set to Troyle's Chant). We had a mossell from *O Isis and Osiris* (from *The Magic Flute* – Mozart). The final act consisted of Verdi's *Force of Destiny* and many other wonderful renderings from soloist and choirs alike, all of whom have promised to return from Gwylad Y Gan, The Land of Song.

24

Poets and Peasants

Standing on top of my 90-year-old English oak writing desk, which Vera bought for me by lashing out £9 at a jumble sale, is a handmade bookshelf containing the literary outpourings of two Orcadians.

Edwin Muir is dead. He died in an East Anglian cottage which stands in Swaffham Prior churchyard, the only English churchyard with two churches. He was born on 15th May, 1887, at a farm called The Folly in the parish of Deerness in Orkney.

My George Mackay Brown died while I was writing this book, a whippersnapper fourteen years my junior, for he waited for birth until 17th October, 1921, in Stromness, Orkney. George was the sixth and youngest child of John Brown, part-time tailor and postman, and of Mhairi Mackay of Strathy, Sutherland. George started his schooling at Stromness Academy but became very ill with tuberculosis and was unemployed for ten years, apart from infrequent forays into local journalism.

The three of us first met in October 1951 in a classroom of Newbattle Abbey College, Dalkeith, situated in the vale of the River Esk near Dalkeith, Midlothian, eight miles from the city of Edinburgh.

I had written a prize-winning essay for the WEA on my idea of a national wages policy. Having attempted to survive on the meagre pittance of a GPO telegraphist, I had personal experience of the paucity of purchasing power. My prize was to be an entry as a student to Newbattle Abbey College for a brace of academic years.

Married, with two young sons, I could not have gone without Vera's help. 'I shall go to work at the EMI factory in their records department. They are advertising for new hands!'

Before I could get my head down to the study of where to put commas and semi-colons, Vera had made a name for herself by causing EMI incalculable expenditure in trying to amend a simple mistake in the King's English. In an important catalogue of their products, already internationally distributed, someone had used a buckshee letter 's' and pluralised *Phil the Fluter's Ball*. Before she could find further atrocities she was whipped off to Richmond, to inspect tapes of recordings of 'Famous Overtures of The London Festival Orchestra'.

Newbattle Abbey, a masterpiece of beauty and design, was a gift of the late Marquess of Lothian. The Abbey itself was founded by the Cistercians in 1140. It shone like a jewel of architecture in its 125 acres of gardens, woodlands and parks. Lions crouched in stone on the pillars of the main gate, guarding the entrance to that main drive which led for nigh on half a mile through avenues of lofty elms and beeches to the handsomely sculptured portico. As I entered I sensed an influence, an atmosphere, a kind of welcome – even before I met the Warden, Edwin Muir and his wife Willa.

They are both dead now. Edwin predeceased her. Willa asked me to take her home so that she could die in Scotland. I did, and in Scotland she died.

Twenty years after her birth and christening as Willa Anderson, this bonnie, brainy lass, graduated with a first class honours degree in Classics at the University of St Andrews. She then studied Educational Psychology, then worked like a beaver to become vice-principal of the London Training School for Teachers.

In September 1918, in a Glasgow flat, she met Edwin Muir.

He had recently graduated as a costing clerk in a Renfrew shipping firm after months of packing seething, wriggly and rotten maggots into plastic tubs and tins for fishing fanatics.

They married within a year of meeting. They worked together, they taught others together, but they did not die together.

On my 'precious' shelf is her book. It is called *Belonging*. It is a memoir. On each of its 316 pages, their love for each other shines through, but the whole story can be read in that first paragraph:

'On the face of things our meeting was unlikely; it was still more unlikely that we should marry in under a year later and most unlikely of all that our marriage would last. Edwin's Glasgow friends, who thought they knew him, prophesied that it would not last six months; my friends in London, who thought they knew me, were of the same opinion.

Yet when he died in 1959, I became aware that I had been assuming that we should die together, when it came to dying, hand in hand. I could not believe it possible for me to be alive and for him to be dead. It did not make sense.

Her inscription reads:

'This book belongs to Spike (RSM C. W. Mays, MA). I hope he will go on liking it and that his wife will like it too.'

(Willa Muir)

Standing next to Willa's *Belonging* is Edwin's autobiography, a third reprint of *Edwin Muir*, dedicated: 'To Stanley Cursiter and Eric Linklater, Fellow Orcadians'. Below that, in his own hand, 'To Spike the Practical'. Those books will stand together for as long as I outlive the authors. Death parted them, but their books will stay together.

Willa took my arm at that first meeting. 'We know about you Spike. You have been a soldier. You were wounded, but you are now our oldest student and you will find peace here, and perhaps yourself. Come, meet the others. We will take tea and heather honey!'

George Mackay Brown was a bit of a puzzler; a craggy, sensitive man, whose strong jaw jutted like the prows of those monstrous Royal Navy ships that jaunted to Jutland and returned to Scapa Flow, hardly a willow tit flight from Stromness, where George first saw the light. With thick jersey cladding and tousley of mane, he looked as though a sea shanty would salvo from him at any minute. Strangely enough, he reminded me of that wonderful Western Isle song *'Turn ye to me'*. When he looked at me, peering with eyes seeming to attempt an escape from bushy, beetled brows, I sensed his sensitivity. When he spoke, in an accent so strange and compelling, I knew I had found a friend, and thought of the Old East Anglian adage: 'As a bird is known by its note, so is a man by his conversation.' We have been friends ever since.

Willa Muir was a marvellous teacher. Herself a writer, poet and translator, she was almost aggressively eager to teach German and Latin.

English Literature and English Language were taught by Edwin, whose object was to foster in us a discriminating taste for, and enjoyment of, English Literature, which he traced from Chaucer to the present day.

Although seriously studying other subjects, most students would gatecrash our classes, thinking they could ill afford to miss even one of his lectures, to be warned in his inimitable style of atrocities we committed in speech and writing upon the world's most lovely language.

We were free-range students with freedom to question Edwin's points of view on writers in general. The week before, we had been informed about vices and virtues of The English Novel. To my surprise he had waxed disdainfully about poor old Danny Defoe's *Treasure Island* – one of my elementary school favourites for that teachers' rest period known as 'silent reading'.

'There is too much chiselling!' said Edwin. 'On almost every page one finds tool-boxes and chisels and more chisels!'

I went to dead Daniel Defoe's aid because I had hoped as a boy to find a desert island, for there was not much future in pulling marigolds with ice in their leaves, for ten bob per 70-hour week. In front of the seminar crowd, gate-crashers included, I informed Edwin Muir that I had worked with chisels and been taught to use them by Harry Wright, our estate carpenter who made the sails for our windmill; that I had met pedantic people who worked only with pens and were unable to bash a wire nail into bits of balsa wood, and continued: 'You see, Doctor Muir, the man who made windmills could hardly write his own name or speak properly. But, if you make a mistake when writing a best seller, all you have to do is grab an ink and pencil rubber, then start off again. Permit me to invite your attention to that fireplace!'

I pointed. There, around the grate, was a magnificently carved fireplace, in one great hunk of wood, about ten feet by five feet. It was a superb grape vine, carved by an Italian. Grape bunches protruded as though offering themselves for wine making. Thick and thin veins patterned every curling leaf; there were even tiny hairs on the bodules.

'I will let you into a secret, Doctor Muir. If the artist who carved that masterpiece made one chisel-slip, his work would have been ruined. He could not tart it up with a mite of rubber!'

Edwin led the clapping, said I was quite right, and that he would save up and buy a tool-box.

After George Mackay Brown graduated, he went on to Edinburgh University on a post-graduate course to study Gerard Manley Hopkins. I wished to do the same, but pennies were few and debts were galloping up our home straight. Edwin came to my aid and recommended me for a two-year Middlesex County award if the GPO would grant me leave, but no cash – the County Council might help if I satisfied an army of inquisitors and answered their questions in a smart and student-like fashion.

There they sat, a white-haired semi-circle of crafty senes-cents, all taking turns to torture me with questions for nearly an hour. The High Priest of the MCC got up on his hinds and asked a leading question.

'Do you think, Mr. Mays, that at your age you will be able to assimilate this vast store of knowledge?'

This put me back a few horses' lengths, so I asked him to repeat his question. He did, and gave me a bit of time.

I looked at each one in turn, making sure they knew I was weighing them up. And then I blurted out: 'Gentlemen, you are my seniors in age, by appearance. Why not give the young 'uns a chance?' Someone gasped. The ancients moved their heads. Some nodded, others shook from side to side. They huddled and whispered as though I was of no concern and the chief of the tribe spoke.

'Thank you, Mr Mays. You may go now, but we will be writing to you very shortly.'

Westminster Hall seemed to turn into a vast echo chamber. My departing footsteps reverberated like horses' hooves on concrete. My stomach churned in protest.

After a couple of stirrups in Hyde Park Barracks, I telephoned Edwin and apologised for letting him down, but he was laughing as I spoke and said, 'Well done, Spike! The Middlesex County Council have already telephoned me. You called them "old fogies". Well, your old fogies are going to award you £300 a year. You will go to Edinburgh University for matriculation.'

Within a month I had matriculated and was accepted at the University of Edinburgh; no mention more will be made of my academic antics in this book for they have been detailed in my earlier book, *No More Soldiering For Me*. Innate modesty compels me to mention an appraisal from a fellow East Anglian, Adrian Bell, who said kind words about it in *The Eastern Daily Press*. Maybe because he used to farm near where I used to live!

'His record is bursting full of his enjoyment of life.'

John Parker of the *Spectator* was pleased:

'It is one of the charms of this thoroughly enjoyable book that it gives a frank picture of a way of life, relatively recent, but totally gone.'

Arthur Swinson seemed to agree, because he said kind words in *Books and Bookmen*:

'An absolute winner ... it is a wonderfully human work compounded of laughter and tears, toughness and sentimentality.'

Without the poets and peasants of Newbattle Abbey College, my books and their words would never have been written.

We shall now return to my good friend George Mackay Brown, on whom I never clapped an eye after we left Auld Reekie (Edinburgh).

George once left Orkney for a holiday in the land of the shamrock, and went once only to London, to collect a prize for a book. We passed, but did not meet each other, on different trains, on the same day.

George was travelling south, I to the north; different directions but with identical objectives. We were on safari to collect awards. My destination was Leeds, where at the Queen's Hotel, I was to receive on behalf of the *Yorkshire Post* Literary Society, and from the hands of The Right Honourable The Earl of Harewood, their award for my *Reuben's Corner* as their book of the year.

George, on the opposite trail for London, was about to net the Scottish Arts Council Literature Prize for his book, *A Time to Keep*.

Without the poet of Newbattle Abbey College, George's poems and books might not have been written. I include a copy of one of his letters. He would have forgiven me for being a mole; everybody is in the 'leak' business today!

16–12–91

'Dear Spike,

Your letter, indomitably cheerful, has just come.

You certainly don't spread gloom around at this dark time of year.

Well done, in spite of all.

May you be able to read and write many a long day yet.

Have a festive dram with the turkey and plum pudding. And may the happy ghosts of Newbattle come thronging about you.

> Your old friend,
> George.'

Strangely enough, when my eyesight failed in 1988, George's eyes decided to have cataracts (later removed, and sight restored to him). He wrote me a poem, to give me hope.

The Lamp
The lamp is needful in Spring, still
Though the jar of daffodil
Out splendours lamplight and hearth flames.

In summer, only near midnight
Is match struck to wick.
A moth, maybe, troubles the rag of flame.

Harvest. The lamp in the window
Summons the scythe-men.
A school book lies on the sill, two yellow
halves.

In December, the lamp's a jewel,
The hearth ingots and incense.
A cold star travels across the pane.

He also sent a note:

'How are the eyes, my friend? May they light you through a few good years yet.

'I am very sorry to hear about your eyes. This is a sad affliction. May light and healing return to them soon. I have included a little impromptu verse which I hope you will "un-stick" and stick anew to the fly-leaf of *Time in a Red Coat*.'

Spike Mays
In remembrance of happy days;
Not on gory fields of battle
But among the pleasant trees and stone
and folk of Newbattle.

'Prolific' is not quite the word for George's contribution to literature; his increasing cascades included an abundance of books and plenitudes of poetry. He blamed his output on ancient Orcadians who had left behind them vast deposits of narrative plagiarised from a long procession of those rapacious rascals who not only conquered but inhabited the Orkney Islands for thousands of years; those rum old stone-agers, early Celts, peculiar Picts, haggis-devouring Scots and those villainous Vikings.

Modern Orcadians should keep a sharp lookout. East Anglia's Anglo-Saxons (of which I am one) might soon be on the prowl. We are getting mighty short of space since our politicians took to spelling '£ove' with the sterling sign, and the bulldozers of their gangs of 'developers' skimmed nature's coverlet from our midden and smarmed the land with concrete, on which to build houses that poets and peasants cannot afford to buy. But I digress!

George laid not all the blame on those obsolete Orcadians. He, too, was guilty and admitted that he felt like old Aladdin in that enchanted cave. All he had to do was use his loaf and imagination to fill in the blanks of the legends, rebuild the obscure places, and this would bring the old stories back to life, make them enjoyable to the readers of the twentieth century.

There's no denying that he made a tidy good job of it. His works have been published in the USA and in Scandinavian languages. Translators are beaver-busy putting the lot into French, German and Polish. His poems are on tapes, reels and cassettes galore, with George reading them. He yapped considerably on radio programmes and was often discerned on the goggle-box. Awards and prizes fell into his Orkney mitts like Blenheim Orange apples to maidens' aprons in late

September. He swiped honorary degrees (by Dundee and the Open University), received an OBE and was elected a Fellow of the Royal Society of Literature.

Edwin Muir began it all by asking George a simple question. 'Would you like me to send your poems to The Hogarth Press? I am more at ease with them than with Eliot and Faber's, and would receive an earlier reply from them, too!'

Hogarth published them as *Loaves and Fishes* in 1959 and published his work ever since. 1959 heralded the beginning of George's recognition – but on the third day of its first month it brought loss, loneliness and grief to Willa. Edwin died in Cambridge Hospital, just after answering his doctor's morning greeting.

Dozens of scilla bulbs had been planted between lavender and the crab-apple tree in their Swaffham Prior garden, to please Edwin. They all bloomed, but Edwin never saw them.

'That was the end of our story,' said Willa, 'but not the end of the Fable, which never stops, so it was not the end of Edwin's poetry or of my belief in True Love.'

I used to visit her at Cambridge, taking with me Vera and my brother Leslie, who had learned German while spending four years in a German POW camp. Willa and Les got on like housen a-fire. By this time Willa had been living in what was dubbed 'A home for intellectual ladies'. Les asked her about it.

'Intellectual, indeed! They are either duffy-lugged or stupid. If you wish them good morning, they pass the salt or the mustard!'

Soon, she left with a cat – to live in a basement flat in Earl's Court. Racked and tortured with arthritis (and grief) this pearl of a woman could totter only inches per step, even with the aid of a metal walking frame.

'Fly me to Scotland, Spike!'

At Heathrow I put her on a flight to Leuchars. She gave a wee fond kiss and two packages. Glenlivet malt whisky for me, and one of Willa's many prizes for scholarship for Vera, a St Andrew's thermos flask. We shall not meet again but, like their books, they are always with me.

25

Band Banners

I had wished to go to Kneller Hall and become a real musician ever since Samuel Sebastian Smith, Bandmaster of the Royal Dragoons, had told me I had the makings of a real musician if I passed the test.

Kneller Hall had a motto, which ran: Sometimes be sharp, never be flat, always be natural. I was seldom sharp, often flat, flat broke, and reasonably natural.

The house and grounds of Kneller Hall were originally the property of the seventeenth century painter Godfrey Kneller, but 'KN', as we old army musicians call it, was swiped by the War Department in 1855, when the Duke of Cambridge posed the first question about its prospective use as a military school of music, for music was the stuff required to soothe his savage breast. The Duke was riled. His rage was inspired when two military bands at a posh Kevee in the depths of equatorial Africa struck up our National Anthem, in different keys. Determined to stop further such enormities, he straightaway helped to form a Military Music Class, formally initiated in 1856. There was need for training. Until then, if a regiment wished to have a band, the officers not only had to find musicians, but pay them and buy their music and instruments.

Bandmasters were usually of foreign extraction. Mostly French or German, they were unreliable and possessed the propensity for vanishing into thin air in times of war.

The formation of the School was an important remedial step and pleased the officers. Each regiment based at home was ordered to submit two men, or one man and an enlisted boy, for instruction as musicians, bugle majors or trumpet majors. Those applying for the latter appointments had to be proficient on an instrument, but should the Commanding Officer suspect such a man to possess the qualities of leadership, his name should be submitted as one 'to be perfected as a Bandmaster'. There was also a reminder, which fortunately did not persist until 1924, otherwise brother Leslie and I might never have been elevated to military musicianship.

'Candidates must be of exemplary character, with some musical ability, able to turn instruction to good account'.

Apart from learning hymns in the church choir, then putting them into good account by yelling and hollering them out to scare rooks, starlings and pigeons from farmers' fields, we were musical nitwits, with not a notion of staves, crotchets and quavers. Nevertheless, in that bitter March of 1924, we created a military music precedent.

With assistance from his schoolteacher, Leslie was accepted as a Drummer, 1st Battalion, Grenadier Guards. Fourteen days later (and he has not ceased to remind me whenever we meet!) I was accepted as a band rat in The Royal Dragoons, aided and abetted by HRH, The Duke of Gloucester, Prince Henry himself, then serving at Aldershot with 'The Shiners' (10th Royal Hussars).

Temporarily withdrawn from drum-bashing to learn the mysteries of fife and flute and piccolo, Leslie suffered a setback when some musical maestro instructor was sufficiently dim of wit as to call Leslie a clod-hopping illegitimate. When Leslie emerged from the Orderly Room and later from the clink, his pay of one shilling per day had been reduced to one shilling per week. It took a long time for him to pay for the repair of a D-flat flute, which disintegrated on contact with the maestro's bonce.

Long before we entered the musical act in 1924, there were peculiar sects and personages by whom military bands were not held in esteem. One was a vocal minority from the Lord's Day Observance Society, aided and abetted by inconsequential priests and prelates who, as early as 1857, reacted violently when Sir Benjamin Hall, then Chief Commissioner of Works, arranged for military bands to play their music on Sundays, in the parks of Victoria, Regent and Hyde.

Priestly protestations waxed so strong that the Archbishop of Canterbury advised the Prime Minister he 'could not be answerable for the religion of the country if the bands were not stopped'.

Whether or not the country's religion has suffered is open to conjecture, but scant regard was paid to the protests and the bands played on, supported most nobly and vigorously by the Press.

In my book *The Band Rats*, published by Peter Davies Ltd, I have dealt more fully with the history of Kneller Hall and military music. The book is now out of print, but now that my own sight is failing, I am very glad to say that it will soon be published by Magnaprint, in large print for those like me who are a bit dim of sight, and also in Braille for the totally blind.

Kneller Hall must be mentioned again for purely personal reasons. The Director of Music, Colonel Trevor Sharpe (who judges all the brass band concerts since leaving the Coldstream Guards as their Director of Music) summoned me by telephone to attend their next monthly concert, where I would receive a surprise.

I was surprised and even more delighted. The first course on their musical menu came from my first book, *Reuben's Corner* and was put to music, as mentioned earlier, by my friend David Shearn, the last Trumpet Major of the Royal Dragoons, now on the staff of Kneller Hall as some kind of professor of composition. Conducting the two suites 'Granny Ford' and 'Nellie' was a smart student wearing the uniform of the Royal Anglian Regiment. He did a good job!

Overjoyed, I asked him to accompany me to the Students' Mess for a stirrup cup. He said he was a Suffolker, his name was Judd and he hailed from Haverhill.

'My brother Les lives there, he plays in the Haverhill Silver Band.'

'I know,' said conductor Judd. 'I was in that band. If it hadn't been for old Les I should never have got to Kneller Hall. Every time I played a wrong note he used to give me a kick up the arse. Small world, ain't it?'

The BBC later asked if they could record the music, but sadly someone had lost the score, and it has never been found to this day.

Much later I learned with glee that Judd had been appointed Director of Music for the 'Death or Glory Boys' (17th/21st Lancers), and had become a pukka 'donkey walloper'.

That same evening I learned from the *East Anglian Daily Times* that a number of Whitehall warriors, who had never set eyes on an angry man, were considering whether or not to permit regimental bands to continue to function, on grounds that they were costly and provided no material benefit to the nation.

Worse still, they were followed by a series of peculiar noises from some pop group called 'Johanne Scouse'. They tried to produce noises they thought might emerge from 'pruned bands' if ever the army suffered from a dearth of musicians. This peculiar collection, like so many of its Liverpudlian counterparts, disregarded a remarkable opportunity for maintaining silence.

Some years ago some other Whitehall warriors tried to shackle down the Royal Air Force, because they are the junior service and had less tradition in music than other arms of the service. I was furious about the Whitehall idiocy, so, in my fortnightly column in the *East Anglian Daily Times* I took them to task.

Questions and criticisms cascaded through my letter box.

'You didn't put the date in your article about disbanding the Bands and when K. H. became "Royal".'

'Why didn't you write about *our* band?'

'What would the Queen's Birthday Parade at Horse Guards be without the bands and music?'

You can't please 'em all, but I tried in the next article.

'In June, 1886, HRH The Duke of Cambridge took most of the top brass to Twickenham: General Viscount Wolseley, Adjutant General; General Sir A. Herbert, Quartermaster General; Sir Ralph Thompson, Permanent Under Secretary of State for War; Major General Sir G.B. Harman, Military Secretary; Ralph H. Knox, Accountant General; Colonel G. H. Mooncrieff, Assistant Military Secretary; the Revd J. C. Edgehill, Chaplain General; and a tidy few more gatecrashers without hooligan tickets.

It was high summer at Twickers. There worn't a rugby ball or football in sight. The Army Council had left their Whitehall desks to take a dekko at Twickenham's Military School of Music, all because the Duke of Cambridge had written a letter to Queen Victoria, and this is how it went.

'Most humbly submitted to Your Majesty by His Royal Highness, Field-Marshal, Commander in Chief...

'That in consideration of the service rendered by the Military School of Music in training Bandmasters and Musicians for the Army, it is most humbly submitted that your Majesty be graciously pleased to confer the prefix of "Royal" upon that Institution.'

Queen Victoria did not take many bars' rest. In General Order 141 of August 1887, it was announced...

'Her Majesty the Queen has been graciously pleased to approve the School of Military Music, Kneller Hall being in future styled the Royal Military School of Music.'

Having answered Taff Evans and hoping to have piped down the remainder, I was taken to task by two ancients of the Royal Horse Artillery – for describing their salute-firing 25-pounders as 'pop guns'.

I was not being unkind, merely making suggestions on how to save a bit of lolly for the nation, and if the Gunners wished to save £90m, why not start at St John's Wood? They have there that wonderful King's Troop. Think of the money we'd save in nonblanco buying. All that whitewash to tart up old guns, limbers, neck-ropes, lanyards and whips. 'Whips over!' Their 'Badgy' (trumpeter) to save another couple of quid, plus the cost of burnishing and blanco for riding grips. Much money could be saved if we stopped them firing salutes in Hyde Park, and blowing regimental lies on their trumpets. We would gain the truth. I used to sound trumpet calls and was compelled to learn the regimental call of every regiment. That call for the RHA, which like all other calls has a jingle to aid the trumpeter's powers of recollection, is the longest regimental call bar one, for the Carabineers.

'The Carbs have got no hilos (Hindi for boots)
No hilos, no hilos.
The Carbs have got no hilos,
They flogged 'em for beer!'
'Tis longer than the Gunners, but true. The Gunners is
   shorter, but false.
'We are the Artillery
The Royal Horse Artillery,
The pride of the Army,
The Right-of-the-Line.'

They are not Right of the Line unless they are 'limbered up' and are trailing their perishing pop-guns, but they took me to task in the Press. One letter came from a fellow Suffolker, a retired Battery Sergeant Major Arthur Digby, Irish Guards, then RHA. He opened his literary salvos in capital letters:

'TARGET – BAND RAT'

'Sir, whilst I've not the slightest intention of having an "up-and-a-downer" with a retired member of another élite regiment, even through the medium of a newspaper, nevertheless I feel that I must fire a round at Spike Mays (*EADT*, 21.1.81). Using one only, of course.

'Simply, I would remind him that, although King's Troop, Royal Horse Artillery, may have only "pop guns" when it takes its rightful place as "Right of the Line and the pride of the British Army", the next in order of precedence must be any other surviving RHA Regiment. Like 7th Regiment, RHA, for example.

'I do assure him that these Gunners are equipped with the latest FH70, a somewhat more effective item than King's Troop's "tarted up" ceremonial guns and limbers. Moreover, I would be the last to suggest that the Royal Dragoons would now go to war using sabres, even though they still carry them on ceremonial parades.

'Then, after 7th RHA, come the rest of the one and only Royal Regiment of Artillery and, eventually, the remainder of the Army. And all this has nothing to do with the Gunners' unique distinction of having Her Majesty The Queen as their Captain General.

'Needless to say, I support Spike Mays to the death in his desire to retain every regimental band for all time, and agree with him that any saving in this direction by the Gunners who, as also the largest regiment in the Army, need all their four or five bands, would not be worth the effort. Though it goes against the Gunner grain to have to suggest it to such an eminent an artilleryman as Brigadier Shelford Bidwell, there's plenty of money to be saved by eliminating civilian dead-wood before any of the indispensable Armed Services are so much as considered for such treatment. As it is, since 1958 the Navy, Army and Air Force have suffered far too many amputations.

'TARGET NEUTRAL!' Carry on writing, Band rat.'
Arthur Digby

This was good news. For once the Gunners were on our side. This was confirmed in February 1981 by the eminent artilleryman himself, another Suffolker.

Brigadier Shelford Bidwell
Woodbridge
Suffolk

'Dear Mr Mays,
    This is a somewhat belated response to your article in the *E. A. Daily Times*, but I must write to say how flattered I am to have flushed out no less a person than the

redoubtable Spike Mays, whose books I admire and, I would like to add in my guise of military historian, are a valuable record of life in that remote army.

And how remote! Forty-five years ago I saw 'C' Battery, RHA, which I cannot refrain from pointing out, saved the bacon of the heavy cavalry on October 25 1854, going out for an exercise at Trimulgherry with its six "pop-guns" shining from paint and brass, with the snowy white cords round the recuperator cylinders, virtually buried in 248 horses, and the detachments armed with swords. Little did I think I was to command it later, when it was armed with eight ugly slab-sided tank-like monsters, or that today it would be a guided missile battery.

I am not really "Ban-the-Bands Bidwell, the demon Brig" – what I said was stone cold sober, in a serious correspondence in *The Times* newspaper concerned with how short we were of essential weapons, air defence, tanks, guns, etc. and I pointed out that before we took the weapons out of successors' hands (yours and mine) you should consider that your lot are expected to cope with odds 3:1 against in tanks, and mine, who should be supporting yours and the infantry, are now expected, division for division, to meet 150-odd guns with 33. Going on from this, I said that there was £90,000,000 spent on a wide variety of activities, only 15m. on bands, which would afford savings.

However, I understand your feelings. Mr Pepper, one of our village postmen, gave me a terrific rocket when he delivered my mail. I didn't know that he was a bandsman, and his son is one now.

With best wishes,
Yours sincerely,
Shelford Bidwell'

I replied to the Brigadier's letter, expressing the hope that his musical postman and his son had exercised the tolerance and courtesy of musicians in general; adding that I, too, understood him and his problem about pennies, but would be using the words of an eminent Royal Dragoon, under whom I had been honoured to serve for many years, at home and abroad. And, as sure as God made little apples, and the Devil guns for the Gunners, I put those words of cavalry wisdom into my next article, and no mention more has been heard from the 'Pop-Gunners'.

'All soldiers who understand regimental soldiering properly appreciate what military music contributes to military efficiency in the broadest sense. Sometimes those in positions of authority who decide on questions of Army organisation have been tempted to see in bands a fruitful source of economy in manpower and money. Usually better judgement has prevailed before much damage has been done. And then in wartime it seems our custom to break up our bands at once, in the very natural desire to produce a few more fighting soldiers in a hurry. How bitterly that precipitate action is regrettable later on.

'No one who lived through the great bombing attacks on this country in the last war is likely to forget the value of a band marching and playing through the streets next day. There are few divisional commanders who would not have given a great deal for a band in spells between battles.

'Field Marshal Sir Gerald Templer, GCB, GCMG, KBE, DSO Chief of the Imperial General Staff, 1955–8 (Gold Stick in Waiting)'

I informed the Gunners, bless their cotton socks, that Sir Gerald Templer's wise cavalry words were swiped by me from the foreword of a book presented to me by the author, Lieutenant Colonel F. L. Binns. It is an excellent book with a wonderful title, *One Hundred Years of Military Music*, and it is all about Kneller Hall!

Now that the Gunners have sounded 'All Clear' and 'Target Neutral', I will wrap myself up in my old stable jacket until the next warning!

26

Seeing Stars

'There's one born every bloody minute!' said a Suffolker when I told him I was a fool. I was the crown prince of fools on an appropriate date, All Fool's Day, 1st April 1980, and had forgotten I had been invited to Blenheim. Not that posh palace in Oxfordshire, the seat of the Dukes of Marlborough, where Winston Churchill was born. I had been there twice and also to Chequers, Churchill's weekend hiding place when he was our Prime Minister during World War Two. With a gang of the Guards Armoured Division, on a Prime Minister's protection party known as 'Exercise Elephant', I used to pop down to Chequers as NCO i/c Wireless – but more of that anon.

Long after Winston left Sandhurst and became a subaltern in the Charsies (4th Hussars), we dashing Dragoons used to soldier with them, drink and sing with them and some-times have punch-ups. Nothing spiteful whatsoever, merely a method of proving and asserting our supremacy! After all, their nickname was taken from a square, low-value Indian coin, the char-anna (fourpenny piece).

The Charsies were the first British cavalry to suffer mech-anisation, an occasion of sadness for us all. Churchill was there at Beaumont Barracks, Aldershot, saying farewell to his horses. He had been a first rate horseman and loved riding. In the press pictures we could see the tears in his eyes. You may well ask, 'What the hell has this got to do with Blenheim?', and rightly so. Here endeth the digression!

My telephone rang. 'That you, Spike? We'll pick you up at Steeple Bumpstead, 1915 hours.'

Smack on time, the car arrived with four fellow Egyptians who, like me, had been born in 'Little Egypt', Glemsford, Suffolk. The natives were friendly. Lapsing into Suffolk dialect we nattered about curry and rice, India, char wallahs, Egypt, Japan and particularly about Orde Wingate, his Chindits and the Burma Road Railway. We also mentioned the pleasant pursuits of shooting mugger (crocodile) near the Marble Rocks of Jubbulpore and excursions into the mysteries of breweries in the Hills of Muree and Nilgiri. A preliminary canter before the gallop nostalgia awaiting us.

'Cum yew on!' said ex-muleteer Bill. 'We've cum hoam. Make for the bar.'

We had arrived, at Blenheim Camp, Bury St Edmunds, the depot of the Royal Anglian Regiment. Some kind of meeting was in progress. On our entry the Chairman addressed his committee. 'The next item on the agenda is "Any other business". Anyone trying that lark will be taken outside and shot. I now declare the meeting closed and passed unanimously! Mine's a pint!'

I felt very much at home. In Suffolk, with ex-servicemen of all our services, there was a brace of that web-footed lot who go to bed in pig nets, the Royal Navy. One Royal Marine had been dubbed 'Nonny-Nonny' because he could sing Shake's warning to ladies:

> One foot on sea and one on shore
> To one thing constant never;
> So sign not so and let him go,
> And be ye blythe and Bonnie.
> Converting all your songs of woe
> To 'Hey Nonny-nonny, sweet lovers
> love the Spring'.

There was a tidy sprinkling of the Per Ardua ad Astra lot, the Brylcreem Boys of RAF Transport Command, who in played-out Dakotas had kept Wingate's warriors in good ammo and spirit throughout jungle warfare. The majority were infantrymen of the Suffolks ('Dutty Dozen' or 12th of Foot), of The Pompadours and Flat Iron (two battalions of the Essex Regiment), the Holy Joes (Norfolks), who flogged their bibles to buy booze, and a number of the services unkindly christened 'Camp Followers': REME ('Nuts and Bolts'), RAMC, ('Rob all my comrades') and the RASC ('Wait for the wagon'), which is their regimental march).

I had only one cavalry companion, donkey walloper Chamber of the Carabineers. The Carbs were Godfearing fellows; unlike the bible-flogging Norfolks, they sold only the India issue boots called hilos, an activity which resulted in that crime being put to music for the longest regimental call, as mentioned in the previous chapter.

When on trumpet training in winter in Aldershot's Long Valley, our lips would split on such long calls – another aid to musical recollection! We did not go much on such a junior regiment with such a posh name. They were known as 'Tichborne's Own' when they managed to get into uniform as late as 1865.

We used to indulge in this inter-regimental rivalry for fun. It was all in good heart, but deeper down there was a reinforcement of personal pride.

That All Fools' Day, 1980, proved that point. Comradeship wrapped round this comparative stranger like soft wings. One felt the honesty, that mutual trust peculiar to comrades in arms who have shared common dangers, that very quality in 'Old Sweats'. One that beats everything to be found in today's money-seeking rat race. More important, the friendship flowed from strangers in Suffolk.

Rain fell and skies were clouded throughout the outward trip. Not a cloud could be spotted coming up the home straight. We sang the old barrack-room ballads. The stars were very bright and I thought they might be giving extra light in support of the one we had left shining behind the bar at Blenheim Camp; a big one, about 18in x 18in, their Burma Star, whose smaller versions had been awarded to pin on manly breasts. But when one looked at the wearers, one could see the prematurely furrowed brows, an empty sleeve or two, crutches and wheelchairs, and other insignia of toil, torture and starvation.

Nearly ten years later, on 10th April 1989, it occurred to me that not one of those old Blenheim braves would be taking a Tokyo trip, with or without HRH Prince Charles.

I'll bet you all the tea in China, or Saki in Japan, that if that other Blenheim boy had hung on a bit longer, instead of being put down in the village graveyard at Bladon, near Woodstock, where his parents and brother Jack were buried, he would not have allowed any of our Royals to attend the funeral of The God of the Rising Sun.

I am very proud that I attended the funeral of the supreme 'Charsie' who was largely responsible for the sinking of The God of the Rising Sun. Not by invitation; I gatecrashed by foiling the police. Over our land and in many other lands, multitudes were parading for that truly magnificent State Funeral. The news moguls of BBC TV thought they might get shots of the private interment at Bladon.

My Indian friend Yavar Abbas was a BBC TV cameraman, working under Roy Fox, Head of News. Yavar was given the job and asked me to join him, and like scalded cats we tore down the A40 in a Zephyr bearing in bold letters above the windscreen 'News – BBC TV'.

Verges were crowded with police cars. We were stopped by a top brass copper in a patrol car. 'Nobody is allowed in the village, not even tradesmen, until after the funeral.'

Yavar produced his credentials. 'Sorry, only people who live in the village!'

We moved to a second class road for cogitation. I suggested that the tell-tale signs should be taken off the motor and that some scruffy garden clobber in the boot be put on before we tried another road to Bladon. This we did and off we went, like a brace of scarecrows.

Almost into Bladon we were halted by another police officer, higher in rank than the first but lower in mentality and manners.

'You can't enter the village unless you bloody well live there.'

Putting on a strong Suffolk twang which I hoped might pass as one proper to this neck of the woods, I bellowed back: 'How the hell can I get my dinner if I can't bloody well get home?'

We were waved on and parked near cottages close to the church, with a good view of the graveyard. Yavar whispered words to a middle-aged lady leaning on her gate and returned for a camera and tripod.

'I can go to a bedroom for pictures. All the curtains are drawn in the village, so we will not be spotted. Stay here by the gate, keep a sharp lookout and use that bloody lingo again if anyone speaks to you.'

I leaned on the garden gate in my borrowed clothes and saw it all and was not spoken to.

This was a very simple, strictly private, family farewell without pomp and circumstance, and most moving. Except for one officer in the red jacket and white plume of the Life Guards, no one was in uniform. We waited until the last mourners of the village had said their goodbyes. We said goodbye. Yavar's camera had captured it all, but the powers of protocol ruled that the film should not be shown in Lady Churchill's lifetime. Will it ever be shown, I wonder?

* * *

I often think about it. The old Charsie had been very kind to me at Chequers. His kindness began one morning there when I was poking about in the soil with an aerial rod.

'Good morning!' said the Prime Minister. 'Are you fond of gardening?'

'No sir, I had enough of that before I joined the army at the age of sixteen!'

He was pleased to talk about the cavalry and asked: 'What do you do here in the evening?'

'We play pontoon, or nap, for cigarettes and matches.'
'Don't you go to the pictures when you are off duty?'
'No. We are confined to Chequers, sir.'
'You will come to the pictures tonight. My pictures.'

After their dinner, some of us were sitting in the drawing room with a mixty-maxty of Cabinet ministers. I sat behind Stafford Cripps, who was so skinny and small-headed that I had an excellent view of the Russians attacking the flanks of the German Sixth Army at Stalingrad. The Jerries were outflanked by what was named 'a splendid Russian pincer movement'. There were pictures of the capture of 90,000 prisoners of war, mostly German. All the Cabinet ministers clapped, but not until Churchill led the clapping. He had a cigar as long as the Maginot Line, and brandy I could smell, but did not taste.

We went often to 'the pictures' and our living conditions underwent a remarkable change for the better.

The old Charsie was stretcher-bound when last I saw him. He was due in from Nice after sustaining a heavy fall in Paris. I was duty PRO for London (Heathrow) Airport. Churchill was flying in from Nice on an RAF Comet, which had been flown out to bring him to an English hospital.

Heathrow was agog; banners blazed, children swarmed, shrieked and waved Japanese plastic Union Jacks, while baggage hands were busy erecting barriers along the Great West and Bath Road. Inside those barriers was a large, reinforced platform, specially designed to carry the bulk of Richard Dimbleby, his sound gear, lighting equipment and a swarm of microphones, all carefully calculated and positioned off with more barriers, just to stop Richard being overworked and could place his live mike under the nose of Winston C. the moment he emerged from the Comet. Not unusually, the calculators put a foot wrong by confusing 'port' and 'starboard'. If they had resorted to cavalry lingo like 'off-side' and 'near-side' they might have got it right, for a change. But no! The Comet taxied in very smoothly to deposit Winston from the port side, and lo and behold, the Dimbleby tower was on the other side and Dick, poor chap, raced breathless beneath the belly of the Comet, holding a hand mike, dragging about 200 yards of connecting cable. Between you and me and the Heathrow gate posts, I was tickled pink.

But I went to meet the Old Charsie and helped him from the Comet and into the car. He gave me a victory sign, all to myself. And that was the last time I saw him, but I heard a lot about him shortly after from one of his lifelong friends. Bernard Baruch had brought from America his housekeeper, Elizabeth. I had coffee with them in the VIP lounge after I had been pestered by pressmen to get Bernard to talk to them.

'I will not talk to them, Mr Mays, but you can tell them that I am an old man, just a minister without portfolio, who has come to see a very dear old friend. When I come back from the hospital I will come and see you again, and perhaps give the press a word or two.'

The news about Churchill was bad for several days, but when Bernard Baruch was about to fly back to America he sent for me.

'I am not going to speak to the press, Mr Mays, but you can give them a message, then come back and have coffee with us. Tell them this. "The bulletins about Winston have not been good, but tonight the bulletin will be a dandy".'

I delivered the message and returned. We spoke at some length about Winston Churchill.

'A remarkably talented man,' said Bernard. 'Bricklayer, painter, horseman, politician, author and soldier. He's also a flirt. When he came to the USA to stay with me I could never find Elizabeth, my housekeeper. When I did find her, she was with him. When I went to Southampton to sail back home – just after the tragedy of Gallipoli, Winston said this to me, with tears in his eyes. "Goodbye, Bernard, you are a great man going back to a great country."

'And I told him this, Mr Mays, "You are a greater man, staying in a greater country."' He continued, 'If you come to America, be sure to come and see us. We will look after you. Thank you for looking after us. We must go now, but I will let you into a secret. I can lick the pants off Winston at Gin Rummy!'

I went with them to the plane. We shook hands. Elizabeth gave me a wee kiss. I had seen more stars, but that bulletin was *not* a dandy!

27

Development!

Eleven years have galloped by since Vera and I struck tent in
Middlesex and moved to Suffolk, hoping to find a mite of
peace and quiet in an East Anglian village. We arrived at
Steeple Bumpstead in 'flaming' June, in a snowstorm, well
away from the din of Heathrow Airport.

Being a 'Taffy', Vera would have preferred Wales, but 'for
once' I did it my way. I reckon I've put a foot wrong!

We had good news from Wales. A brace of technocrats, one
from Swansea, one from Lowestoft, had put their inquisitive
and highly intelligent heads together, investigating the problems of *pophra*.

Now this is not a Welsh Trade Union or a sinister secret
service society, but a health producing, succulent seaweed
grown in the waters of the Gower Peninsula. It has a high
iodine content supposed to increase the height of those who
have become a mite cretinous through stooping a lot in the
labyrinthine coal burrows of the Rhondda. It is wholesome,
cheap and absolutely delicious when fried for breakfast with
hunks of Welsh bacon, but quite revolting to look at. Welsh
women camouflage or disguise it with liberal sprinklings of
oatmeal. It can be bought in its raw state by the sack, wagon
load or shovelful in the markets of Swansea and Carmarthen,
and in shops and market stalls, already disguised. When raw
it looks like cow pats from bovines over-fed on rich grass or
clover, and it is called 'Bara Lawr' which means 'larva bread'.

With 'Edwina's Epistle to the Egg' and the ministerial soft soap on soft cheeses, and mad cows, I am quite surprised to have survived for nigh on eighty-nine years.

When I was a boy, we all sucked eggs, of fowls of all kinds, including those of game birds, pheasants, partridges and plovers, to the consternation of Uncle Jasper; the game-keeper. We gulped down quarts of rich, creamy, non-pasteurised milk, still warm from Bella's udder, and we are still living, to be exploited by the 'developers'. Old Granny was right. If her rice pudden had been scorched, and we would not eat that 'owd black bit', she'd put us in our place. 'Git on with it. Eat it up. Yew gotter eat a peck 'dirt afore yew die!'

Harking back to that peace I knew we would find in dear old East Anglia – and even wrote a book about it *Return to Anglia* – it now occurs to me that I might *well* have put a foot wrong; that we should have gone to Vera's Welsh Wales, where people have a knack for preservation. Not only for *pophra*. People of the principality are not easy prey for grabbing developers and they did a good job about the Gower Peninsula. Their Swansea Councillors had enough oil in their lamps to put the kybosh on that fat, red jacket-dad Canadian Billy Butlin's plot to churn the lovely bays into yet another garish holiday camp, to destroy Bracelet, Caswell, Three Cliffs and Rhosilli.

Vera and I used to board the old tram and rumble to Mumbles and then tour the bays on Shanks's pony. Thanks to those Councillors, it may still be done!

On Worm's Head, Rhosilli, we watched the languid swell and gentle lapping of the white-maned rollers as they seemed to queue to kiss those sweeps of golden, untrodden sand. From overhead came the plaintive mewing of gulls. These were the only sounds, for our feet were muffled by short, fine grass that thrives on sandy loam and provides a sound-deadening carpet for the whole of the Rhosilli Downs – the highest point of Glorious Gower, right to the edges of the cliffs, so sheer as if about to parachute themselves into the sea.

Development!

We walked there for solace. We had lost our son, little Glyn. Not quite four years he had been evacuated; then from the London bombs, but now from us, for ever. Vera taught me a Welsh love song. I sensed that it was inspired by Rhosilli.

> Ar Lan y Mor
> Ar lan y mor mae rhosys cochion;
> Ar lan y mor maed lili gwynion.
> Ar lan y mor mae 'ngariad inne
> Yn cysgu'r nos a chodi'r bore.

Some of the beauty is lost by translation. It is better heard than seen, and in the music of the Druids. It's more than 'fair t'middlin' in English.

> By the Sea Shore
> By the sea shore are red, red roses;
> By the sea shore are whitest lilies.
> By the sea shore my love is pining
> Asleep at night, at dawn awaking.

Let's get back to Anglia for a bit. They owd Essex boys ain't as daft as they look. One night in the hamlet pub, at the Horkey Supper, the labourers' thanksgiving for a successful harvest, our old horsekeeper got up on his hinds about Essex place names. Places are due for bulldozing before long. George only knew about our villages, he had never clapped eyes on the sea in his 65 years of clod-hopping.

> Willingale Doe and Willingale Spain,
> Bulworth and Bobbinworth Colne Engaine;
> Wended Lofts, Beaumont-cum-Rose, Bung Row;
> Gentingthorpe, Ugley and Fingring Hoe.
> Helions Bumpstead and Mountnessing,
> Bottle End, Tolleshunt D'arcy, Messing;
> Islands of Canvey, Foulness, Potton,

Stondon Massey and Belchamp Otton.
Insworth, Inworth and Kedington,
Shallow Bolws, Ulting and Kelvedon.
Margaret Roothing and Manningtree –
The better yew sound 'em the better they be!

They'd have to be sounded 'tidy loud' to drown the racket of the bulldozers, some already turning up to skim off the top soil to flog to the new City Horticulturists. If only the laboratory lads and sagacious councillors of Swansea could come to the aid of North-West Essex! If we do not extract our conservation digits our villages will be 'promoted' to runways and taxiways. Consider the extension for London (Stansted) Airport. Consider what happened to poor old Hounslow Heath.

We will start with Stansted, Essex. Geoffrey Rippon had been ranting through his titfer about the creating of Maplin, an extension of Stansted and the prosperity it would afford to our villagers. 'Men of Essex want to enjoy the prosperity of the east.' Has he asked the North-Easterners? Has *anyone* asked them?

They said something without being questioned: 'To hell with Maplin and Stansted.'

Over 40 years ago I watched the rape of Hounslow Heath during its artificial mutation into a hideous Middlesex city of air and earth congestion. I worked there for 15 years. But long before that, we trained our cavalry horses there, on that self-same heath where Dick Turpin and other highwaymen had ridden before me. There are many 'highwaymen' operating there today. Their operations are acceptable (to me) under the dubious classifications of development and progress. I witnessed what happened. Devastation and laying waste of horticultural and agricultural small holdings. Where once grew carrots, carnations and cabbages, there are Comets, Caravelles, Concordes, all queueing up to wing with nerve-shattering blastings through the stinking paraffinny clouds of their own making. Air France Caravelles used to come in handy when the beer in the bar of No. 1 Passenger Building was rather warm; Johney Freully used to whip me off to Orly Airport and back, for iced champagne. Is that progress?

Our beautiful birds that once flew in large flocks, and some in RAF-like formation, have been ingested by old Whittle's now mostly Rolls-Royce jet engines, causing flight hazards for the jet set, and surviving birds have changed flight patterns and earthly habits. Some squat on runways and taxiways, to warm their cold bums on the jet-heated concrete, now that the hedgerows have been uprooted and our trees chopped down.

The British Airports Authority once had a brainwave and engaged an ornithologist to look into the birds' behaviour pattern, to find some method to shoo them away. He made recordings of birdy distress signals, amplified them and played them on the runway through some tannoy system. More birds attended, just to listen. His next wheeze was the employment of some unemployed people armed with a brace of dust-bin lids, which they clouted together cymbal-licly, but this was too expensive because the cymbal bashers demanded extra lolly for night work. My suggestions were completely ignored. First they should transmit a popular recording, that Scouse lot, The Beatles and their 'yeah, yeah, yeah'. The ornithologist, a Scot, didn't go much on that – but even less on my second. They should borrow from BBC TV one of their female news readers, any one of the several with a Glaswegian accent, which, I assured them, came in handy to scour rust from my ex-cavalry spurs.

Before the age of Beeching, the Great Train Robber, North-West Essex had suffered a severe setback in this wonderful field of development.

Audley End boasted a small rail junction which connected a single line track to Haverhill, Suffolk, Ashdon Halt and diminutive Bartlow, where we used to entrain for the Colne Valley Line to visit Constable country, but never again! The junction functions mainly as the village bus stop, but also as a 'stopper' for undergrads *en route* to Cambridge to be taught 'Planning and Development'.

When we village yokels caught the train at Ashdon Halt – if we were in funds and could rustle up the fare to go 'swaining' – we would train trip to Audley End Park, a place where housebound house maids were released from bondage once a fortnight, in the evening. The whole day off was on Sunday, but swaining worn't allowed on the Sabbath!

No one can go there now.

George Sutton, the trim-bearded guard with a permanent thirst, will never blow his whistle or wave his red and green flags again. His track is overgrown, his trains, four a day in both directions, have been broken up – for development. But I shall never forget when he blew his little whistle in vain after his emergence from the pub at Audley End, and rushed into his guard's van. The engine driver steam-tooted his usual reply.

The tank engine chugged off to Saffron Walden, leaving George in his van, wondering how he had failed to notice that the one and only passenger coach had not been coupled to that departing tooting engine.

Wild strawberries still grow on the deep wooded banks of that old sociable line, with hosts of wild flowers, and jungles of weeds between the tracks where George was once an important link in the life of our country community.

George is long dead, but The Planners are much alive and are not yet finished with Audley End.

In 1970 an Essex County Council plan stipulated that Audley End Park was of such exceptional value that it should be preserved for all time, at all costs. There was a reason! Way back in the eighteenth century, the park had been most magnificently landscaped by Lancelot 'Capability' Brown. It was always a joy to go there, irrespective of the results. But the edict of 1970 is very old, and has given ample time for the 'planners', who become restless if they do not occasionally emerge and do something socially disobliging to justify their deplorable existence. The Local Authorities planned their masterpiece. To erect a vast sewerage works (with pagoda roofs, mind you!) smack in the centre of old 'Capability' Brown's fine park. They were quite specific. It will be built between one stately home, Audley End Mansion and Saffron Walden's fine church, where the Bishop patted my head when I was up for confirmation.

Architecture has been defined as a social art – one requiring the ready skills and full co-operation of many trades and crafts – to build for the people, those who pay the price.

Much of today's building is coming under public control. Our towns and villages are largely under the control of local authorities, who are supposed to be directly in touch with, and under the control of, the electors.

They are *supposed* to be under the control of the electors, but in Steeple Bumpstead they are not. We, the electors who pay the price, cannot call the tune. We are muzzled at Local Council meetings. Only the 'elected' can spout. Words from the 'electors' are permitted only at Annual General Meetings without an agenda provided there is time after the Minutes of the previous AGM (page upon page) have been gabbled by a self-appointed Secretary unable to speak English. I am angry. I will describe The Rape of Steeple Bumpstead.

Bow Lodge, our Bumpstead bungalow, faces south. When first we entered, we heard the dawn chorus. The birds sang every morning whether the sun beamed or skulked behind clouds. Smack opposite was undulating meadowland, surrounded by hedgerows interspersed with trees of oak, elm, sycamore, and towering chestnuts, all conker bearers. A stream ran through the meadows, Bumpstead Brook. Kingfishers winged their rainbow way along its banks, unless small boys and girls were fish-netting tiddlers.

Planners and profiteers huddled, consulted their treasury departments and decided that Church Fields was such a glorious place that many more people from our capital city should share this beauty. Then they skimmed off the top soil, uprooted the hedges, cut down the trees, built concrete roads and a concrete bridge. Just to make space to build houses for the poor people of London who wished to live in the place they had just destroyed.

Before they smarmed the area with concrete and tar, the gentle rain that fell upon us from heaven to the earth beneath had the natural habit of seeping its way through the earth beneath. But nevermore!

We were flooded six times in less than three years. The planners had not planned for 'drainage' ... water cascaded down from roofs and concrete roads. From my study window I watched it pouring down the main road to our Water Lane, flooding the lane before little Bumpstead Brook, the natural drainage, became half-filled.

I conformed to the norm by complaining first to the junior Parish Council, progressing next to Braintree District Council, then Essex County Council, Anglia Water Board and finally to Alan Hazelhurst, MP for Saffron Walden. Many letters passed many hands before our MP gingered up the laggards. A few experts arrived, but always after the flooding, when they could see the effect but not the cause. They had not enough oil in their dim lamps to perceive that the natural seepage had been bull-dozed and sold, that storm water is not stormy enough to penetrate concrete and tarmacadam.

They brought cameras, theodolites, measuring rods and note books. One said they were preparing notes for an impending Board Meeting, but lacked a board room. He was displeased when I offered them six board rooms, each devoid of carpet, and under the floorboards five and half inches of flood water they could use for further analysis.

Help came in the crucial hours from Suffolkers with sense who knew about handling water – the Suffolk fire brigade, who lugged out our carpets and furniture, after wading through the wet stuff up to their armpits to reach us, and stayed to help for five hours.

I made but one attendance at our Parish Council meeting and was not at all surprised to be told I could not speak; it was not an Annual General Meeting. I was first on parade at the Annual General and first to speak by telling the Chairman he should apologise to the village and resign. I walked out.

Something has been achieved. Bumpstead's little brook is no longer a brook and is now promoted to 'riverhood'. This promotion permits the Anglian Water Board to regard it with respect and consideration; the Anglia water frogs are stirring in their mud, but their thick crusts do not accept a simple fact. If our Water Lane gets flooded before our little brook gets half filled, it is not the fault of our little brook that Water Lane floods. Our brook has always been a well behaved one, not at all naughty, for it is quite grown up, quite content and can hold its water. Plenty of the new people in the new houses can vouch for that. We have christened their estate 'Colditz', because those living on it when the floods start can't get out. Those outside can't get in.

Alby came to see me one day, a village ancient dubbed 'butterfly' because he only came out when the sun was shining. He looked to the new Church Fields and put it all in a nutshell.

'Dew yew know, Spike, I ain't bin down this end o' the village fer years. I uster stand here, look across there an' see the fields. Cattle, sheep and a hoss or two. Flower an' nettles. Children playin', shriekin' an' hollerin' in the grass. Ain't room ter swing a cat there now. No gardens, jest flower boxes. So close together too. £45,000 a-piece an' all, fer bloody chicken coops!'

Three of my former neighbours have gone, one from each side to Dawlish, plus one who replaced one of the leavers. Bill was born within the sound of Bow Bells and is now in Suffolk.

I wonder if the enlarged Stansted Airport will make flights to Rhosilli!

28

Remember, Remember – Bangers!

'Please, Mr Spike, please!' said nine-year-old Paul. 'Come with me and see the bangers. They are like flowers falling out of the sky, and my mum says I can stay up late if you take me.'

Paul's eyes twinkled like electric sparklers. He came often to my workshop. He could use tools quite well and talk. He seldom stopped talking. Talking, watching and learning. It was very intelligent talk.

Paul reckoned he had 'growed up' now that he was nine. I had to chair a meeting of our branch of the Royal British Legion and was buffing up medals by lathe for the impending Remembrance Parade. I tried to work Paul a flanker.

'That's a lot of rot!' said I. 'How on earth can anyone see a bang? It's a noise m'lad. You don't "see" bangs, you "hear" them!'

'Rubbish!' said Paul. 'You didn't listen. I said "bangers", not "bangs". You see bangers when they go bang in the sky. You can eat them as well!' said Paul, somewhat reflectively. 'Bangers is also sausages as well!'

Because he had put me in my place, I took him early. We saw bangers, heard bangers and scoffed a couple on sticks. I took him home, only three cottages away, and raced to the Red Lion, just in time to open the meeting by reciting the exhortation, 'They shall grow not old...'

Throughout that meeting my mind jangled with thoughts

about Paul and poppies, fireworks and Flanders, solemnity and sausages. After a jar or two with fellow Legionaires I strolled homewards through Church Fields under the star-jewelled November sky, still thinking. Very soon, at the eleventh hour of the eleventh day of the eleventh month, we would be 'gonged up', standing stiff as ram-rods with banners drooped. We would be listening. Listening to villagers' names being read, names permanently etched in the grey granite of the Steeple Bumpstead War Memorial. Family names, names of two generations, for two bloody wars! Thoughts took me back to that Armistice of 1918, and the Peace Celebration of 1919 in Park Mede, Ashdon. I was then eleven years of age and it was more than 75 years ago. Years beyond our allotted span of three score years and ten. Unforgettable!

Although the senseless slaughter had finished in Flanders, other battles were being waged in Park Mede to celebrate the outbreak of Peace. In a comic, beflagged boxing ring, old men were bashing the living daylights out of each other, 'Blacks versus Whites', and were garbed accordingly. The shanks of the Whites were covered by white tights and Long Johns, the bums of the Blacks in passion dampers (black bloomers borrowed from wives and grand-mums) and the black and white linen boxing gloves filled with flour and soot.

Two bands played nearly all day, at the same time but with different tunes. Old men and maidens, young men and children raced one another in wheelbarrows, up and down wagon ropes, under tarpaulins, with legs tied together, with hands carrying eggs and spoons and lips blowing up balloons.

There were bottle and cake stalls, beer tents and a kind of teepee in which one's fortune could be forecast from playing cards and tea leaves; there was even a Hokey Pokey stall.

A comic parson umpired a comic cricket match and a real parson, even more comical, supervised an intervillage tug-of-war. Urged on by the inn-keepers, the permanently thirsty minority queued up for the beer drinking competition. They had got dry, bowling for a pig and hurling balls at the coconut shy.

After four years of madness and sadnesses the old village seemed to have taken on a mantle of madness and happiness. A remarkable transformation.

De-loused and demobbed, the able-bodied were now back at work on the fields and farms, with a long overdue increase in wage.

That old squirearchy system which had been in bloom in the compost of its own making, began to wilt and droop. Old Quim Walls, who lived in Collier Row, a cottage near the school, put it very neatly: 'Never sin anything like this afore. Even the owd farmers are a-laughin'. Thasser a bloody caution, there's no mistake!'

In the evening, at dimmit light, the other lights faded and sounds of revelry became hushed; we had two kinds of bangers, just as young Paul described so many years afterwards. Fireworks galore and sizzling sausages on little sticks from Goddards of Saffron Walden, reckoned to be the best sausage maker ever.

All at once there appeared in the sky a blinding white light which scared the living daylights out of old Joslin, our Bible-bashing hot-gospeller and thatcher.

Joslin was one of our 'characters', one who used to go to his thatching in a frock coat 'tails' and a top hat. Each time he had finished thatching a stack, he would stand on his hands on the stack ridge and bellow out a hymn of praise whilst upside down. He 'saw the light' in more ways that one that evening. He jumped on his hot-gospelling bike and pedalled like fury round the village, ringing his hot-gospelling hand bell and hollering: 'Cum yew on out an' be saved, dear brothers an' sisters. Cum yew on out! Retribution hev copped us. Cum yew on out!'

That blinding light was not part of the fire and brimstone we all deserved. Ashdon had got itself lit up deliberately with the aid of a 'government surplus' naval flare. All fixed up, it was said, by the Reverend Hartly, our C of E parson who once had served the Royal Navy as a chaplain.

That was certainly the brightest non-banging banger of our Peace Celebrations. Liza Coote said, 'That were so bright I could see to read my *Christian Herald* in the bloody dark!'

Harking back to Paul's other bangers, I can recall those hard times when we had little to take to and used to look forward, perhaps once a month, if mother could raise the wind, to a feed of sausages.

Duggie Batemen and Sonny Pearson were our village butchers and pig killers. They served us sausages from their shop next door to the Fox and Hounds pub. Both are no more!

There have never been before, and never will be again, such truly succulent sausages. Even better than Goddards! They fair sizzled their superiority and smelt of rich pork, not today's spiced breadcrumbs pumped into plastic hides!

Sonny was the comedian and Lothario who winked at the gals. His straw hat was always at a jaunty angle, and his blue and white apron, all bloodstained after a kill, was held round his goodly girth by a leather surcingle stuffed with steels and gadgets for sharpening his wicked-looking knives. He would raise his eyebrows in feigned shock and indignation, and glare with scorn into the very souls of small boys and girls who asked for a pound of sausages.

'POWNDS, m'dear, POWNDS!' Then, in whispers, 'Didn't yewer luvly Mum say yards or miles?'

If the children wondered who was right, Sonny would open the secret door and display his masterpieces, pale-pinky, and looped over shining steel hooks, chains of bangers!

'There they be, m'beauties! Miles an' miles on 'em. We sell 'em b'the mile in towns an' cities. B' the rod, perch or pole in other villages, but on'y in yards an' feet in hamlets like you'rn. Cum yew on, now yew just weigh a POWND yerself, m'dear. I dunno how!'

It all came back again. I was so pleased that Paul wanted to see and hear the 'bangers'.

29

Horus the Horse

For a dozen years I was truly delighted to write a fortnightly column for an excellent newspaper, the *East Anglian Daily Times*. Not only did I enjoy the writing, which really was the incentive to writing nine books of autobiography, but because my scribbling made me many friends. My postbag became so heavy that I now have tea chests chock full of letters, greeting cards, photographs, and even ballads with musical notation in pukka manuscript form.

In writing about my cavalry capers in India, I quoted the first two verses of The Hon Mrs Norton in her moving poem 'The Arab's Farewell to His Steed'. Because I am a bit on the soft side, and like being emotionally moved, I shall now type them again and try not to have a frog in the throat or damp in the eye.

> 'My beautiful, my beautiful!
> Who standest meekly by,
> With thy proudly arched and glossy neck
> And dark and fiery eye,
> Fret not to rove the desert now
> With all thy winged speed;
> I may not mount on thee again,
> Thou'rt sold, my Arab steed.
>
> Fret not with that impatient hoof!
> Snuff not the breezy wind!

The farthest that thou fli-est now,
So far am I behind.
The Stranger hath thy bridle rein,
Thy master hath his gold.
Fleet-limbed and beautiful, farewell!
Thou'rt sold, my steed ... thou'rt sold!'

Letters poured in from lovers of horses, hunters of foxes, writers of verses, ancient troopers, grooms, ostlers, two ex-cavalry galloping majors (both from Woodbridge) and a very angry lady who replied in the Letters to the Editor column and fair took me to task by stating that the horse was not sold; that I had missed out verses proving that it was not sold; that I had sold readers down the river by not writing it all, thus giving a false impression. Others trotted along, asking if I knew the poet, the composer of the music, and where could copies be obtained. This old Arab steed seemed to be permanently stabled in the *East Anglian Daily Times*, and Donald Simpson, then Editor-in-Chief, sighed with relief and wrote to thank me for putting a stop to column canterings about this mythical, much-loved, sand-trotting Arabian nag.

Lo and behold! Eureka! That which was lost was in my postbag. A kindly Suffolk horsewoman-musician who could play the piano bareback or quit stirrups, sent me an original manuscript, all tatty and faded but containing every lovely line and every verse of The Hon Mrs Norton's poem, all underlined below the musical score of the long dead composer, John Brockley. All the verses were published in my next column. Sold or not, the Arab steed was put out to grass. No mention more was made of him.

* * *

My Arabian antic began long before that. Not on the sands of the desert, but on Hounslow Heath. We were then stationed at Hounslow Barracks, the usual jumping-off course for cavalry regiments about to proceed overseas and safeguard the remnants of the British Empire. As usual, not a soul knew where, but conjecture was rife until Lieutenant Lonsdale let the cat out of the bag just as we finished riding school on the Heath. Some had reckoned Rawalpindi, Trimulgherry, Peshawar. Shoey Thornton, the farrier corporal, reckoned it was our turn for Timbuctoo. Lonsdale said: 'It's Cairo!' He was right.

In the permanence of the typed word it became official. Part II Orders proclaimed that Royal Dragoons would be Cairo-bound on 27th September, 1929.

New jobs were found for old horsemen, packing stores and equipment wanted and not wanted on voyage. The departure and voyage I have described in my second book *Fall Out The Officers*, but before we left Hounslow our adjutant, The Right Honourable G. Browne, OBE, found an unusual job for Lieutenant A.D. Wintle, MC, FRSL.

'You will lecture to the men about Egypt. Warn them of the dangers. Tell them how the Pyramids were built and so on.'

'No one knows how the Pyramids were built! retorted Wintle.

'Find out! said Gerald. 'If you can't find out a simple thing like that, you're not fit to be a cavalry officer!'

Lectures began with full attendance. According to our newly created Social Anthropologist, the primary racial characteristics of the Gippos were drugs and dope peddling, pimping and whoring, dirty postcard flogging, lying, thieving and homosexuality. We much enjoyed these preliminaries but got a bit foxed when he extended his thesis into the peculiar realms of Egyptian mythology, a subject on which he appeared to be an authority. Trooper Woodroffe, his batman, let the cat out of the bag. Wintle had bought books to ginger up his research. He had a quick wit and a great sense of humour. We revelled in his racy description of the anatomical details and activities of a host of gods. Ptah, Baast, Ammon Ra and others. In particular of Osiris, Protector of the Dead, and his son Horus, the god with the body of a man and head of a kite. Each of these gods had been almost as efficient as Royal

218

Dragoon troopers of our day. They had possessed miraculous and supernatural powers and had enjoyed the special favour of kings, who considered them their divine ancestors. Like troopers and common mortals, the gods had wives and families, and as they were also celestial sovereigns their jewel-crusted courts brimmed with soldiers, servants and slaves. For dirty weekends they had palaces, not country cottages, built high in the sky, in the great mountains of the east, and deep down in the dirty depths of the wicked underworld. Vivid descriptions were offered of their pets, the sacred animals, bulls, rams, cats, snakes and even frogs, fishes and birds. 'Like all good Dragoons,' said our professor, 'the gods grew daily drunk with drinking, their bodies strong, lusty and joyful, they shouted aloud and sang and were exultant.'

Our hearts began to exult with thoughts of what might lie in store for us, but we eventually arrived at Main Barracks, Abbassia, Cairo – without horses – for we were taking over horses from the regiment we were about to relieve, The 3rd Royal Hussars.

Like every cavalryman, every horse is given a regimental number, which is tattooed on the lower gum. Horses are also given a squadron number, branded by hot irons into the front of the off-fore hoof. All our horses could readily be identified by document, for each had a Veterinary History Sheet on which was recorded in detail height, colour, weight, character, virtues and vices. A kind of equine crimes sheet, giving useful tips such as: 'Bites when grooming', 'cow-kicks on mounting', 'blows out on girthing', 'rears and rolls on soft going'. Everything known about our faithful steeds was recorded. There was not a syllable about names. Names were fickle and could be changed from regiment to regiment, from rider to rider. When all the other information had been gathered in, logged and counter-logged, and the handover had finished, the rider could pick a name for his gee-gee and it would be painted on in regimental colours. The trooper could name his horse, all by himself, without a font, Holy Water, Chaplain or christening ceremonial. And Lo, it came to pass, after the feast of Take-Over, and in less than one Egyptian month, that all horses were named and name-board painted. All spick and span for the GOC's inspection. Passing through one stable at the tail end of a crocodile of Top Brass, Wintle looked up to a name board and saw on it the word Horus, the name of a mighty Egyptian god, with the body of man and head of a kite, son of Osiris, Protector of the Dead. With tremendous appreciation he looked down to the man grooming that well-named horse.

'Capstick,' said Wintle, screwing in his monocle and taking more appreciative glances at the name board.

'Sir!' Ginger stood to his horse, ram-rod stiff.

'Are you interested in Egyptian mythology, Capstick?'

'Jest a bit, sir!'

'Have you been reading about it?'

'Nossir!'

'Is there much talk about it in the barrack rooms after my lectures? About the pyramids, the sphinx and the gods?'

'Not as I've noticed, sir.'

Ginger was the last man to remember a word of any lecture, but he could box and play football. His answers were hardly those Wintle expected from a man who had named his horse after an Egyptian god.

'Tell me, Capstick. Why the devil did you name your horse "Horus"?'

'I see what you mean, sir.' He patted his horse affectionately. 'Old Horace, sir. I named him after my brother. He's Corporal of Horse in the Life Guards!'

That reminds me. I've remembered those missing verses:

> When the dim distance cheats my eye
> And thro' the gath'rin tears,
> Thy bright form for a moment
> Like the false mirage appears.
> And sitting down by that green well
> I'll pause and sadly think
> 'Twas there he bow'd his glossy neck
> When last I saw him drink

Horus the Horse

They tempted me, My Beautiful
For hunger's power is strong.
They tempted me, My Beautiful –
But I have loved too long.
Who said that I had gi'en you up?
Who said that thou wert sold?
Tis false! Tis false, my Arab steed,
I fling them back their gold.

Thus, thus Heap upon thy back
And scour the distant plains
AWAY! Who overtakes us now
Shall claim thee for his pains.

Name boards can't be hung up in the desert, and I've often wondered what the Arab called his steed. 'My Beautiful' ain't bad. I'll settle for that!

30

Softness

Most men and mawthers who have passed our allotted span of three score year and ten by a further ten, should have developed a tidy few idiosyncrasies, more personally welcomed as convictions and beliefs.

No matter how hard one has tried to avert it, all that lovely soft malleable clay of our early impressionable years, like the ruins that Cromwell knocked about a bit, gets pounded into quite different shapes.

Before we can holler a couple of boos to a gander, our innocence and softness has 'gone off', like quick-drying cement. We become things of angles, corners and spikes, grating and jarring upon others who do not hold our point of view, and this is particularly true of those three subjects which are not supposed to be mentioned in pubs but remain the chief topic of conversation. Religion, politics and sex.

Now and again it is delightful to remember the soft clay of peasants, that stuff that poets rant and rave about, and I was more than a mite pleased when a fat, jolly man (who looked a bit like our Suffolk Punch), on a chat show in November 1977, reminded us so innocently of our first loves.

Sir John Betjeman did a wonderful job. He reminded us of our lovelorn lunacy and the beauty of it before sex entered into the old, old pattern, when life and love were new.

For almost a year, until August 1921, when I was 14 and had left my elementary school, I had fluctuated between peaks of exhilaration and troughs of despair. I was blithesome as a bird when she smiled, dull and dismal as ditchwater when she seemed not to notice me. We hardly spoke, we were so shy, but knew we had something to share, sometime.

When first our eyes met and played havoc with my mind I became acutely aware of inferiority, of mental and physical shortcomings. I felt that I needed gayer plumes. A new suit might do the trick. A general rejuvenation of my outward appearance; a reinvigoration of my wit, and the aptitude swiftly and accurately to answer my schoolmaster's most tricky questions when he orally tested our class in the 'big room', might also help.

Whether or not I knew the answer, my hand had to be the first one raised. When the schoolmaster was sufficiently misguided to pick someone else, I prayed the answer would be wrong, that he would come to me for the right one.

She was never out of my mind. Because of her I lived in a realm of constant day-dreaming, hallucination and fantasy. I was her hero, her professor, her, Sir Galahad and St George. Every one of those questions was a dragon, ogre, or wicked knight to be slain with the sharp swords of my wit for my lady.

I knew the extraordinary scenes I conjured up were not and never would be 'experience'. Although they were more vivid than life itself, I knew full well that I was merely hoping and wishing, a cunning device fully generated by my yearning to impress her.

I was in love. *She* knew. Her face betrayed her. I did not dare to tell her. For months we were equally evasive and elusive. We led each other a pretty dance – until that letter came.

She had gone to London for the summer holidays.

Before her letter came I had got into the habit of staying up very late, sometimes getting up again after going to my bed – just to walk sorrowfully and soulfully past the cottage where she lived. Walking very lightly, always on grass verges so that none should hear. In my crazed mind she was 'up there', in 'that' room, but she was not, she could not be, because she was away from our fields and woods in smoky London. She had slipped deep into my heart, my life, forever.

Her letter was short. 'Back to Ashdon next week. See you in school. Love, Nellie.'

I tore to my tiny bedroom to read my first love letter, a thousand times. Each time it seemed different and even more wonderful.

I could, and should, have spoken to her when we broke class, but she was not alone and I was shy. I skulked along the allotment patch path, screened from the road by dense hawthorn. She looked back, loitered, then halted smack in the middle of the road, opposite the only hedge gap. I stepped through that gap and stood, like an oaf.

She came to me.

She came so close that the light wind tickled her hair into my face like an angel's kiss. For one surging, tumultuous moment we stood face to face, an inch apart, and looked into each other, not saying a word. There was no need for words. I could see by her eyes that our minds had been adjusted to love.

Later, we walked together endless measures of foot-pathed fields, hipped hawed hedgerows and emerald meadows, clutching, as forever, their old beauty to our new young hearts.

There were halts for kisses, for long looks into each other's eyes, intervals for inspection of faces and souls, troths and promises by the bushel, carving of hearts and Cupid's arrows in the olive green bark of the soft willow, initials etched into sturdy stunted oak and towering elm, to outlive us.

My arm would encompass her willowy waist, her hair tendrils zephyring to my cheeks with electric shocks. There would be a sinking to the green of the meadows to fashion for my Lady's dark tresses a golden pagel chain as the sun sank in its own fire of scarlet and orange to herald the next fine day.

Then butterfly kisses would be exchanged, like thistledown and dead leaves meeting in the wind. More promises, more majesty! There are not poet's words, nor is there maestros' music, to tell how our hearts sang when we were young and so in love.

Sir John Betjeman did us all a power of good, as have so many others of his ilk. Perhaps Robert Southey summed it up way back in 1810 in his 'The Curse of Kehama'.

> They sin who tell us love can die.
> With life all other passions die
> All others are but Vanity.
>
> In heaven Ambition cannot dwell,
> Nor Avarice in the vaults of hell;
> Earthly these passions of the earth,
> They perish where they had their birth.
>
> But Love is indestructible;
> Its holy flame for ever burneth,
> From heaven it came, to heaven returneth
> Too oft on earth a troubled guest,
> At times deceived, at time oppressed.
>
> It here is tried and purified
> Than have in heaven its perfect rest
> It soweth here with toil and care,
> But the harvest time of Love – is there.

31

'Peggy' Lawrence

As choirboys, we used to bellow out music in our Sunday School on very important practice nights in the tail end of July and sometimes through August, if the weather was unkind. We were getting our tonsils in trim for the tricky anthems of Harvest Thanksgiving. Handel, aided and abetted by biblical words, used to play Puck with my emotions. My eyes would water like old land drains. 'The valleys stand so thick with corn that they laugh and sing.' But lest I became unduly emotional in the choir stalls about the annual garnering, I would counter emotional onslaughts with other unsaintly parodies. 'Wicked parodies' as mother used to call them.

> 'All is safely gathered in
> But if it ain't, it oughther bin.
> All upon the barnyard floor,
> For the rats an' meece t'gnaw.'

I recalled those words in August 1977, those heavy incessant rains and flattening of the uncut corn. It looked as though we might never get the bumper harvest that non-agricultural forecasters of BBC TV prophesied on that day when the sun shone for a good ten minutes. As usual, the farmers were griping about the weather and the potential lack of profit, but they are a resilient bunch and mastered the problem before the choristers had learned the new 'modified' harvest hymns.

I thought I had put a foot wrong during that harvest time. Not in church or harvest fields, but in a Haverhill dub room as an after dinner speaker for the Round Tablers. Four parsons were present, all wearing dog collars. I began by a flank attack on the dog collars and told them a story about a man who went to church but once in 25 years. He sat himself in the front pew, smack under the pulpit and was literally looking right up the parson's nose throughout the sermon. The parson was delighted to see a new face among his steadily diminishing congregation, and quite entranced that the stranger's eyes never strayed from gazing at him. Service over, the parson raced to the porch, determined to get a new sheep to his fold.

'Good morning! I have not seen you in our church before.'

'There's a reason fer that!'

'Oh, indeed! What is the reason?'

'I ain't bin afore! I were hoss-keeper an' hosses want feeding on the Sabbath, my owd met!'

'Of course! So you have a holiday, perhaps?'

'Hellabit! I got the bloody sack. They got a tractor, don't want hosses no more. I got bugger-all ter do, thought I'd come t'church!'

'Oh, I see! Did you enjoy my sermon?'

'Didn't know what the hell you were a talkin' about, metty!'

'But you seemed so interested. Your eyes never left my face!'

'I were very interested and still be interested. I've bin a wonderin' how the hell you got that great fat head through that little white collar!'

The Round Tablers of Haverhill applauded and roared with laughter as the four parsons rose, whipped off their dog collars and waved them furiously. Later they asked me to talk to some of their members, mostly the Mothers' Union and the Jerusalem jam-makers of the Women's Institute. I still do it today and find it a worthwhile and heartening experience.

One week after the dog collar display, I found myself in a

Parish Hall at Dunmow, Essex, where, once upon a time the inhabitants would hand over a whole flitch of bacon to a married pair of their community who had a row every day for that year and told a pack of lies about it.

I knew the landlord of the Dunmow pub, The Queen Victoria. Wally Lawrence once lived at Springfields, Ashdon, and I went to school with him. His father had been nick-named 'Peggy' Lawrence because he had a wooden leg, but more of that anon.

Some years before the 1914-18 war, an experiment was conducted on the farmland soil of parts of Ashdon. Roderick Charlton, fresh from college, conceived the notion of growing fruit on his smallholding, Springfields, where for years only cereals had been planted. Tall, thin and studious looking, he wore a surgical boot.

First he planted apple and plum trees, then between the rows, strawberries and goosegogs. While the hard fruit was being established on the trees, the planting and harvesting of soft fruit provided employment for the women of our village.

Bumper crops were sent off regularly to market. Had Roderick's health matched his zeal, his business would have expanded, but his health failed and he had to give up.

Over the nearby hill at Sprigg's Farm, old John King Desborough, who had watched the horticultural activities with interest, followed Rod Charlton's example. Acres of his farm, which had previously grown corn, were planted with saplings of apple, pear, plum and, between the standards, long rows of strawberries. A new industry was founded in our corn-growing community.

A newcomer arrived at Springfields. Walter (Peggy) Lawrence returned from Australia where he and his wife had built themselves a house with their own hands. Our local Ashdon builders built them a new one to the same design. One living room, two bedrooms, and, when things began to pick up a bit, a kitchen and another bedroom were added.

Peggy lost his leg in Australia. He was knocked down by a railway engine as he walked a mere 20 miles along the track to find a doctor because his wife was ill. A forthright character, full throttle of speech, he was held in high esteem and was renowned for cursing fearlessly at all, in all presences. Had he not been able to swear at a good volume he might not have survived. Fortunately, after the engine had knocked him down, another train came along on this single line track on which only one train per day was the schedule, but Peggy's cursing was heard by the driver and he was saved.

His flaxen-haired son Wally, with the wide grin and 'Aussie' accent, helped Peggy to run the smallholding which Peggy the practical had christened 'Fruit Farm'. Part of it had reverted to its original name 'Eight Acres'.

Peggy was justifiably proud of his fine strawberry fields and orchards. A place of back-breaking industry, but of great beauty. Seven lofty elms towered at the back, hawthorns and blackthorns practically surrounded it. Stallentyne Hill bounded the right flank, and in springtime an ocean of apple blossom billowed to the left and cascaded down the hill.

His children, seated on the five-barred gate, greeted my old friends, the Thakes, Cornells and Downhams, on their way to Goldstone Farm for 'tater pickin'. (Later, these women were employed by Peggy to reinforce the fruit pickers from the village with whom I went to school, Polly Webb, Beat Chapman, the Heards and others).

Fruit farming, like cereal farming, is liable to disruption by the vagaries of weather. When strawberries are in full bloom a late frost can wreak havoc.

Thus it was with Peggy. One May night he had seen the telltale signs in the sky and prayed on his knees all night. The rich dark green leaves of his most promising crop were capped with waxy, golden-eyed blossom. But next morning, on his wife's birthday, he found the cruel fingerings of frost. Instead of blossoming life there was dark, depressing death.

His daughter had seen her father's tears but once before, when after the accident he was told that his leg had gone. In the ruin of his fine crop followed disaster, the beginning of the end for a courageous man. His 'Lawrence' strain of 'Sir Joseph Paxton' had won him high award, but now his occupation had gone. He sold his fruit farm and his beloved 'Eight Acres'.

When the elder Desborough died, his children John and Nell, who kept house, carried on the good work. The fruit acreage was greatly increased and Sprigg's Farm became famous for huge Monarch plums, Early Rivers and Czars, which grew in equal profusion to the fine black damsons and succulent greengages.

Strawberry production was intensified and provided employment for many throughout the village, for the strawberry jam makers of Tiptree bought the 'Lawrence' strain of 'Sir Joseph Paxton.'

Although the greater part of the farmland was still under the plough, fruit and cereal production was conducted concurrently and successfully until the end of the war, with the help of Bill Mizern, whom Nell married.

Basil (Brisk) Fisher, one of the Desborough regulars, took some responsibility from the ageing trio and stayed on when the farm came under the management of Major Bill Mallet, an ex-paratrooper. Bill further expanded the fruit growing area and respect from his employees. To work at Sprigg's Farm today is not only a way to earn a living, but a horticultural status symbol.

'Eight Acres', or 'Peggy's Owd Place', changed hands several times. There was not the acreage or scope for further expansion, but the trees which were planted by young Rod Charlton still bear good fruit in due season.

Fruit pickers of today have filled the place of the old corn gleaners of my childhood. Unlike us, they are gaily and comfortably clad in coloured slacks and sweaters, but the old dialect, badinage, talk and laughter is heard from prettily painted mouths.

Mineral waters, Coca-Cola and steaming flasks of tea and coffee have replaced those old cans of cold, milk-less, sugarless tea. All owe their presence in those lovely orchards to two courageous men, the tall, bookish, skinny pioneer, and 'Peggy' ('that owd Orstralyun'), both crippled in body, but not in spirit – despite the frost and rain.

32

Iddy Umpty

''Iddy' is for dots and 'Umpty' for dashes!' said my father, John Mays. 'Remember that a dash is three times longer than a dot!'

He was pretty slick as a signals instructor. Shortly after his discharge from hospital, after old Kaiser Bill's war, with five wound stripes on his blue tunic sleeve, he worked as a farm labourer for twelve shillings per 65 hours at Ashdon Place Farm. Long before that he had been a signaller in the Suffolk Regiment at Rawalpindi and was also a telegraphist for the East India Company at Peshawar. This was long before he clapped his Suffolk eyes on mother, but he established full marital communication with her and had two sons and one daughter. He seemed fully determined that brother Leslie and I should tread one of the paths he had trod and used to sing an old music hall ditty to inspire us.

> 'I don't know where I'm going,
> But when I get there I'll be glad.
> I'm following in father's footsteps –
> I'm following me dear old Dad.'

Before we were twelve we could send and receive Morse and semaphore. Lacking Post Office donkey-sounders, we improvised with table knives and forks, tapping the blade through the fork slots, usually at meal times. Mother was not amused by 'That old clicketty-clattering'. Possibly because this was a 'secret language' in which women and girls could not chip in or contradict.

Father and Captain Reville were largely responsible for the formation of the first troop of Ashdon Boy Scouts, and father was appointed as Signals and PT Instructor, not only to the Scouts but to other children in our village. Even the Squire's daughter and her companion he put through their training on the front lawn of Walton's Park, the village mansion. He made trips to Langley and Home Woods to cut slender, straight sticks of nut-hazel for flag-poles. He washed, stitched and dyed old sheets and cast-off choir surplices to make the flags, one blue, the other blue and white, using little cubes called 'Dolly Dyes', recommended by Mrs Reckitts, who was pictured on each cube. Each boy needed at least one flag to make 'Iddy Umpties' for Morse signalling. If the distances were not too great, boys' arms were ideal for semaphore.

Pretty soon the fields and meadowlands of our scattered village were dotted with prospective signallers, flag-bashing like fury, transmitting messages of vital village gravity. 'Tell father to get a rabbit', 'Look in my mole traps', 'Choir practice is cancelled', 'Get Doctor Palmer, Mrs Fitch has just had a baby', and 'Tell Walter Bricklayer's Arms, not Rose and Crown'.

Although these news flashes had advantages in an area singularly lacking in communication, some village elders ridiculed us and we were suspect.

'I reckon they boys hev gone start starin' mad. Trapsin' round the fields, flappin' owd rags like a lot of bird-scarers! Tellin' tales about us to the farmers, an all!' added Wuddy Smith.

Years later I became a regimental signaller, entitled to wear crossed flags and crossed rifles above the 'dodger' on my left sleeve, a single chevron denoting that I had been a pukka cavalryman, on man-service for two whole years. This meant a picture had to be taken to send home and boast. So off we went to Gale & Polden, the Aldershot military photographers. The prominent feature was our left sleeve, all twisted so that our badges of efficiency were not overlooked.

Our skills were never fully appreciated by non-signallers. Not only did we flag-wave in Morse and semaphore, we pumped out Morse on the keys of Aldis and Lucas lamps, by day and night, on heliographs by day (if the sun shone) and clapped it out on shutters, donkey sounders, buzzers, hooters and most noise producing instruments. Even on motor horns and ship sirens! We spoke a different language as well, and had to learn the alphabetical language which was shortly to be changed.

Instead of the nice little ABC we had learned at home and school, a new name had to be used for every letter:

Ack, BEER, CORK, DON, EDDY, FREDDIE, GEORGE, HARRY, INK, JUG, KING, LOVE, EMMA (or MONKEY), NUTS, ORANGE, PIP, QUOD, ROGER, SUGAR, TOC H, UNCLE, VICTOR, WEDNESDAY, X-RAY, YORK and ZEBRA.

Numbers remained unchanged, but we had to emphasise the vowel sounds to eliminate errors caused by men with different dialects. I much preferred the old letter names, for they reeked to me of ancient history. Father had told us these had been used in the Boer War, the Boxer Rebellion, and in strange places named Bloemfontein, Spion Kop and Colenso. They had been used by 'The Suffolks' to transmit messages over 90 miles by heliograph, resulting in wholesale slaughter of countless Zulus and Fuzzy-Wuzzies. Since then I have had to learn many more signalling alphabets, appropriate to teleprinters and such, and dislike the pedantics of 'ALPHA, BRAVO, etc. I felt inclined to use FOXTROT OSCAR when told I must learn the Civil Aviation versions, conjured up by brain-drained boffins of the Ministry of Civil Aviation for whose teleprinting and tape recording gadgetry we had to swot up a host of new conventional signals. To my delight, an old favourite for real signallers escaped molestation: 'INK EMMA INK'. This is not an exhortation for some junior female clerk to top up the odd dried-out inkwell, but an important command that part, or maybe the whole, of a message should be repeated, and is bashed out in the Morse code as IDDY, IDDY – UMPTY, UMPTY – IDDY IDDY!

Ill-spacing, misspelling and indifferent enunciation on live telephone circuits can prove fatal under active service conditions. There are a couple of examples still used to prove the point.

A message was telephoned in the heat of battle, and in a Glaswegian accent, to GHQ: 'Send reinforcements, we are going to advance.' It was received as: 'Send three and fourpence, we are going to a dance.'

The other, far more likely to jeopardise human lives, was poorly spaced and read on receipt from an advanced Observation Post: 'Enemy nowhere in sight', but should have been 'Enemy now here in sight.'

Another old favourite has been retained but was never mentioned in our Signal Training Manual. It is the signaller's word for 'chuckle' or 'laughter' and is exactly opposite to INK EMMA INK (UMPTY, IDDY, IDDY – UMPTY, UMPTY).

I last saw this used by heliograph signalling in Meerut, 40 miles north of Delhi, when it was used in conjunction with another signal known as 'TOCK ORANGE LOVE' meaning 'Turn off extra light'.

Shining objects like burnished sword-scabbards, polished mess-tins and even steel spurs can distract the reading of the heliograph. On receipt of 'TOCK ORANGE LOVE' shining objects are moved or masked. On this occasion the 'extra light' was not turned off until the signal sergeant put on his Cawnpore topee (sun helmet) and masked the shine off his balding pate! Then both stations 'chuckled' by sending 'MIM', the appropriate signal – 'EMMA-INK-EMMA'.

After our repatriation to the United Kingdom, having spent over five years in Kipling's 'shiny', two of us had left Meerut and qualified for a six months' course of training in Teleprinter Operating and Maintenance at the GPO, Cardiff. After a monastic, celibate life in a land where we were not allowed to look at women, in the telegraph Instrument Room we were swamped with them, of all ages and sizes, but most with a chilling contempt for 'common soldiers'.

We lived in 'civvy digs' dressed in new civvy suits and were clean and tidy always, for old habits die hard, and we had been dragooned into the importance of personal appearance. 'I reckon we must still smell of bloody horses!' said Squash.

Halfway through the training we had found favour with most of the telegraphists. They were charitable at heart, but the rigid Post Office discipline was not unlike a Guards Depot; there seemed no time for extra-mural activities, at least not with us.

We passed the examinations five weeks before the course was due to end and were 'allowed' to sit on live circuits, to send and receive telegrams to and from the most important stations: 'MF' (Milford Haven), the fish market of Wales, 'NP' (Newport) and even 'TNS' (the London Stock Exchange) and were warned against misdemeanours, two examples of which have never failed to cheer me. Talking was not encouraged. Smiling was suspect and, with the exception of a witty comment by the Telegraph Superintendent, laughter was out.

Consternation had reigned when a telegram came from the pneumatic into the hands of Kitty, who shrieked with laughter, handed it round to provoke more laughter, and even more laughter when it was read aloud:

'Unto us a child is born six feet long and four feet wide'

The Superintendent did not join in. He was concerned. If ever there was an 'embarrassing telegram' (which were not allowed to be transmitted, according to the Post Office Rule Book) this was one.

Enquiry from the office of origin revealed that it had been handed in by two charming ladies dressed in the uniform of the Salvation Army for transmission to a firm of banner makers in Aldersgate. 'Unto us a child is born' was to be the inscription; the remainder, the dimensions.

The other was a telegram which had been transmitted without question. On the face of it there was not one iota of ambiguity or embarrassment:

'Report death and position 0300 hours'

This was a 'Greetings Telegram' at a special rate, on an ornate form, and was addressed to a sub-mariner of the Royal Navy on the occasion of his wedding to a lady in the WRNS, and was sent by his fellow sailors, of both sexes.

We much enjoyed our intensive training and the friendship which developed with those intelligent and dedicated telegraphists in the capital city of the Principality, and were more than delighted when the Telegraph Superintendent addressed us before them all:

'You have all attained a high degree of proficiency. You have helped us on live circuits when staffing was difficult. If you are thinking of a career in telegraphy with the Post Office, I can guarantee you all established posts at Cardiff. If you prefer offices nearer to your homes, I shall be glad to recommend you for any telegraph office in the Kingdom.'

The words of my father rushed to mind, but I made alterations:

'I do know where I'm going
And I haven't done too bad.
I've followed in father's footsteps...
I've galloped past me dear old Dad!'

* * *

We returned to our Units, later to become GPO Telegraphists in civvy street, and we all joined the Post Office Territorial Army Reserve. As an 'OWL' (Operator Wireless and Line) I was posted to No. 2 Line of Communication Signals at Balham, but worked at the Central Telegraph Office.

It is not given to all good telegraphists that they should go to the aid of the nation by direct messages on their own teleprinters, but I was, when war was declared in 1939.

'Report Balham HQ 0900 Hours Field Service Marching Order 48 Teleprinter Operating Section.'

A few days later a dozen of us reported to Heston Airport and were Paris-bound in an ancient four-engined Albatross laden with much telegraph equipment. Due to some unprecedented oversight by the War Office, we had the most comfortable billets in military history, the lounges and bars of Le Bourget Airport. Our mission was to strip the Pans Postale Telegraphe Telephone system of telegraphy, in which pretty persons perched on high stools and operated a kind of piano keyboard complete with black and white keys, and substitute our own teleprinters: 3As for tape and 7Bs for page printing.

Mission accomplished in Paris, our reinforced L of C was broken into smaller units and repeated the drill throughout major garrisons, towns and seaports, but we became static at Cherbourg for a few months of the 'phoney war'.

Active operations began in May 1940. By the 11th, German shelling had demolished our land lines and the balanced cables of our teleprinter system. Having worked with the French during the phoney war in the famous Maginot Line, and heard the oft-repeated postulations of the inhabitants, 'Ils ne passeron pas', we were astounded by the breakthrough.

From the beginning, the Frogs had little faith in wireless communications with high power or medium power transmitters, as they were thought to be a high security risk. German direction finders could pinpoint the position of GHQ, but when the balanced teleprinter cables were destroyed there were frantic calls to resort to wireless, and a great witch-hunt for key punchers was begun.

In less than 24 hours half a dozen of us old GPO and Army wireless operators were whipped off to Le Mans, in the vain hope of restoring lost communication. We were too late, almost too late for evacuation from France altogether, but we managed it three weeks after the débâcle of Dunkirk, skulking in ditches and hedgerows by day and slinking towards St Nazaire by night. We eventually arrived for re-training at Murrayfield, Edinburgh.

One morning I was summoned to Scots Command HQ to be interviewed by Major H. V. G. Bloodworth.

'Mays, I have a job for you. How would you like to be a wireless instructor in the new "hush-hush" regiment, The Phantom?'

Phantom was composed of highly mobile squadrons of 'officer patrols' to be deployed among forward units equipped with light armoured cars, medium power radio transmitters and, in the last resort, hampers of carrier pigeons. The drill was that the Commanding Officer of Phantom remained with the battle commander and sent messages to the nearest Phantom squadron to the battle area to discover what was cooking. This was quite a new approach to battle procedure and had been hatched out by a Colonel Hopkinson. After Dunkirk, he realised that if the top brass did not receive information from the front line, they could do little towards helping the outcome.

'Their official title is GHQ HQ Liaison Regiment,' said Major Bloodworth. 'They wear a white letter "P" on a black shoulder tab. Fast armoured cars, machine-guns and wireless. No teleprinters and, like the cavalry, they work in troops and squadrons. What do you think about it?'

'When do I start?'

'Good! You will be promoted today and go to London tomorrow to fetch the wireless trainees for "E" Squadron. You have a great responsibility and there will be plenty of work for you to do. We shall need well-trained wireless operators before we are very much older. Good luck!'

We swapped salutes. I left the office feeling 40 feet tall, thinking how pleased my father would have been had he lived.

At Richmond, Surrey, next door to the Star and Garter Home for seriously disabled ex-servicemen, GHQ Liaison Regiment had its HQ. We paraded for a pep talk and in the evening I collected my batch of wireless operators-to-be and took them back to Edinburgh. An odd bunch; butchers, carpenters, motor mechanics, two machine gunners, one officer's batman and a pioneer. Not one regimental signaller.

I complained to my new CO, Major Mervyn Vernon, Grenadier Guards, and was swiftly put in my place.

'You were a professional soldier and know that orders are to be obeyed. Get on with it!'

He brought with him a brace of Grenadier Sergeants, Les Cullen and Sandy Powell, for drill and discipline. They soon got on with it. Within a week our key-punchers-to-be crashed down their feet like steam-hammers, saluted everything that moved and blancoed all things static. But they also progressed more quickly with Morse reading and sending than their commissioned superiors, one of whom wore the uniform of the Rifle Brigade. He boasted that he had read one letter 'E' in a Morse reading session of 20 minutes, one little 'Iddy', one solitary dot! Then added: 'There is but one reason why I cannot read the Morse code far better than our instructor!'

'And what may that be?' asked the Major.

'It is my total incapacity to distinguish between dots and dashes!'

Very amusing, but not quite true. The comedian was an old timer, an ex-professional soldier who had been gazetted at Sandhurst at the age of $18^1/_2$. When asked to complete a form, to indicate preference of regiment, he gave three options:

1. The Argyll and Sutherland Highlanders
2. The Black Watch
3. Anything but the Highland Light Infantry.

Another comedian lurked in the War Office, for his nibs was promptly commissioned into the Highland Light Infantry.

The young HLI officer served at home and abroad (Malta), getting into scrapes, incurring the wrath of his superiors. He hated the army life and left it by surrendering his commission, mainly to avoid being tried by court martial. He borrowed the fare and sailed off to Canada. Then, in the USA he became a bootlegger, barman and an organiser of Indoor Pony Races. By an extraordinary stroke of luck, he barged his way into the film studios of Hollywood and there he remained from 1935 to 1939, starring in many an heroic film and winning wars on celluloid, aided and abetted on occasions by Errol Flynn.

The Royal Air Force would not accept him and neither

would the Scots Guards, but he was accepted with open arms (and a bit of wangling) by the Rifle Brigade. He then came to us, GHQ Liaison Regiment, and became OC 'A' Squadron, 'Phantom', and obtained his majority.

We had fun and games at Richmond. He laid on peculiar parties for the other ranks, punt trips down the River Thames, after victualling up at the Roebuck Hotel, filling hampers with ham and cheese rolls, hard-boiled eggs and exotic liquids, various and plentiful to cater for every taste. He was asked to name the best gal he had ever laid hands on.

'Undoubtedly, dear sir, none other than Claudette Colbert's maid!'

When the balloon went up for the second time, we both went into Normandy. He managed to stay the course until they reached the ruin of Berlin. I managed to reach Falaise, then back to Blighty as blind as a bat for treatment at Moorfields Eye Hospital. I used to call him 'Iddy', the one dot reader, but never saw him, again. He sent me a copy of his first book, *The Moon's a Balloon*, with the inscription:

To Spike
In memory of many *very* peculiar days directed by very peculiar people.
> Yours aye, David Niven

There followed a letter, in reply to my acknowledgement:

> Cap Ferrat
> 14th September, 1973

Dear Spike,
What fun it was to get your letter and how many memories it brought back.
Please forgive such a short acknowledgement of all the kind things you said, but I'm only home for 24 hours, between Greece and the United States.
All good wishes to you, fellow author, and take care of yourself. There ain't many of us left!

Yours very sincerely,
David Niven

Rum owd business, this IDDY – UMPTY lark!

33

Forgive and Forget

Telephonic instructions came to my ear late one Friday. My old troop officer was still ordering me about. We had long left the cavalry and had almost got to grips with the peculiarities of civvy street.

'Come to dinner tomorrow. The Cassons are coming and Sybil Thorndike has something for you. Bring your tape recorder. I will meet you at Wrotham Bull for a stirrup cup and explanations. Your luncheon will be poured in readiness.'

We met. We stirrup-cupped.

'I have to do a special talk for Lance Corporal Cradock and wish to take a preliminary canter through your recorder.'

Bob Cradock was 'Head of Talks' at the BBC, Portland Place, but he had been a lance-jack in the Army Pay Corps and now worked in the cackle shop inscribed 'Nation Shall Speak Unto Nation'. Wintle agreed with the principle, but not the continuity, and said that Cradock had to wax cautious because the talk concerned Royalty. Not long before, a professional broadcaster had put a foot wrong by saying 'Nigger' instead of 'Niger' when about to begin a programme called 'The Land of the Niger'. The professional was our friend, the late ex-Major Jack de Manio, he who seldom broadcast the right time on Auntie Beeb's dawn-break programme, 'Today'.

De Manio is as dead as death and so is Wintle, but I have relics or souvenirs to remind me of the pleasure of knowing

242

them. Above his name, on the fly-leaf of his book *To Auntie With Love* (in which Wintle is mentioned), is an endorsement: 'To Spike Mays ... Bless you for buying a copy. It's good to know I've sold one!'

Wintle left me his typewriter, the diary of his solitary confinement as a prisoner of the Vichy French in Fort St Catherine, Toulon, the book from the BBC programme 'This Is Your Life', a bowler hat which featured on the programme, a number of his books, and his old cavalry spurs. But recently when digging out my den, I came across the tape we made at Coldharbour, Wrotham, on the day he was taken ill through drinking from a misleading bottle.

We started in 'Crystal Palace', his glass-covered scribbling den, where I tested him for sound with a question:

'How many beans make five? Speak up!'

'Two in each hand and one up the Quartermaster's orifice!' replied Wintle. I played it back to him. He adjusted his monocle, took a prodigious pinch of Golden Cardinal snuff, glanced at his script and said: 'You had better listen to this, Mays, it will do you the power of good, so here we go!'

* * *

'Forgive and forget! Our little Queen is safely home. Safe, thank God.

Undismayed, erect, splendid, she went over the top as so many of her grandfather's and father's soldiers did in two world wars, into the face of the enemy and came back triumphant, the lone survivor of a very great battle with a splendid victory, and many trembled for her, into the face of the enemy on a State visit to Germany. Eleven whole days during which every second was an opportunity for some madman to ... ? But it didn't happen. So now we must learn to forgive and forget.

A new generation of Germans has sprung up who know nothing of what has happened in the past, whose characters have altered radically and have all been transformed into a lot of English public school cricket-playing chaps. Splendid!

243

There was once upon a time a King of Prussia who became Frederick the Great. His grandfather had been a mere Margrave but acquired the title of King. His father was a military madman, who condemned his own son to death for some comparatively trivial military misdemeanor and would no doubt have carried out he sentence but for the intervention of the Emperor of the Austrian and German Empire. The Emperor had no male issue, but promulgated a law known as the Pragmatic Sanction, which ensured the imperial crown passing to his daughter Maria Teresa. This sanction was subscribed to by all the Imperial Powers, including Prussia.

When Maria Teresa became Empress, from no quarter came more fulsome and enthusiastic assurance of goodwill than from Prussia. At the same time Frederick the Great of Prussia was preparing to attack Maria Teresa and rob her of Silesia. 'We must not and we cannot believe such a thing,' said the Governor of Genoa when the proceedings were reported.

Frederick attacked Silesia without any open declaration of war and as a result precipitated the Seven Years War, which set the whole of Europe alight. During this war he betrayed his own allies three times as suited him. The outcome was the whole of Europe was exhausted. Prussia alone gained. She gained Silesia. Still, all that was a long time ago and is all forgiven and forgotten; a new generation has arisen.

In 1860 Prussia, without reason or excuse, attacked Saxony, then in 1866 she wantonly attacked and annexed Holstein. In 1870, by means of a forged telegram, she annexed Alsace Lorraine.

But all this was a long time ago and a new generation of Germans has grown up. All was forgiven and forgotten, particularly by the British, who suffered nothing.

In 1914 Germany instituted the Kaiser's War by means of that scrap of paper. After that war, a new generation of Germans sprang up who knew nothing of what had happened before; whose mentality had completely changed. So everything was forgiven and forgotten until Adolf Hitler reminded them, and once again they remembered to attack

Czechoslovakia and Poland until finally we had to go to war with them.

Still, Hitler's war has now been over for more than 20 years. A new generation of Germans has sprung up who know nothing of what went on in the past, whose characters have altered radically and have tried to develop an urge to play the game. Splendid! So we must continue to forgive and forget.

While we are on the subject of forgiving and forgetting, there is one man who has never done anything but good for the British. For many years he devoted his whole life to his country. The Duke of Windsor. He is now slowly becoming an old man and before it is too late it would be seemly for him to have a home of his own in England. There again, and with better reason, might the precept of Forgive and Forget be applied? It would of course be difficult to forget him. But who knows? The time may come when the people of this country will learn to forgive themselves for the shabby way they treated him.

* * *

I watched him as he listened to the 'play-back'. His words came crystal clear into his Crystal Palace. He pretended not to be moved, but did not fool me. We had both been war-disabled by the Germans.

In the Kaiser's War he had lost one eye, bits of a leg and fingers from his left hand. In Corporal Adolf Hitler's dust-up he was captured and imprisoned for eighteen months in solitary confinement. He had fought for England and well merited his Military Cross and the citation for gallantry of a high order.

'What do you think of it, Mays?'

'It's far too good for the BBC ... They won't broadcast it!'

'We shall find out. We will now go to The Bull and drink to the health of the Duke of Windsor.'

'I shall drink to the Duke of Gloucester, his brother Henry of "The Shiny 10th" (10th Royal Hussars) as well. They both rode in the point-to-point at Tweaseldown, Aldershot and

Prince Henry won. He was responsible for my enlistment into the Royal Dragoons in 1924.'

We popped in to see Sybil Thorndike, who let me hold the play that George Bernard Shaw wrote especially for her, *Saint Joan*. It was a joy to behold, in Shaw's own handwriting.

Much later, after drinking health to all present and absent, Wintle telephoned Sybil. 'Bring some whisky, we've run dry!'

We heard Sybil before we saw her. Rain was bucketing down and she was blasting out *I'm singing in the rain*.

She wore a transparent, colourless plastic raincoat and was carrying useful looking bottles.

'Is that whisky?' asked Wintle.

'No, it's gin. Lewis is bringing the whisky.'

'Where is he?'

'Up a ladder, moving a tile. The rain is coming through.'

Much later Wintle went to his secret liquid cupboard and returned coughing like a broken down cabhorse and foaming at the mouth. He addressed Mrs Wintle.

'Who has been messing about with the Crème de Menthe?'

'We have no Crème de Menthe!'

'What the hell is in the green bottle?'

'Oh, I forgot to tell you. It's the dog's shampoo!'

I am so pleased that I found that old tape. I shall now forgive myself for forgetting it!

34

Major R. G. Tomlinson,

BA, FTCL, ARCM, LGSM, psm.

Director of Music, The Blues and Royals

I first met Roger Tomlinson at Angel Hill, Bury St Edmunds, in the tail end of the Band Coach, just as it was leaving after a music and marching concert. I later wrote expressing my disappointment and regret in being unable to take up his invitation to attend the International Military Music Festival, Hyde Park Barracks, and informed Roger that I would be keeping a critical eye on him I throughout his first Trooping the Colour on Her Majesty the Queen's Birthday Parade at Horse Guards, and I did.

He made a first class job of it. When I asked about his reaction he beamed and said: 'Fulfilment!'

'One word is not enough,' said I. 'You are a composer, you read and write music, you have a BA degree, so get cracking and compose a letter about your fulfilment for my next book. And he did – and this is it!

FULFILMENT
'Household Cavalry Bands – in Sections of Eight –
Right Wheel – Walk March'

So this was it. After nearly an hour of just sitting there,

watching the Foot Guards do their thing. It was at last the turn of the Household Cavalry, and here was I, live on television, leading the Household Cavalry Mounted Bands across the hallowed square of Horse Guards Parade. Nervous, yet wonderfully elated; taking part in the ceremony of Trooping the Colour for the very first time.

'Massed Bands – Stand at Ease!'

That was my cue. I signalled to Corporal Major Marsh riding The Blues and Royals Drum Horse, Belisarius, to bring the ready and to begin the drum rolls for *Aida*.

The bands struck up. Now then, the right wheel ... and suddenly there, she was, Her Majesty The Queen, right in front of me on the saluting dais. So close, and taking in every detail of a parade she knew so well. I pray that nothing goes wrong – please, Petronella, be a good girl – please don't fidget or get excited when the other horses go by, or go into one of those tantrums of yours.

Petronella is my charger. I'd previously been riding Dunfermline, a very reliable and experienced horse, but he was now becoming too old for this sort of thing, and I had been on the lookout for something a little younger. Consequently I'd only been riding Petronella for a few months, but already she was showing every sign of being ideal for the Director of Music. Steady, quiet, easy to manoeuvre, and above all, not afraid of the awesome drum horses immediately behind her. However, she does have one serious problem. She finds these parades so terribly boring and adopts one of her poses ... sometimes a foreleg stuck out at a jaunty angle, sometimes her rear legs crossed, occasionally both poses simultaneously. Unfortunately I can never tell when she's doing it. There I am, sitting perfectly in the saddle, head erect, chin in, back straight, legs in the classic riding position, feeling incredibly proud and important and then I see a photograph of myself taken at that moment, and discover that old Petronella has (once again) completely let me down. Excuse me, I must concentrate for a moment... The Household Cavalry Walk Past has been completed and the two Squadrons are about to break into the trot.

Major R. G. Tomlinson, BA, FTCL, ARCM, LGSM, psm.

There, that's successfully negotiated! Out of the corner of my eye I can see the rear of the Life Guards Squadron, bouncing up and down as they begin the long circuit of Horse Guards Parade. Thank goodness she doesn't have to play at the trot, especially the sitting trot. What an uncomfortable and undignified motion! It takes me back to my days in the riding school.

'Congratulations Roger. We've just heard that you've been selected to be the next Director of Music for The Blues and Royals!'

'That's marvellous,' I thought. 'When do I start?'

'Oh, not until June of next year,' said my Commanding Officer. 'However, you need to report on January 6th to begin the Household Cavalry Equitation Course, it lasts five months.'

Five months! How can it take five months just to teach you how to ride sedately into the middle of a parade square, sit still for a while and then ride quietly off again? I couldn't believe it, but then I knew very little about horses and riding.

'Quickest and best – Mount.' The first thing you learn is how to get your body into the saddle of a horse seemingly standing about nine feet tall, without using the stirrup irons. It may be easy for John Wayne; it may be relatively easy for the fit young troopers who make up the rest of the recruit ride, but it certainly wasn't easy for a geriatric 46-year-old Director of Music. Actually, the whole stirrup iron syndrome was something of a culture shock. For the first two months of the course we were not permitted to use the stirrups at all in the riding school. The idea is to strengthen the muscles of the seat and legs to a very high degree, and I rapidly became painfully aware of several muscles I didn't realise I had before.

The training develops a finely tuned sense of balance which in turn is supposed to give us a good posture, or seat. In this precarious manner we progressed from walking to trotting, then cantering and finally to jumping. It was the jumping that literally brought me down to earth. Not only did we jump without stirrups, but without reins as well. In the initial stages

249

we had to knot the reins and go over the cavallettis with our arms folded across our chest or, as a variation, upon our thighs, or just to make it really interesting, taking off our jackets along the way.

This is where I began to bite the dust with some regularity. The experience of coming off a horse while travelling at 30 miles an hour across a series of fences is one that doesn't stand up to many repeats. After each asphyxiating and bone-jarring fall, I was quite determined that that was the very last time they would get me up on a horse's back. There was nothing about it in recruiting posters, nothing to prepare us in the Kneller Hall Student Bandmaster's course of psm classes. Could it possibly be right, at my age, to have myself subjected to this physical abuse?

The only exception to the non-stirrup rule was when the ride moved down to Windsor and we were able to ride in the streets or most pleasant of all, in Windsor Great Park, where we learned to gallop for the first time. Some of us unintentionally! Consider that these long-suffering horses of ours spend week after week after week trotting round the riding school, or at best, trotting the busy streets of London or Windsor. Then, all of a sudden they find themselves with grass under their hooves and a wide open expanse in front of them. Their initial reaction is to go mad. On our first visit to the Great Park we managed to have several of our rides disappearing in all directions in scenarios similar to many Western film chases.

Actually riding a charging horse, though at first somewhat alarming, is quite easy to do. You simply raise your seat out of the saddle, crouch like a National Hunt jockey, and wait for the horse to run out of steam, which in most cases lasts only a few hundred yards.

The problem is that these horses are not used to this sort of activity. The spirit is willing but, fortunately, the flesh is weak, otherwise some of us might not have halted until we hit some shoreline.

After regrouping, the ride settles down, and we begin to make the most of Great Park. For me this was the most pleasant aspect of learning to ride. The simple pleasure of riding in such beautiful surroundings gave me a deep sense of joy and contentment and, for the first time in many weeks, I actually felt happy. This was not to last long. Having shortly 'passed out' (in Khako, by the dreaded Riding Master) we began the final and most difficult part of the course, the 'kit ride'. The kit consists of helmet with plume, gauntlets, stiff buckskin breeches, thigh-length jackboots, and for troopers (not musicians) the cuirass – a solid metal chest and back plate. Not only did we have to learn a new set of riding techniques, we also had to learn to look like soldiers of the Household Cavalry, the Sovereign's Escort, professional, competent and, above all, incredibly smart.

The last four weeks are probably the most demanding part of the whole course. At times I began to lose faith in my ability, but I survived. The Full Dress Pass Out Parade is performed with great ceremony before the Commanding Officer and his entourage. Parents, relatives and friends are invited to witness a ceremony lasting all morning and consisting of detailed inspection, a series of manoeuvres and drill exercises in the riding school and another series in Rotten Row in Hyde Park and – finally – a formal parade, complete with the mounted band on the square at Knightsbridge Barracks.

Excuse me, I must break off now. The Household Cavalry 'trot past' has been completed and here comes my next big moment.

'Household Cavalry Bands – Head Half Left – Walk March – Eyes Right!' and it is nearly all over.

What a fantastic experience! My first Trooping. Well done, Petronella, old girl. I feel elated and proud, with a tiny hope that the television cameras got us both on our best sides!

35

Cum Yew On – Last of The First

Having dodged the undertaker for over 80 years I did not think to write another book, but I was 'dragooned' into further literary action by Christopher South, Officer in Charge at BBC Radio Cambridge.

In his hush-hush studio, where only breathing is permitted, he purred into his microphone to countless East Anglians, 'We have Spike Mays with us again today, and we are going to talk about his last book, *Return to Anglia*, which is a sequel to his first book, *Reuben's Corner*.

'Oh no it ain't, said I loudly and ungrammatically.

'That's what it says on the jacket,' said Chris, a mite frostily.

'The publishers did that, not me,' I said.

'In that case, you had better write another book and call it, *The Sequel to the Sequel*. We shall then know what we are going to talk about,' Chris replied.

Two days later I entered the Black Boy, at Sudbury. An old mate greeted me. We had both worked on the land and were born in 'Little Egypt' (Glemsford, Suffolk). 'Wotcher, Spike, heard yew on the wireless. Yewer goin't write another book, called *The Sequel to the Sequel*. That aint much cop as a title... Why don't you give it a good owd Suffolk title?'

'You're a good old Suffolker,' said I, 'you give it a good owd Suffolk title.'

Then, as some Suffolkers do when asked to do something a

bit out of the ordinary, he blurted out the usual protest, 'Cum yew on!'

That means, in other words, 'Get on with it!', 'Get going!' All my life somebody has been telling me to 'Get on with it', 'Get going' or 'Cum yew on'. One of the first times this happened was of course in 1925, when aged 16, a band boy in The Royal Dragoons, and in the Cambridge Military Hospital, Aldershot, I was ordered to get well by Lieutenant A. D. Wintle ME. In other words, 'Cum yew on'. I did so, it was the straw to clutch on to, and I recovered. I had to. One does not disobey an order from a Royal Dragoons officer!

I then spent two months at an expensive convalescent home in Hunstanton where, with careful nursing and nourishing food, I made a full recovery. It was not until 19th January, 1959, when I appeared on the TV programme of Wintle's 'This is Your Life', did I discover that Wintle had paid for my stay at Hunstanton from his own pocket.

It was while I was attending Edinburgh University, that I had renewed my friendship and association with Colonel Wintle. I had believed him dead, as rumours had abounded that he had been killed in the war. A chance reading of an article in the *Weekly News*, while returning home by train from Edinburgh made me aware that Wintle was alive and well. I wrote to him, and received a reply by return of post, which led to a long and firm friendship.

Having watched 'This is Your its Life', and being rather bored with some of its victims, I thought it would be a good idea to have a 'real' person as the programme's subject. In 1958 I telephoned the producer, T. Leslie Jackson at the BBC, and suggested that he have Colonel Wintle as the 'victim'. 'Jacko' not only agreed, but was bursting with enthusiasm, and gave me the job, along with two of his investigators, of rounding up about a dozen of Wintle's acquaintances. Within a week we had rooted them out.

One of the guests who agreed to appear was Prince Aly Khan, who had worked with Wintle in Military Intelligence during the war. Also attending would be Lt Molia, who had been one of Wintle's guards when he was captured in Vichy

The Last of the First

France, and imprisoned at Fort St Catherine, Toulon. Molia had complained to him that because of Wintle's numerous escapes, all the guards' leave had been cancelled. As a result, Molia was in danger of losing his sweetheart to a rival. Wintle then agreed not to try to escape while Molia was on leave. The agreement worked, and Molia reported to Wintle that he and his girl had become engaged. Wintle was delighted, and gave Molia a gold sovereign, which he had hidden in his cell, to make into a wedding ring.

Molia was so impressed that he later deserted from the Vichy regime and joined the French Resistance, becoming the leader of 280 Maquis.

The problem remained, however, how we were to get Wintle into the Shepherd's Bush studio without him suspecting that something was afoot. Wintle was, at the time, writing stories for the *Evening News* and the *Evening Standard*. Ramsden Greig, the editor of the *Evening Standard*, solved the problem for us. He persuaded Wintle to go to the dockside at Hays Wharf, overlooking the Pool of London, where he might pick up a story as the TV cameras would be there for a new feature entitled 'Slice of Life', on 19th January, 1959.

I contacted Mrs Wintle, telling her I would pick her up at her home after Wintle had left to catch the London train. I had a BBC car and driver, and we hid in the woods and watched. Mrs Wintle told us that the Colonel had left, but we checked at Wrotham station, before dashing back to London.

When Wintle arrived at Hays Wharf, the cameras were rolling, but he was unaware that they were trained on him. Ramsden Greig met Wintle as his taxi drew up, and introduced him to Eamonn Andrews. 'Colonel Alfred Daniel Wintle, ME soldier and fighter for the freedom of the individual, *This Is Your Life*,' said Eamonn, proffering his hand. 'I'll let you into a secret,' said the Colonel. 'My life is not yet over.'

He was then driven to the studio for the rest of the programme. Eamonn Andrews, thinking that Wintle might be nervous, tried to calm him, but Wintle, thinking that it was Eamonn who was nervous, said, 'Don't worry. Everything will be all right.'

254

During the programme, Wintle's life was revealed by people who knew him. The Sister who had nursed him when he was blinded. A black man, whom Wintle had befriended in prison. A King's Counsellor, and a fellow Officer of the 'Gunners'. Then Prince Aly Khan, who unfortunately could not be there in person, due to a United Nations meeting in Geneva, spoke to Wintle by the Eurovision television link. 'Nothing would have given me greater pleasure, mon vieux, than to have been present in person,' he said. Quick as a flash, Wintle replied, 'I don't see why you could not come, mon vieux. After all, it is not that you cannot afford the fare.'

Just before the end of the programme, Mr and Mrs Simpson came on stage. With a baby in arms they had stood in a Stockwell street in 1945. All day they had searched for a house in vain. They were very dispirited, when a car stopped and the driver offered them a lift. 'We didn't know it was Colonel Wintle then,' said Mrs Simpson, 'because he wasn't in uniform. I wish he had been, because when I got in the car, I sat on his bowler hat. It was ruined.'

Minutes before the show, Eamonn had sent out for a new bowler hat, so that Alan Simpson (the baby), now 14 years old, could present Wintle with it. I had once tried on one of Wintle's hats and it fitted, so I gave them my size.

Alan Simpson, trembling with excitement, presented the hat to Wintle, who put it on. It was two sizes too small, and looked like a pimple on a haystack. After the show, I was accused of a trick to get myself a new hat. Eamonn offered to have it changed, but Wintle declined, and to my surprise took the side of my accusers. 'Mays knows perfectly well that I have two bowlers and he has none. I should expect a man of my regiment to find himself a hat if he lacked one. Mays shall keep it.' On its white silk lining Wintle wrote, 'Dear Mays. This is Your Hat from This Is My Life. A. D. Wintle, The Royal Dragoons, 19 January, 1959.' I still have the hat and shall always keep it.

In April 1944, I had a letter from Colonel Roger Tomlinson. Rogers, former Director of Music of the Blues and Royals, instructed me to 'Cum Yew On'. He invited me and Vera to a

Concert at Kneller Hall, to celebrate my birthday and also Roger's last day in the Army after 37 years' service. I told him that I was too ill to travel, which brought the reply, 'The Army will pick you up, and the bloody Army will take you home'. Sadly, I was too ill to attend the Concert and I deeply regret that I could not be present at such a wonderful occasion.

Last of the First – Now what is that all about? Well it is true, and I am the last of the First. I am now the sole survivor of my old regiment, The First The Royal Dragoons. The Royal Dragoons were formed by King Charles II in 1661, together with another regiment, The Royal Scots. These two regiments were the first of the Standing Army of Britain. The Royal Scots were nicknamed, 'Pontius Pilate's Bodyguard', and the Royal Dragoons had several nicknames, including, 'The Bird Catchers'. This was because they captured a French Gold Eagle at the Battle of Waterloo. I joined the Royal Dragoons in 1924 and served with them until 1931, when I transferred to the Royal Signals. The Royals survived without me until 1969, when they were amalgamated with the Horse Guards (The Blues) to become the Blues and Royals who, together with the Life Guards, make up the Household Cavalry. I am the last of them, the last of the First.

By Our Deeds We are Known – *Spectemur Agendo*. That is the motto of the First The Royal Dragoons and, if you ask me, a damn good motto for us all to live by. When my time comes, I hope the Almighty will overlook the many misdemeanours committed during my long life, and concentrate on the few good deeds I have attempted. I trust that he will smile at me benignly and say, 'Cedric Wesley Mays – cum yew on'.